WHAT MAKES A SOUTH DAKOTAN?

South Dakota Stories

40th Anniversary Special Edition

Edited by
John E. Miller
Lenora Hudson

South Dakota Humanities Council
Brookings, South Dakota

i

Library of Congress Cataloging in Publication Data

Miller, John E. and Hudson, Lenora
South Dakota Stories

John E. Miller and Lenora Hudson

1. South Dakota—Anecdotes
2. South Dakota—Social life and customs—Anecdotes
3. South Dakota—Biography
4. South Dakota—History
F651.6W42 2012
978.3/03—dc23

ISBN 0963215787

First Edition
Manufactured in the United States of America
by Mailway Printers

Compiled and Edited by John E. Miller and Lenora Hudson
Design, Photo Editing and Layout by Sherry DeBoer and Mailway Printers
Text and Technical Assistance by Jennifer Widman, Carolyn Marshall, and Ryan Woodard
Indexed by Bang Kim

Front Cover Image Illustration by Evan H. Yoo, based on a photo courtesy of SDSU Archives & Special Collections, Hilton M. Briggs Library, South Dakota State University, Brookings, S.D.

ii

PEOPLE ARE SAYING . . .

This volume bursts with song — a collection of voices honoring homelands unlike any other. South Dakotans sing with pride, anger, joy, sorrow, and strength of lives shaped and nourished by this sacred plot of earth. It is a whirlwind of stories that do justice to a remarkable territory.

Susan Power, author, Standing Rock Sioux

South Dakotans are proud of their heritage. They welcome challenge, greet visitors with open arms, embrace hard work and remain optimistic during adversity.

Governor Dennis Daugaard

This may be the most audacious publishing effort in state history. The amazing thing is that I think the publishers succeeded. We always attributed being South Dakotan to too much walleye and Wall Drug doughnuts (as if you can ever have too much of either), but we were wrong. There's more to it than that and taken altogether — blizzards, homecomings, love of the land, cows and the rest — the stories in this book do show how we differ from folks in the other 49 states.

Katie Hunhoff, South Dakota Magazine

While there are many different types of people in our great state, South Dakotans share the value of hard work. Whether it is a farmer, rancher, teacher, small business owner or any other profession in our state, South Dakotans work hard and get the job done. This has been the case since my great-grandfather homesteaded in what was then the Dakota Territory. Our hard work ethic is one of the many reasons I am so proud to call South Dakota home.

Senator Tim Johnson

Sometimes, I think the best definition of what makes a South Dakotan may be an appreciation for the subtle beauty of the land and the sky that's rushing past the car window on a trip between Sioux Falls and Rapid City. Yes, the Black Hills are scenic and the

Badlands are stunning, but anyone can see that. When you can see the prairie's gifts, you see with a real South Dakotan's eye.

Mary Garrigan, Reporter, Rapid City Journal

As immigrants settled the fertile prairies and miners staked their claim in the Black Hills during the gold rush, South Dakota became a state of great diversity. From this vast diversity grew close-knit communities which yielded a state filled with citizens dedicated to building and strengthening these communities. What makes a South Dakotan is hard-work, the ability to thrive when faced with adversity, a sense of community, and an undying loyalty to their state and country. Distance does not change the fact that we are all neighbors in South Dakota.

Senator John Thune

South Dakotans are unbreakable, resilient and have a deep understanding of what's truly important in life. We find limitless beauty in the spectacular sunrises and expanse of prairie and farmland. We feel such a deep connection to the land, it is difficult to adequately express. Our rich heritage of faith, family, hard work and determination has created a community of people that are as tough as we are generous. I couldn't be more proud to call South Dakota home.

Representative Kristi Noem

When reading this volume of South Dakota stories, so rich in history, culture and humor, countless enchanted hours will pass by for the reader. Hearing stories told by individuals who have enjoyed so many similar experiences will make them even more special. This is a work that will be handed down to future generations of South Dakotans, maintaining our state's legacy through storytelling.

Bob Sutton, President, South Dakota Community Foundation

Rarely do we find a book on South Dakota that attempts to integrate immigrant and tribal perspectives. Only the inclusion of strong tribal voices, from the writers to the editing, can correct the amnesia most South Dakota narratives contain. This brave book attempts to do just that. South Dakota deserves nothing less.

Tasiyagnunpa Livermont, editor, West River Eagle

South Dakota is all about place, but it's all about people, too. The stories illustrate that in warm, rich tones that convey the deep affection the writers have for this place that - no matter their 'temporary' residence - they call home.

Terry Woster, Public Information Officer, South Dakota Department of Public Safety

EXCERPTS

Oh, you'll hear a lot of glowing attributes describing a South Dakotan. Not unlike Captain 11 (and every true South Dakotan knows who that is!), a South Dakotan "must be kind. He must be fair. He must be brave." But let me put a spin on this topic and tell you what a real South Dakotan isn't. A South Dakotan isn't a Snow Bird!

From "What A South Dakotan Isn't" by Maxine Swanson

I will awake again ready
ready this time
to cry out the words
alive on my tongue
Mni Sose you are my home
and it is I, I am South Dakota
born on these banks
made visible by truth.

From "Dreaming South Dakota" By Mabel Picotte

Almost twenty-four years ago, I walked into the tiny Centerville, SD, post office with my five-month-old daughter in my arms. When I asked to buy stamps to mail some letters, the postmaster asked me if I needed a weight.
"No, thanks," I said. "Just the stamps."
"I mean the baby," he said kindly. "Do you want me to weigh your baby?"

From "Postmarked in South Dakota" by Jean Patrick

It was a dark and stormy Tuesday night throughout the whole state of South Dakota. Off an old dirt road in rural Hartford, my family sat in our living room watching the evening news. Suddenly all the electricity went out, and the sky began to turn greenish. The world seemed to stand still.

From "Tornado Tuesday" by Danielle Eldredge

The graveyard lies at the edge
of a cornfield by the edge of town,
along the highway ditch,
the tombstones among sunflowers nodding
at the moaning tires going by.

From "Dakota Town" by Doug Cockrell

In South Dakota, getting the guyshed is pretty much a prerequisite for getting your mancard punched. It's sort of a shedmitzvah.

From "The Guyshed: a South Dakota Institution" by Lee Schoenbeck

It has something to do with "belonging." South Dakota is a state of the nation and identified as a geographic location. I like the term "homeland," which just happens to be in South Dakota. As the homeland, it precedes statehood, and its roots go deeper than settlements, towns, counties, land demarcations, and ownership. When my feet touch the soil, it connects me to my ancestors and my mother earth, and I have a comforting feeling that someday I will rest in her bosom.

From "My Ancestral Homeland" by Elden Lawrence

Traveling on business to Singapore, I attended a local Rotary Club meeting during which the president of the club introduced me and asked me to talk about South Dakota. I stated that the reason I lived in South Dakota was because of the four distinct seasons of the year—June, July, August, and Winter! To which he replied "It's the same for us here in Singapore; only here it is hot, hotter, wet, wetter!" Weather is a South Dakota character builder.

From "Weather, weather, weather" by Larry Fjeldos

You say you recognize your neighbors as your kin—the very few in this wide world who'd ever care to claim themselves to South Dakota—sturdy, stubborn, close and open, mostly straight and true, familiar, dear and often maddening family? Perhaps you are a South Dakotan—fewer than the needles on a Ponderosa Pine. You'll know if you belong to this rare breed— your heart will tell you so.

From "Your heart will tell you so" by Cindy Kirkeby

CONTENTS

INTRODUCTION

CHARACTERISTICS

DIVERSITY

RELATIONSHIPS

TOWNS

WEATHER

ACTIVITIES

MEMORY

CULTURE

By Greg Latza. Used with permission of Greg Latza.

By Tom Dempster. Used with permission of Tom Dempster.

INTRODUCTION

The Many Sides of South Dakota

South Dakota, like other states, has meant many things to many people. To the Arikara Indians, the area that later became South Dakota provided fertile ground for planting crops. For the Dakota, Nakota, and Lakota, it contained abundant hunting regions for following the bison and other animals. To early French fur traders, it meant animal pelts; to Lewis and Clark, a base for exploration. To eager homesteaders in the 1860s and later, the rich soil held immense allure. Small-town artisans, store-keepers, shippers, and elevator operators mined profits from their customers and clients by shipping in manufactured articles and marketing farmers' grain and livestock. Churchmen sought converts, schoolteachers yearned for willing pupils, and newspaper editors wanted readers.

The initial pattern of European-American settlement east of the Missouri River, in place by 1890, established a template for development and expansion in later decades. The West River region, meanwhile, once entirely set aside for the Native American population, quickly witnessed reservation boundaries shrink by various land acquisitions and ruses, as whites streamed into the region, hungry for land and gold. The Black Hills—the sacred "He Sapa" of the Lakota—eventually became a popular playground for tourists, sports enthusiasts, and retirees.

No single essay or book could possibly capture the full extent, variety, or direction of South Dakota culture in its totality. In truth, asking the question "What Makes a South Dakotan?" presents an impossible task. The range of possible answers and opinions is as expansive and diverse as the individuals who attempt to respond to it. Thus, the purpose of this book is not to provide simple or definitive answers to the question but rather to offer up a range of opinions that suggest the wide variety of realities and understandings that have existed in the past and that continue to prevail today. The collected essays and poems operate as sort of a kaleidoscope providing a spectrum of views revealing just how diverse and complex is the culture that has evolved over time in South Dakota.

The state's amazingly beautiful topography and copious natural resources have inspired observers to refer to it as "the land of infinite variety." In similar fashion, South Dakota might be called the "society of infinite variation." From the rich, well-watered, slightly rolling farmland in the eastern tiers of counties, settled mainly by people from the Midwest and of northern and western European descent; to the short-grass prairies running from the James River Valley to the Missouri River; to the vast open plains of West River cattle country, which contain most of the Indian reservations in the state; to the magnificent and mysterious Black Hills, the South Dakota landscape has both fostered multiple sorts of social adaptations and in turn been shaped and influenced by the peoples who have been centered in and drawn to those places. While in many ways the residents of the state have comprised a more homogeneous collection of people than exists in many other states, the mix has been greatly complicated and enriched in recent decades by in-migrants from all over the United States and all over the world. The continued presence and expansion of the American Indian population provides a distinctive coloration to a state where the indigenous population traces its history back not just centuries but millennia.

Against this varied and vibrant backdrop, the South Dakota Humanities Council (SDHC) envisions a South Dakota "where we fulfill our essential human need to tell our stories, satisfy our curiosity and take action in response to our vision of a better world." Implicit within this vision is the need to provide tools for citizens to participate fully in the cultural and civic life of our communities. In recognition of the 40th Anniversary of the SDHC, and because democracy demands wisdom, trainers from the Project on Civic Reflection convened with SDHC staff, board members, partners, and scholars in Chamberlain in October 2011. The civic reflection model would serve as a central focus of the statewide effort to collect journey stories for the fifth book in the "South Dakota Stories" series. This 40th anniversary edition will serve as a legacy to enhance the civic and cultural life of all South Dakotans.

The editors, after participating in the conference, formulated some notion of what they might expect to receive when the call went out for essays responding to the question of "What Makes a South Dakotan?" None of us, however, fully anticipated the variety, ingeniousness, insight, and plain delightfulness of the submissions that were sent in. We expected to read many stories about family, friends, acquaintances, and iconic individuals who were considered to embody the kinds of traits that people often associate with the state . . . and we did. The humanities are especially geared to story-telling. In the words of social psychologist Jonathan Haidt, "The human mind is a story processor, not a logic processor. Everyone loves a good story; every culture bathes its children in stories." The volume you hold in your hands is replete with such stories about ordinary South Dakotans, as well as several about more noted ones, such as Laura Ingalls Wilder, George S. Mickelson, Robert Lusk, George McGovern, and Karl Mundt. Heartfelt emotions of admiration and respect, joy and heartbreak, inspiration and loss also run through the book's various depictions of environmental features, weather disasters, fires, concerts, celebrations, ball games, travels, family happenings, community gatherings, wartime, peacetime, buildings constructed, and buildings demolished.

Many of the essays bypass story-telling to directly address the question of what kinds of qualities or characteristics South Dakotans are thought to embody. The list is extensive and not internally consistent. State residents are observed to be hard-working, tenacious, generous, good-hearted, helpful, creative, patriotic, and self-reliant. The list could be considerably extended. Not surprisingly, most of these depictions are laudatory, but now and again a writer reminds us that not all South Dakotans have been exemplary in their actions. Moreover, the types of people who exhibit these traits are becoming more and more varied as time goes by. While it once may have been somewhat accurate to characterize the state's white population as being heavily German and Scandinavian in nature (while acknowledging that many other nationality groups were also present), today that notion becomes less and less relevant as the populace becomes more and more diverse. One of the essays in this book notes that this year fifty-seven languages and more than a dozen separate dialects will be represented in the Sioux Falls school district alone. Always, our culture has been enriched and strengthened by the large presence of the first Americans in our midst—the American Indians. This and all the groups that contribute to the diversity of South Dakota invite readers to reflect more deeply upon their own identity, the values that motivate them, and the aspirations that inspire them.

Obviously, reliance upon well-worn stereotypes and long-disproved generalizations about what makes a South Dakotan will not do in a book of this type. The essays contained in this volume, we believe, point the way toward a complex, diversified, and sometimes contradictory image of the state's residents. In the end, we are a people beholden to a variety of dreams, desirous of improving our own lot and that of others, and united by a democratic vision of how we as a citizenry can thrive together peaceably and fruitfully. If one of our greatest challenges lies in bridging our differences and diversity, those very factors also rank among our greatest strengths and accomplishments. No one has ever made a convincing argument that South Dakotans should all be of one stamp.

Our requirement that writers encompass their thoughts in an essay or poem of between 100 and 600 words has forced our contributors to focus their attention upon only a small piece or pieces of the larger puzzle. We have grouped the submissions into somewhat arbitrary categories; many of the submissions could just as easily have fit into other categories. There are many great stories included here about people, groups, places, events, activities, the land, history, memory, institutions, relationships, ideas, and other elements that speak to the subject at hand. Admittedly, these brief writings do not encompass everything that might be said about the state and its people. Notably sparse, for instance, are treatments of education, religion, politics, business, art, architecture, music, and literature, as well as of a number of other subjects that might occur to readers. What we do have before us, however, is a splendid array of thoughtful, colorful, and insightful vignettes that go a long way toward answering the question of what makes a South Dakotan.

In sum, we, the editors, are highly pleased by the results of our inquiry and would like to express our gratitude toward everyone who participated in the project in any way. Thanks especially to Sherry DeBoer, Ryan Woodard, Jennifer Widman, Steve Binkley, Carolyn Marshall, Stephanie Frank and the entire staff at the South Dakota Humanities Council; to the Board of Directors; to the National Endowment for the Humanities and all of the other contributors to humanities programs in the state; to all of the humanities scholars who held meetings, worked with contributors, and in other ways helped make this book possible, as well as to all of the other scholars and friends of the humanities who carry on their work every day; to the writers who sent in their poems and essays, whether they were included in the book or not; to all of the people who will read this volume; and to the entire citizenry who are a part of the subject addressed in it. A particular note of gratitude goes to the South Dakota Community Foundation, celebrating their 25th Anniversary this year. A very generous grant from them has allowed us to form a unique partnership in publishing this special edition. As we recall the past forty years of the South Dakota Humanities Council and its many achievements, we look forward to the public's continued engagement in and energetic participation in the civic culture that lies at the heart of a democratic society.

John E. Miller, Brookings and Lenora Hudson, Rapid City

PRELUDE

Hocokan: Within the Circle of Home

everything in the circle has a song
songs like fine transparent threads
spin dreams in countless galaxies
and in rainbow colored places
sing away ragged feelings
caught inside
like a river glistening, the milky way
flows with songs from those waiting
on the other side
songs of silent things
caught in the orange swirls of sunsets
in the colorful flower shadows
before the last traces of day
slip away in slivers of light
and dreams emerge in the songs again
on the iridescent wings of dragonflies
within the circle of home

Lydia Whirlwind Soldier, Rosebud

Tipi Tatanka (Buffalo Tipi), Summer Solstice, the beginning of the Sundance Season, Porcupine. By Nick Estes. Used with permission of Nick Estes.

OBSERVATIONS

Bridge north of Gettysburg on the Missouri River. By Tom Dempster. Used with permission of Tom Dempster.

_⚜_

The Cadillac Caper

We had a good laugh after reading a story in the March 27 edition of the _Wessington Springs True Dakotan_. They learned about the incident in the _Plankinton South Dakota Mail_, and now we're retelling the tale to you.

It's said that criminals often return to the scene of their crime. That was true on March 9, when the Aurora County Courthouse in Plankinton was the scene of a brazen daytime theft. Larry Unruh had parked his red Cadillac out front while he took care of some official business inside. When he left the building, the Cadillac had disappeared.

Luckily, Deputy Preston Crissey was on the scene. He sprang into action, running upstairs to the Sheriff's office to issue a stolen car bulletin and alert the Highway Patrol, then back out to patrol the streets of Plankinton and track down the culprit.

Mr. Unruh headed up to the Sheriff's office to make a report of his own. When questioned by Sheriff David Fink, Unruh reported that the vehicle was full of gas and his girlfriend's purse was inside, full of money.

"While the investigation continued, Sheriff Fink looked out the courthouse window to the north and surprisingly saw a vehicle fitting that description traveling east very slowly on Fifth Street," read the _South Dakota Mail_ report.

Unruh looked out the window. Yes, it was the missing Cadillac . . . and it was pulling back into the courthouse parking lot. The two men went into the Clerk of Courts office to get a better view from their window.

Two figures got out of the pilfered Caddy. The getaway driver was a young high school girl. Her passenger was a man with a clipboard—driver's license examiner Dale Steffen.

"According to Sheriff Fink, the young girl's parents dropped her off for her driver's test and drove away. Not knowing this, Mr. Steffen believed that was the family's vehicle, while the nervous young driver assumed it was the test vehicle."

"Mr. Unruh told Sheriff Fink, 'I'm not pressing charges!'" said the *Mail.*

We hope that the teasing has died down in Plankinton for all parties involved. Thanks to the *South Dakota Mail* and the *Wessington Springs True Dakotan* for sharing the story.

By Gayle Van Genderen of the South Dakota Mail *in Plankington*
This essay appeared on the South Dakota Magazine *website.*

Reflections from a Distance

Six of us, all travelers, just happened to be sitting at the same table for supper. Before the food arrived, we discovered that three of us were originally from South Dakota, both east and west of the river. The kicker is that we were in India.

We talked about what it means to be South Dakotan. Our eyes were damp as we reminisced about what we had learned from family, friends, and neighbors. Among those qualities were courtesy, curiosity, and an appreciation for the earth and sky. We marveled at the dazzling but sometimes understated examples of creativity and problem-solving skills that were all around us and helped shape our lives.

Growing up, most of us learned to cope with a scarcity of material things. At the same time, we were blessed with an appreciation for sunrises and sunsets, life-giving rain, birds, and the whistling of the wind. People who grow up on the land are natural environmentalists. We instinctively care about what is now called the balance between economic growth and development and quality of life.

We shook our heads a bit as we observed that, while understanding how to live with scarcity can be a survival skill, it has sometimes been turned into a badge of honor. Progress can be tough when we become overly proud of living with scarcity and give too little attention to solving the problems that cause it. We expressed some regret that polarization in our country often spills over into our state. Occasionally, we even gang up for one reason or another to short-circuit things that could be in our own long-term best interest. In this fast-changing world, our state and nation need the wisdom of the plains to help us find a clear path into an even brighter future.

Laura Ingalls Wilder, through her writings, and Harvey Dunn, in his magnificent paintings, held up a mirror to reflect the pioneering character and spirit of people who grew up on the prairie. Mount Rushmore connects us to leaders and great ideas that helped shape our democracy and set an example for nations everywhere. The emerging sculpture of Crazy Horse reminds us of our closeness to nature and the perseverance of so many others who came before us, whose names we might never know.

Back to the encounter in India. Even though we sat across a table in a desolate part of Rajasthan, we declared that each of us will always be a South Dakotan. Wherever we live, in this country or somewhere else, that's who we are. Yes, there is a Greater South Dakota that reaches far beyond our state's geographic boundaries. The seeds are planted each and every day across the nation and world.

Gary Marx, Vienna, Va.

A South Dakotan Abroad

It is my favorite part of meeting someone new. As the used-to-be stranger and I work through common areas for our acquaintance, I wait for the question. I practice saying it in my head and load anecdotes and facts for further discussion. I wait and wait, and finally it comes. "Where are you from?" the other person tosses into the air. Without hesitation and a prideful smile, I say, "South Dakota."

During the last two years, I've served with the Peace Corps in two different African nations. While being exposed to unfamiliar cultures, I've learned more about Americans as I've worked alongside volunteers from all parts of our country. Until that point, South Dakota was just a square on the map and a place I had long wanted to escape. Growing up, like many youth in our state, I had dreams of big city lights and distant oceans. South Dakota was fine, but I desired something more. As I told others about these ambitions, especially those who did leave and came back, they told me the same thing: "You'll never meet people like South Dakotans."

The Rushmore state was the backdrop for my first twenty-five years of life, except for a seven-month stint in Idaho. Eventually, though, I said goodbye and pursued a life outside the state. Through my work, I've met Americans from Hawaii to New York and from Michigan to Texas with varying backgrounds and experiences. We shared stories of home and life in our part of the United States. They were nice people from great places, but through these interactions I realized what a special breed South Dakotans are. We help another person without being asked and never let a compliment or good deed go without a "Thank You." We work hard each day and stick to our word. We offer our beds to those in need and never shoulder work onto someone else. We respect the land, and family is our highest priority. We are good people. I know that good people exist elsewhere in America, but in South Dakota, it's our way of life. The things that I value about myself—hard-work ethic, willingness to help others, and understanding of what is right—aren't qualities I possess because I am a good person. No, they are qualities I possess because I am a South Dakotan. When people ask me, "What is in South Dakota?" or "Why would anyone ever go there?" I always reply in the same way: "The People." You may not find a sprawling metropolis or endless oceans, but you'll find down-to-earth, generous people. For that reason, above all else, I am proud to be a South Dakotan.

Heather Mangan, Pierre

Four Haiku for the Land and People.

I
Towering mountains shadow
the endless prairie.
Nurturing people of strength.

II
The Old World was ours.
American land called us.
South Dakota's home.

III
Independent, yes!
We integrate dependence
to support each other.

IV
Resolute names us.
Molding the open prairie.
The hungry world waits.

Micaela E. Nelson, Mitchell

Dakota Luck

I think South Dakotans are lucky. We're lucky to live in a state like this, one that's not too small, but not too big. There is so much beauty here that the rest of the country seems to overlook. When everyone else has cut down every tree and covered up every spot of empty land with metal, we have miles and miles of fields filled with crops, green grass, thriving trees, bright flowers, and animals. Look up into the night sky, and you'll see millions of bright stars that you can't see in big cities. I think the balance of modern and natural things is perfect. In nearly every teenager's room, you'll see cell phones, iPods, and every other kind of technology they have in big cities. Schools use laptops and other technology to improve the students' learning experiences. But we still have small towns, close-knit communities, and miles of farmland. We in South Dakota have learned that modernization can be a great improvement to life, helping us with everything from cooking, to school, to work. But we haven't lost sight of the wonderful things that we are already blessed with, and we've learned to appreciate the beauty around us.

Ali VanPelt, Mitchell

Homecoming

The first time I came to South Dakota, I was on a family vacation to the Black Hills. Having been a Colorado girl originally, the Black Hills felt like home to me. We stayed in Custer and did all the touristy things in the Hills. We had never seen Mount Rushmore or Crazy Horse, the Badlands or Spearfish Canyon, the Passion Play or Sylvan Lake. As we visited the various attractions, my heart filled with pride and patriotism as I gazed at the faces of Mount Rushmore, admiration at the vision of the Crazy Horse Monument, awe at the drama and grandeur of the Badlands, and a sense of wonder and peace at the beauty of the Black Hills. While we were traveling around the area, a vision formed in our minds of moving to this place that seemed to be calling us home. In six weeks' time, we became South Dakotans, new South Dakotans. South Dakotans who were not related to anyone who lived here, a rarity we found. Not only were we not related to anyone, we didn't know anyone.

As time went on, I fell in love. In love with the drive from Belle Fourche to Spearfish, as the Hills rose up before me and the valley below offered her bounty to animals and humans alike. I fell in love with the confluence of the Belle Fourche and Redwater Rivers, as they joined behind my house, the rivers changing with the light and the seasons, never the same, yet always rushing with the musical sounds of the waters.

I fell in love with the people, their history, and their stories. Although they were sometimes a bit hesitant to accept an outsider, with time, smiles, and offers of friendship, I found the people trusting, caring, and hard working. Like the weeping willow trees we planted near the river, as time went on, I found my roots growing deep in the friendship and support of a community—a community of South Dakotans. In time, that community entrusted me with their stories and their history, the very essence of who they are. Sometimes a person is born a South Dakotan, and sometimes South Dakota calls us home.

Rochelle Silva, Belle Fourche

Welcoming and Acceptance

Normally the question of "What Makes a South Dakotan?" would invite only positive things to be said, and no doubt many will emphasize the good things about being South Dakotan. It is a more complicated question than that, however, as I do not believe there is a unique set of qualities associated with being a South Dakotan that makes us stand out among all the other states. I've found many South Dakotans to be hard-working people, regardless of income level, class, or race. People exhibit strong faith and a willingness to help others, regardless of who they are or what background they have. But while I have found that South Dakotans are welcoming, acceptance can be a different story. I have a sense that South Dakotans don't openly accept or embrace the kind of greater diversity that would make our state a better one. Many say they are welcoming, but acceptance is not always practiced. Without acceptance accompanying welcoming, there will be fewer people who can truly be defined as being South Dakotan. And that's something that we South Dakotans need to work on together as a community.

Patti Martinson, Rapid City

Grace Freeman, who transplanted to Westreville in 1997, with her friend Salem Waters after kayaking on the wild and scenic stretch of the Missouri in the rain. Used with permission of Grace Freeman.

Transplanted

My husband and I were spending a pleasant winter in Florida assisting my 90-year-old grandmother in her home while he looked for research or university jobs with his recent Ph.D. We were appalled by news stories in December of 1996 of blizzards in South Dakota and thought out loud, "Who would ever live there?"

Five months later, my husband, Harry, was called to interview in Vermillion, South Dakota, and by August, seven months pregnant with our first child we were moving into a 125-year-old farmhouse in a small community northeast of Vermillion. It's a community that still exists on maps because weathermen refer to it especially during tornado season. In 2005 there were twenty-five tornados in the area, and you would hear, "A tornado has been spotted heading southeast through Clay County and is headed toward Westreville. . . ."

A native South Dakotan explained to us that in South Dakota you don't have captivating oceans or majestic mountains, you have events—like the monarch or dragonfly migrations, the birds of prey migrations, the Flood of 2011, or the Christmas blizzard that shut everything down for three days in 2009. You have the world turn into an ice palace; you have blazing Vermillion-pink sunrises over the Missouri River; or you have waves of green when the corn is high and healthy. One day you feel close to the edge, like you can barely stand the bugs or the weather, and then some moment comes along like a night when the Milky Way appears to be pouring out of the sky and stops you in your tracks, and you feel so honored to have witnessed it. It makes you feel dignified and lucky to say, "I live in South Dakota." Southeast South Dakota isn't a hot spot for international tourists, and I'm really glad it isn't, because that might destroy these rare, beautiful beyond words moments. I don't know how many times we were kayaking, skiing, or hiking a wild and scenic stretch of the Missouri and thought, "Pinch me. It's so quiet and beautiful, and I have it all to myself!"

After we arrived in South Dakota and before I began to appreciate the landscape, I was very depressed. I found none of the progressive coffee shops, art galleries, health food co-ops, contra dances, etc., that I had had in Florida, Seattle, Wisconsin, or Cincinnati. So I decided I would take my newborn daughter, Elena, to the local nursing home and find someone to fill in the void of family and familiar activities.

First I met Clifford Johnson and then soon after his friend, Clady Lloyd. They were Norwegian bachelor farmers who had farmed in Westreville. They filled me with stories and history of my neighborhood and of homesteaders from Norway. Clifford's grandfather had built our house and the Pleasant Valley Lutheran Church. They told us that our house had always been called Grace and Harry's place, because Clifford's cousin Harry and his wife Grace lived there thirty years before us (there's some destiny for you!). There were stories of dances, horse races, and outlandish April Fool's Day tricks. Clifford said one time he and his buddy pulled farm implements onto every avenue in Meckling, blocking traffic in and out of town for half the day!

Clifford and Clady were two of the most open-minded, good-hearted, non-competitive, and good-humored folks I have ever met. I have learned so much living in Westreville. You have to be tough, have a good sense of humor, be able to see the joy in little things, and appreciate every moment that comes your way.

Grace Freeman, Vermillion

Walworth County By Christian Begeman. Used with permission of Christian Begeman.

By Tom Dempster. Used with permission of Tom Dempster.

SOUTH DAKOTA*

Producer of What's for Dinner and The Other White Meat,
Corn Idolater, Wheat Grower,
Cowboy, Indian;
Wind—leathered, tenacious, resilient,
State of Great Faces Places:

They tell me you are bigoted and I believe them,
for I have heard you and even your young
speak ugly words of racial intolerance.

And they tell me you expect hardship, believe you deserve little,
and view progress with a wary eye.

My reply is: Your teachers are underpaid
    and too many of your schools are old and leaky.
Too many children crouch in the corners of poverty.
I have seen you grieve the loss of so many bright young
minds
    gone away to make a living.

And they tell me you—you up there by Fargo, right?—are
provincial and unsophisticated
    and I answer: You betcha!
It is true that dinner is really lunch,
    that vacationing "out west" often means a Rapid City
weekend
        at the Ramkota so the kids can swim.

And having answered so, I turn once more to those who sneer at
this my state,
    and I give them back the sneer and say to them:

Come and show me another state where geese fly high above the
white–domed capitol
    in a sky so clean and so blue and so pure:
    A place where your heart wells up in your throat as you
watch
        and, for just a moment in all your humility, you are
        unable to speak.

Come and show me another state that comes from hardier stock:
    The fierce and proud Lakota warriors
        defending to the death their lands and their people;
    the pioneers burning dung in their sod houses
        to stay alive in the deep freeze of a prairie winter;
    the shack–sheltered gold miners
        existing on nothing but hope and beans.

You are adaptable as coyotes hunting jackrabbits in a wet summer,
        shriveled berries in a cinderbox fall; bantamweight
        but scrappy,
    building sinew and muscle through hard work and pluck.

Plowing, Planting, Harvesting,
Improvising, Jerry—rigging, Making Do,
Rodeoing, Powwowing, Watching Basketball on Friday
Nights,
Sticking Together,
Hunkering Down.

You are seduced and betrayed again and again by that fickle harlot
who brings you bouquets of pasque flowers
and braids of fat timpsila,
then summons the blistering winds to suck your land dry,
the howling blizzards to ice your newborn calves.

Even so, you grit your white teeth and kiss her again in the spring
because deep in your gut you love her and you will never give
up.

Pulling your cap down lower against the sunset, you will remember,
though you are small, that you are bound to greatness:
Sue the Magnificent with her five-foot skull
and twelve-inch serrated teeth;
woolly mammoths and giant bison long gone;
the massive heartbeat of He Sapa.

And like the great leaders who watch over you with granite eyes
and point the way to destiny,
you will greet the future with fortitude:
with the subtle wave of an upturned chin,
with a raised index finger on the steering wheel
as you meet a stranger on the dusty road.

*The concept and structure of this poem are based on "Chicago," the well-known poem by Carl Sandburg. The line "And having answered so, I turn once more to those who sneer at this, my state, and I give them back the sneer and say to them:" is a direct quote from Sandburg's poem with the word "state" substituted for "city."

Sandra Bacon Gaspar, Spearfish

_SV̲_

South Dakotan Likes and Dislikes

What we like most and least about South Dakota provides insight into the state's character, and our passions about these preferences provide bookends to who we are.

South Dakotans appreciate the land and environment of the state. The wide-open spaces in particular have a great appeal. These spaces, coupled with the cycles of the seasons and beautiful sunsets, nourish the South Dakota spirit. The open spaces provide the stage for numerous outdoor activities and habitat for wildlife, while the diversity of landscapes and changing weather add spice to the environment. The Black Hills in particular provide a welcome contrast to the cropland and ranchland of the rest of the state. East River South Dakotans daydream of leaving the flat lands for visits to the Black Hills and bemoan the absence of closer places with expanses of public land where they can spend time outdoors.

South Dakota is a rural state with few people relative to its size. Rurality is part of our character. The open spaces minimize traffic issues and provide opportunities for the solitude that often eludes people in other states. The slower pace of life provides a blanket of peacefulness that many appreciate. The people are friendly and have social values that are appreciated by their friends and neighbors. Many South Dakotans would not consider living anywhere else, and many out-migrants return home for retirement or so their children can be close to relatives and have opportunities to acquire South Dakota values to guide them through life.

South Dakotans generally see the state with clear vision and realize that living half way to the North Pole provides hardships and sometimes denies opportunities. The state's weather tops almost everyone's list of things to dislike. South Dakotans tend to recoil from rather than embrace winter, as our neighbors in Minnesota often do. Adapting to the chill of midwinter and the extended season of long nights sandwiched between frosts that appear too late in the spring and too early in the fall are part of

15

what makes South Dakotans who we are. Complaining about the wind, cold, snow, and abruptly changing extremes of weather provides fodder for conversation when meeting both strangers and friends.

The wide open spaces and paucity of residents limit economic and career opportunities and contribute to the low wages that are an unappreciated part of the cultural fabric of the state. Limited job opportunities, a lagging educational system, and a modicum of innovation alter everyone's life. These are often blamed on the state's political and cultural climate. Many South Dakotans associate their neighbors' conservative economic and political views with the state's slow progress, and it seems that many citizens bask in a recession mentality that is proud of hardships.

The relative isolation of South Dakota and generations of out-migration have also limited the cultural diversity of the state. Many South Dakotans crave more diversity, from having neighbors who have different ideas and cultural backgrounds, to acquiring more opportunity to experience big city entertainment. Though South Dakotans like their neighbors as individuals, they often perceive stagnation in thought, especially in small communities. This results in people being closed to new ideas, timid in the face of new opportunities, reluctant to invest in the future, and ignorant of other places and peoples, especially foreigners and international affairs.

South Dakotans live a paradox. Many of us simultaneously love the State's open space and the small population that makes virtually everyone a neighbor, while wishing for the opportunities and diversity that are common in more populated areas.

Proud of our stoicism in the face of hardship, we nevertheless grumble about those same hardships. Proud of our state, often to the point of harboring unrealistic beliefs about it, we nevertheless ask what other states have done about problems we face. Fleeing the state when we are young to find good paying jobs, we nevertheless long for the day when we can return. What an interesting bunch of people we are!

Darrell Napton, Brookings

Forces and Factors Making the Modern South Dakotan

A South Dakotan is a unique combination of history plus cultural and physical geography that has produced an individual and a society that brings to the contemporary scene an outlook that is different from those of people living in surrounding states. Most, if not all, of modern day South Dakotans can trace their personal histories from European-descended ancestors who settled and developed the Upper Midwest in the later nineteenth and early twentieth centuries. Their presence can be tracked to decisions made to occupy what was then a new territory. But it is worth remembering that there were other Americans here first. These first peoples have a somewhat divergent perspective on the historical developments that have produced today's South Dakota. Additionally, others have moved to the state who weren't represented in the region's demography until relatively recently.

The factors and forces which have made the modern South Dakotan may be summed up as follows. Historically, we are an amalgam of the choices that several previous generations made to establish themselves in first the territory and subsequently the state. These people organized the land according to their ideas of appropriate development. This was played out against a backdrop of the physical environment in which there exists a division between East and West River, as both the climate and the landforms change across the state. In addition, the Black Hills provided a special degree of history and geography.

Perhaps the most significant events that molded the philosophies and the psychologies of the state's residents in the twentieth century were the Great Depression and the Dust Bowl; the first catastrophe was human-caused, while the other was a synthesis of natural and cultural factors. People were sorely tested during the decade of the 1930s, and that period still casts a long shadow across the land. A number of both rural and urban residents left the state permanently. Remarkably, many stuck it out and were able to rebuild their lives and livelihoods in succeeding decades.

The net result of population increase, in-migration, economic development in non-traditional sectors, and periods of favorable weather conditions for agriculture has been the enhancement of the state.

The contemporary South Dakotan reflects his or her personal and family history as well as the changes that have occurred in the state's geography and economy. South Dakota's population is proud of its standing in the fabric of American life—its citizens are living in an environment of their own choosing, one which was shaped by the decisions of the past, but one that will be contoured by their collective judgments concerning the way forward into the future. While the majority culture's worldview will continue as the prevailing model for the state's community, South Dakota has become increasingly diverse from the perspective of its minorities, most of whom will develop support for the societal norms. These contributing elements include first and foremost the state's Native Americans, now about 10 percent of the population, increasing numbers of Hispanic/Latino origins, and those arriving from Eastern Europe and Sub-Saharan Africa. Many who have moved to South Dakota manifested the same motivations that brought earlier populations to Dakota Territory and, later on, the state—a chance at improving their economic status, an opportunity to live a free life, and a sincere desire to achieve the American dream in all of its wonderful outcomes.

In sum, what makes a South Dakotan is very similar to what many other people in the United States have sought to do with their lives. In our situation the essential difference has been the geographical stage upon which this human drama has taken place. South Dakota represents a physical and human landscape that is distinctive from other states because of the cultural imprint placed on the land by successive waves of people and their histories. People, place, and history are intimately associated and define what it means to be a South Dakotan.

Donald J. Berg, Brookings

_\V/_

A Commitment to Social Order

I am not a South Dakotan. I moved here from South Carolina in 1983. When I arrived, I instantly noticed a difference between the South (I am originally from Georgia but had lived in South Carolina for many years) and South Dakota. In the first week I was here, the *Sioux Falls Argus Leader* prominently featured a murder that had just occurred in the city. It treated this one murder as an important story for the entire state.

I found the treatment of this murder as a story of state-wide importance odd, since Atlanta—the capital city of Georgia—at the time was suffering about one murder every day. This comparison was my first clue that South Dakotans have a strong commitment to social order. They share and are committed to many societal values and guidelines dealing with social order.

I have not found my first impression to be wrong. I think those shared values and guidelines help explain the strong emotional responses of South Dakotans throughout the state to the 2011 killing of the young police office in Rapid City and of the prison guard in Sioux Falls.

I do not deny that bad things happen in South Dakota. There are numerous small crimes and acts of deviance. And every once in a while there are heinous crimes like rape and murder, but those seriously bad behaviors stand out because they are so exceptional. In general, South Dakotans are committed to social order.

I often represent South Dakota State University in talking to high school students visiting the campus evaluating South Dakota State University as a potential university they might attend. After talking to the students about our programs, I turn to the parents, who often accompany the students, and explain that I have never worried about the safety of my family. I did not worry about my son as he grew up in South Dakota, and now I do not worry about my grandchildren.

My brother once told me he had moved his family out of Athens, Georgia—the city in which he and I grew up—to a much smaller town because of his fear of crime. Several years ago, my wife's brother and his family visited us from their home in Alabama. They were amazed, and envious, of our lack of concern about the possibility of crime.

Social scientists often talk about "culture," what others mean when they talk about a society's "way of life." It seems to me that a core part of South Dakota culture is a strong belief in social order.

Ron G. Stover, Brookings

Used with permission of Children's Museum of South Dakota.

～ӱ～

Our Place on the Prairie

Whether they grew up on a farm or lived in town, all South Dakotans have been shaped by the land in one way or another. I'm not really the outdoors type, and, unlike most South Dakotans, I have absolutely no sense of direction. Still, I find driving through the expansive prairie to be incredibly peaceful, and wide, open spaces are where I feel the most creative. Although I have an appreciation for the varying landscapes of the world, there is nothing more beautiful than the prairie—green, golden, or brown.

Like many of my classmates, I left South Dakota for better horizons. I soon realized I couldn't really separate myself from this place. So when my family decided to create the Children's Museum of South Dakota, I knew I wanted the museum to help children discover their appreciation for the uniqueness of South Dakota.

At the beginning of the adventure, we envisioned a children's museum representative of the values of our family, of our community of Brookings, and of our special place on the prairie. We wanted to give children a sense of pride in their heritage and hope for their future as South Dakotans.

After my family and the museum board compiled our list of exhibit ideas, we gathered focus groups from the community to tell us what they'd like to see in the Children's Museum of South Dakota. Through these discussions, we discovered a list of shared values: the importance of children, family, and community; a love for learning; a strong sense of cooperation—working together and helping each other; an appreciation of the Lakota Culture; an ease with change and adaptation; a desire to make a difference in the world; a high regard for hard work and entrepreneurship; independence and self-sufficiency; a respect for nature; and an admiration for the arts. Above all, we expressed a shared commonality to create a sense of place, a sense of belonging, and an appreciation of being South Dakotan.

The board desired a place that sparked the imagination; a place that fostered a love of nature and an appreciation of diversity; a place that empowers children to make their own choices and decisions; and one that instills confidence that they can accomplish anything. Museum exhibits encourage children to develop their sense of wonder, to create, and to explore. The exhibits celebrate South Dakota's history, culture, and landscape.

Children's museums often have a grocery store, but the Children's Museum of South Dakota has a farm-to-market exhibit. Children tend tomatoes, corn, and pumpkins on the South Dakota farm next to the grocery store. Vegetables are placed on the conveyor belt and sorted into bins before being carried to the store. Some vegetables find their way to the sod house modeled after my great-uncle's prairie home.

The mini-explorers exhibit invites toddlers to explore the various landscapes native to South Dakota such as hills, rivers, and prairie. The outside beckons visitors to wander through native prairie grasses. Children maneuver through the Cloud Climber, painted with the gorgeous colors of the South Dakota skies. The museum's Cafè Coteau, with its artistic mobile of critters found in the Coteau des Prairies, introduces children to the plateau of prairie flatlands in eastern South Dakota.

I've been to many wonderful children's museums around the country, but as I played in these amazing spaces, I realized I could be anywhere—Chicago, Philadelphia, or San Diego. Visiting the Children's Museum in Brookings, children know where they are; it couldn't be anywhere else but South Dakota.

Maree Larson, Brookings

Weather, Weather, Weather

What is a South Dakotan? I'm first generation American, my father having immigrated from Norway. Our family moved from northwestern Iowa to eastern South Dakota, and this has been our family home now for over thirty years. My son is a realtor, and he continues to talk about the three most important things in real estate: location, location, location. Translated into South Dakota lingo, it becomes, "weather, weather, weather," with some creative spelling permitted, to wit, "wenther," "we there," and "whether."

"Weather" here is so unpredictable and extreme that it is hard to explain to those not in the know. Traveling on business to Singapore, I attended a local Rotary Club meeting during which the president of the club introduced me and asked me to talk about South Dakota. I stated that the reason I lived in South Dakota was because of the four distinct seasons of the year—June, July, August, and Winter! To which he replied "It's the same for us here in Singapore; only here it is hot, hotter, wet, wetter!" Weather is a South Dakota character builder.

"We there, yet?" This is the familiar question from the back seat passengers to the front, to which the standard answer is, "We're half way," no matter how much distance to travel remains. Years ago, my ten-year-old daughter, remembering past camping trips traversing the miles from Brookings to Custer State Park, spoke up at our family planning meeting asking if she could fly to Rapid City. She promised to wait at the airport for us. Geographical distance is part of the South Dakota thought pattern.

Finally, there is the word "whether," which is summarized by the choices that we make. Mitch Albom defined this as "the tension of opposites." South Dakota is a hotbed of choice—in politics, religion, culture, and society—all the time fighting against entropy, which is defined as "the natural tendency of the universe to fall apart into disorder." Consider that despite all of our encouragement and good intentions, my kids' rooms evolved eventually into a natural state of clutter. My children are now parents, and as parents they continue to fight the good fight. With regard to the tension of opposites discussed by Albom in *Tuesdays with Morrie*, when asked which side wins in the classic struggle between good and evil, Morrie responds, "Love wins, love always wins." South Dakotans choose to make choices, not leaving our future to the natural force of entropy.

Larry Fjeldos, Brookings

CHARACTERISTICS

Tatanka (Bull Buffalo), Custer State Park. By Nick Estes. Used with permission of Nick Estes.

୬୧

To Be a South Dakotan

To be a South Dakotan, one must know where "here" is. To be a South Dakotan, one must know that "here" is beyond the long lines of wire along the state's many roads. One must know that "here" is corn rows that shuffle vertically like book pages; shelter belts; hayfields with great, green round bales; expanses of black cattle grazing; country churches standing against rolling clouds in the blue distances; sunlit summer lake shores; and flocks of blackbirds bobbing over ripe late summer fields.

To be a South Dakotan is to also know the stress of high interest payments for mammoth high tech farm equipment; to know the impulse to look to the sky, The Great Above, for the drops of rain which do not always fall when needed; and to be jolted by two lumps over a bridge above a creek.

To be a South Dakotan is also to have some sense of the deeper history of this place—to be able to imagine the aboriginal landscapes, the thriving villages, and the slow-moving brown masses of their relatives, the buffalo.

To be a South Dakotan is also to know of the past and present battlefields, to feel the need for reconciliation between peoples, and to understand what native peoples have always known about where "here" is and understand that "here" is both a physical place and the spirit within and above that place.

Doug Cockrell, Sioux Falls

Photo by Christian Begeman. Used with permission of Christian Begeman

Your Heart Will Tell You So

It seems to me, you get to say yourself if you're a South Dakotan. Do you call the prairie buttes your home, the plum draws or the gumbo, the Badlands or the flatlands, the glacial lakes or prairie potholes, Black Hills, mountain meadows, rolling grasslands, reservations, bluffs or breaks or lowlands of the Mighty Mo or many river country? Do you call a little town your home, a mansion or a studio apartment, a ranch house in the cottonwoods, a cabin in the aspen and the pines, a busy city near the borderlands or in another state or on another continent? You call yourself a farmer or an artist or a teacher, a parent or an elder or a Jack or Jill of all that may intrigue you, and you know it doesn't matter where you live or who you are or what you do—it's how you resonate.

You say you left a long, long time ago and now you live far away, but some of who you are comes back again, again in reverie to catch the summer wind and evening light and then the crickets and the fireflies and find some comfort deep within your dear familiar patch of starry sky? You say you first arrived from otherwhere to take a job in this far unknown place and never gave a thought to really living here in South Dakota 'til it happened—driving into town you recognized these people as your own and—still amazing as it seems—you somehow knew that you had found your home?

You say you and your sister both were born four blocks away and left and lived around and came back many years ago and now you've lived here almost all your lives—best friends and confidants and neighbors in this little town of friends and confidants and neighbors—every spring you decorate the graves of generations—greats and great-greats, grands and mom and child—and you feel a long and deep and wide belonging with these people and this place? You say you recognize your neighbors as your kin—the very few in this wide world who'd ever care to claim themselves to South Dakota sturdy, stubborn, close and open, mostly straight and true, familiar, dear and often maddening family? Perhaps you are a South Dakotan—fewer than the needles on a Ponderosa Pine. You'll know if you belong to this rare breed—your heart will tell you so.

Cindy Kirkeby, Vermillion

You Wanna Be a South Dakotan, Do Ya?

People are increasingly realizing that South Dakota is a great place to live. Some people move to South Dakota for the fishing, the hunting, or the boating on our four great lakes that run from

Yankton clear to North Dakota. Others come because of the beauty of the Black Hills. Many are drawn to the economic opportunities that followed I-90 and I-29 into the state. The new residents invariably compliment South Dakota for its friendly people. Their friendliness makes every newcomer want to become a South Dakotan—a real South Dakotan. If you are one of them who is hankerin' to qualify, complete the following application to see if you make the gate cut.

Help a neighbor in need
South Dakotans are helpful folk. If we drive down a country road or an isolated stretch of highway and come across a stranded driver, we stop. "Need any help?" Every South Dakotan has helped at least one elderly lady change a tire. Many a farmer or self-trained mechanic has rolled up his sleeves and stuck his head under the hood. Stop in any small-town cafe and you can hear a story of someone who was befallen by a calamity. While the man was recuperating in a hospital, his neighbors combined his 640 acres of wheat, or daily milked his 50 dairy cows, or put up 320 acres of hay. That is what we do here in South Dakota.

☐ If you have helped a neighbor, check the box and continue.

Make your handshake good
South Dakotans don't have anything against lawyers (well, we try not to), but we don't use lawyers much to make agreements between ourselves. A South Dakotan's handshake is good. Million-dollar ranches are often bought and sold on a handshake. Two hundred head of cattle are put out on lease on a handshake. If a South Dakotan closes a deal with a handshake, that deal is iron clad.

☐ If your handshake is good as a lawyer's contract, check the box and continue.

Be honest
South Dakotans are an honest lot. One story makes the point. Back in 1910, Jake Olson, an old bachelor, walked three miles from his homestead into Interior. Jake bought a sack of groceries

from Johnson's General Store and then walked back to his soddy. When he got home, Olson looked over his itemized bill and the change he had gotten back from three dollars. Louie Johnson had made an error, giving back a nickel too much. Jake turned right around and walked the three miles back to town and gave Louie Johnson the overpaid nickel. Louie was pleased but surprised, "That is quite the effort for one nickel," Louie remarked. "Can't let dishonesty take root down here along White River," Jake replied. "If we do, it will come on like weeds."

☐ If you are honest, check the box and continue.

Be a good neighbor

South Dakotans are good neighbors. We are respectful of our neighbor's rights and lifestyle. We recently had a new neighbor, one who came from North Dakota with his oil royalty check. He bought the house just to our west. Only one problem: His dog did not understand what it meant to be a good South Dakotan. Every morning, the dog went into our backyard and left his calling card. Seeing this, the neighbor came over and apologized. He immediately had a contractor build an attractive fence to keep the dog out of our yard, demonstrating that he knew what it took to be a good South Dakotan.

☐ If you have been a good neighbor, check the box and continue.

Stewards of the land

South Dakotans understand that their ownership of ag land is temporary. The land will still be there after the present owner is long gone. Realizing that, South Dakotans, especially those whose roots run deep, take care of their land. We don't overgraze our pastures. We do no-till farming. But you don't have to own a 10,000-acre ranch to be a good steward of the land. You can be a good steward of your .3 acre lot and the house that sits on it. You can be a good steward to your house or the apartment you rent. Whatever you own or are responsible for that is part of the landscape should appeal to a passerby's eye and enhance South Dakota's beauty.

☐ If you are a good steward of your holdings, check this box and continue.

Be a villager

South Dakotans know that it takes a village to raise a child. Fred knows this. You see, when Fred was a child, his parents were dirt-poor. They were so poor that they could not afford to feed their child, much less clothe him. Seeing that, a neighbor couple said, "Would you like us to take Fred in until you get back on your feet?" It was the beginning of the dirty thirties drought followed by the Great Depression. Fred's parents lost what little land they had to taxes. Their hand-dug well went dry. Their garden withered. The family never got back on their feet. The neighbor family raised Fred, giving him not only a home, but love. Years later, Fred made a 50-mile, round trip drive twice a week to the nursing home in New Underwood to see and comfort his mother the woman who reared him.

☐ If you occasionally shoulder the obligations of a villager, check the box and continue.

Don't sell out

Tried and true South Dakotans resist the temptation to sell out for the almighty dollar. A decade ago a developer from Minneapolis came to South Dakota intent on promoting ranchettes in Red Canyon, a particularly beautiful, picturesque area of the Southern Black Hills. His intentions offended Jesse Sunstrom. Jesse set out to stop the developer from ruining Red Canyon, and she did. The development never got off the ground. South Dakotans understand that if we sell our wild and beautiful and scenic areas, where do we get more?

☐ If you promise not to sell out for the almighty dollar, check the box and continue.

Leave it better than you found it

South Dakotans live their lives such that when our day of reckoning comes, we will leave more behind than we took. South Dakotans take pride in contributing to those things that improve the quality of life for those who come later. Sometimes it is the little things. As you drive the byways of South Dakota, you are apt to see couples walking in the early morning or late evening. Look close, and chances are you'll notice that they are carrying a plastic sack. Why the plastic sack? They fill it with every beer bottle, aluminum can, and paper cup they find in the road ditch. At the end of their walk, they leave that particular South Dakota byway prettier than they found it.

☐ If you can intentionally do things to leave South Dakota better than you found it, check the box.

If you have checked all of the boxes, welcome to South Dakota, pardner.

Philip Hall, Spearfish

South Dakota Pensées

Some thoughts and notes on what makes a South Dakotan, from a non-native, long-time resident who chose to retire in South Dakota.

A South Dakotan is someone who:
Appreciates a crystal clear night sky that allows you to see every star.
Enjoys watching thunderstorms build and perform over a seemingly endless prairie.
Rides a bicycle the length of the Mickelson trail and enjoys the uphills as much as the down.
Sees a mountain lion near the Missouri River below Vermillion.
Has deer come down to the hot tub on the back deck in Deadwood.
Watches a state football championship indoors at the DakotaDome.

31

Survives a tornado south of Sioux Falls and a forest fire in Deadwood.
Remembers using counter checks in a café in Faith.
Visited a Minute Man II missile silo and toured Ellsworth Air Force Base.
Did the Volksmarch to the arm of Crazy Horse.
Raises three daughters to be successful, accomplished women who all felt the need to leave the state to prosper.
Discovered the great food at most sales barn cafes.
Has flown in a light plane to every corner of the state.
Has been caught in a cattle drive on the highway near Bison and has been stared down by a buffalo on the Custer game loop.
Climbed to the top of the heads at Mount Rushmore and rode to the bottom of the open cut in Lead.
Believes that 20-mile-an-hour winds are a mild breeze.
Gone crazy looking for a corner to pee in in a round barn.
Skipped through the rattlesnakes around the Fort Randall Chapel.
Seen Deadwood evolve from Wild Bill and Calamity Jane to casinos and buffets.
Gone for a morning run in two states while staying in Lemmon to visit the Petrified Wood Park.
Read good books by Kathleen Norris, Jerry Wilson, Tom Kilian.
Been to Sturgis for the Rally, Deadwood for Mardi Gras, Sioux Falls for the Empire Mall.
Notices the differences between East River and West River and wonders how they can ever work together and realizes that they do.
Admires the pride and joy that people take in their small-town hometowns.
Knows that the one and only Mitchell Corn Palace truly is unique and worth visiting.
Realizes that "fly over country" is really a compliment.
Discovers that there is an incredible amount of talent, knowledge, and expertise scattered around the state. This is generally accompanied by passion and a desire to share with others.

Jim Wilson, Vermillion

What Defines Us as South Dakotans

We are strong – Let me explain:
Steadfast – in living our checkerboard lives with miles between,
yet never far when a need arises
Tough – not as mean, but as pliant to weather and circum-
stances
Revitalize – following the peaks and valleys of our economy
Optimistic – next year will be better—the calf crop, the planted
seed, the weather
Naïve – in our simplicity, perhaps, but truthful and savvy of
happenings in the world
Grateful – for this sacred state, which our Native American
brothers and sisters have always treasured

Lois K. Howe, Rapid City

The Many Sides of a South Dakotan

South Dakotans are weathered, resilient, proud, and
stubbornly in love with the dirt beneath their feet. South Dakotans
are friendly, optimistic, have a can-do attitude, and will give their
last dollar to a neighbor they think needs it more than they do.
South Dakotans have a talking relationship with God, a thankful
heart for a drop of rain, and the undying belief that next year will
be better than the last. South Dakotans will wave hello to the man
across the street, vote for the man across the river, and send their
sons across the world to die for the freedom to do so.

How does a South Dakotan become all those things? By
surviving blizzards in January, riding in rodeos in July, outliving
five-year droughts, greeting neighbors on Main Street, cheering

for grandchildren on Friday night, and thanking God on Sunday. By helping a brother brand cattle, proudly displaying the purple ribbon won at the County Fair, and flying the red, white and blue flag of our nation.

A South Dakotan cries unabashed tears when a friend is diagnosed with cancer or loses a house in a flood or when hail pounds his crop to smithereens, but a South Dakotan survives with humility when the same thing happens to her. South Dakotans are rock solid in their beliefs and respect those who don't always agree with them. South Dakotans have respect for truth and are faithful to those they love. South Dakota's motto "Under God the People Rule" is embedded on their flag and in their heart.

That's what I think makes a South Dakotan.

Betty Downs, Black Hawk

Ninety-One Years of Thankfulness

After ninety-one years of living, I owe many attributes to my native state. As a stock-dealer's daughter growing up on a farm north of Artesian, I had no idea how many of my prairie experiences would influence my life-long values. Having been a grade-school girl during the Great Depression, I shall never forget the optimistic outlook on everyday living that my parents, Leo and Bessie Rowan, exhibited. Evenings, the hired men and we would sit on the grass, which was kept green by water from a wooden water tank, which Dad filled at another well two miles away. We couldn't run a hose from the home water tank to the lawn, as the cattle needed all the water that artesian well produced. These evening conversations were not about the 100-degree temperatures of the day, the withering grass, the anthrax devastation, or the grasshoppers clinging to the fence posts. They were light-hearted jokes or plans for the future. Every summer for about five years, Mr. Smith, a hobo, lived in our barn loft. His tales of travel in box cars across the continent enthralled us during these evening gatherings and inspired me to learn about the world away from Artesian.

During my early years, the Rowan Brothers' homestead two miles away became my home whenever my mother was ill. Evenings, we would sit on the back porch, gazing over the rolling prairie, watching the sheep bedding down and the outline of another farm in the distance. There never was arguing among the five brothers and their sister, as we listened to the news of the day or to people's reminiscences. They taught me to listen to others and to respect other peoples' opinions. I never heard a cross word between the siblings, but there was an unwritten family rule that politics and religion would not be discussed.

During the Great Depression, the Glenview Congregational Church, five miles north of Fedora, became my social life. In our flour-sack dresses and hand me downs, a group of us ten- to fourteen-year-olds learned to play the harmonica. Then, when we entered high school, Mr. Best formed an orchestra. In the summer, our group swam together and played volleyball; in the winter, we enjoyed playing Gossip, Spin-the-Bottle, and Post Office inside and skating outside. Thus, I learned how to communicate with my cohorts, to be happy with inexpensive pleasures, and to appreciate whatever I possessed. Although my folks did not participate in the WPA (Works Progress Administration), they taught me a lesson that served me well in post-World War II Germany. In the 30s, neighbors who received grapefruit and other supplies from the WPA shared with our family. My mother taught me to enjoy these special treats, but to be discrete about receiving them. When I moved to Germany in 1946 to be with my husband, George, we left meat on the pork chops or on the ham bone so that our servants could have enough food not only for themselves but tidbits to take home to their families. No foodstuffs were ever thrown in the trash; I knew that men and women were scrounging in every garbage can for any particle of food or cigarette that they could garner. South Dakota is a state where neighbors share and look out for each other. Even though I lived in many different states and overseas with my Army family, I learned one truth: the South Dakota values I absorbed growing up traveled along with me.

Eleanore R. Moe, Rapid City

Yielding

It happened just the other day. My car and three others reached the four-way-stop intersection at the same time. Our polite, expectant smiles to each other only resulted in the driver to my right shrugging his hands off the steering wheel with a questioning gesture of, "Who is going to go first?" After more nodding and you-go-first hand-waving, the woman across from me ventured into the intersection. Now I was free to drive on to my meeting, where, after the hostess announced, "Breakfast is ready, please help yourselves," at least five minutes passed before she herself finally began the progression through the generously supplied breakfast table.

Yielding. We South Dakotans do it well. We are more comfortable with deferring to others than with being first. It is not that we don't like being first. We can be hard-driving and competitive to get the most corn harvested so that we can be first to the grain elevator. Our young people dutifully practice and hone their skills to earn first places. It is just that we celebrate inwardly. On the outside, we acknowledge our accomplishments with modest smiles. Too much boasting or bragging is a dead giveaway that you are not a born and bred South Dakotan.

Perhaps our frequent inhospitable and extreme weather has contributed to our internal natures. What does one do about below freezing temperatures, life-threatening wind chills, mountains of snow, too much rain, unrelenting wind, or drought? If we fussed, stomped our feet, got mad about it, what good would it do? Weather has its own way. Better to teach yourself to say, "It's not that bad."

Yes, we South Dakotans are good at yielding. In fact, the yield from our crops, the land, and our farmers is something to brag about, that is, if we would brag. Even though it is true that South Dakota has for decades had low hourly wages compared to the national average, and even though our teacher salaries are the lowest in the nation, you would never know it considering how hard South Dakotans work. One would think we were all being paid top dollar by the reliable, conscientious, high-quality, steady labor that is produced in this state every day.

Native Americans in South Dakota seem to embody a certain aspect of what I am referring to as yielding. It's not that they did not bravely defend the land they inhabited. Today, unfortunately, four of the ten poorest counties in the United States are associated with our very own Indian Reservations. Perhaps we are waiting, maybe too patiently, for a Rosa Parks, a bus boycott, or the dream to be proclaimed from the (Black Hills) mountain top.

I hope all this yielding talk is not picturing us South Dakotans in a bad light, because yielding can be a very good thing. It is a necessary skill of life.

Life can be hard, the weather uncooperative, relationships strained, people we love dearly die too soon. Life too often turns out differently than we thought it would, so I am thankful for my South Dakota ancestors who taught me the valuable skill of yielding. We South Dakotans can relinquish our needs, wants, or expectations. It is modest recognition that in the end, do all that we might, we must yield the palm to Wakan Tanka—The Great Mystery, The Great Spirit.

My South Dakota grandmother responded to her doctor's diagnosis of terminal cancer with equanimity and the gentle words, "I always wondered how I was going to die." She could yield, knowing she had worked hard, given selflessly to her family and community, enjoyed the simple things of life . . . that she had "a good life" here in South Dakota.

Colleen A. Natalie-Lees, Aberdeen

Survival

After milking chores,
The hired man was the first to notice it.
Carrying the buckets from the barn,
He heard it bearing down across the fields,
Grinding its dizzy way directly toward him.

He dropped the buckets and ran to the root cellar,
Pulling the door shut behind him,
Staggering down the steep, crooked steps
Into the musty darkness.
Outside, the tornado, mulching
Buildings and trees,
Tossing tools, boards, machinery
Like a demented, furious giant.

Then . . . silence.
No one else was home.
He waited, trapped.
A fallen tree had blocked the door.

The farm of four generations' growth
Lay twisted and shattered.
The sturdy barn—gone.
The animals—scattered, wounded, dead.
The machine shed—vanished, but
Leaving two bicycles
Standing upright, untouched
On the naked foundation.

A tractor inside the granary was rotated 90 degrees,
Like a child's plaything,
Nose now pressed immovable against a wall.
A green wagon from the west farmyard
Traveled, somehow,
To a field east of the buildings.

Later, someone would notice the green paint-scrape
On the chimney of the two-story house.

Mysteriously, the house itself was intact,
Save for a porch wrenched from the wall,
And the aged chicken coop merely sagged
Slightly more than usual, exhausted by the ordeal.

In hours—no, minutes even—
The farm gradually began to breathe again.
In disbelief, the family returned.
The hired man was released to a scene of devastation.
Concerned neighbors, even complete strangers,
Began to appear in the yard,
Began to sort through the rubble,
To clear away broken branches,
Scraps of boards, twisted wads of metal.
They searched the fields and brought back offerings
Of tools, and parts, and anything that still looked useful,
Retrieving pieces to put a farm back together.

Some would return day after day,
Week after week,
Until the farm resembled
What they had remembered.
But on that first day,
With nothing the same as it had been,
The wife began to wash her windows.

Sharon Olbertson, Beresford

Courtesy of SDSU Archives & Special Collections, Hilton M. Briggs Library, South Dakota State University, Brookings, S.D.

_⊻_

Next Year I'm Gonna

What makes a South Dakotan? Perseverance, hard work, self-sufficiency, and faith in a loving and merciful God. "Next year I'm gonna . . . ." When we were first married in the '70s, my husband would laugh at me when I prefaced each new garden strategy with the words "Next year I'm gonna . . . ." When he stopped by me working in my garden, he always called me a true South Dakota Farmer when I said, "Next year I'm gonna . . . ." After all, he was a town boy from Iowa, where it rained and all you had to do was fling some garden seeds out the back door and they would produce bushel baskets full of food. The basket would pop out of the dirt already filled with vegetables. I grew up near Iroquois, where my optimistic, hard-working father would look longingly at the cloud-filled sky, knowing that there wouldn't be any rain, even when he had hay down. As a young married woman, I would day dream about next year's abundant vegetable garden while trying to feed four ever-hungry sons and several other children that I took care of, and then change my menu to reflect whatever had actually grown. I became a master at making lemonade out of lemons when they were plentiful, although it was more likely to be deviled eggs at a church potluck. My, how those hens could lay! We once went to a reunion in Wisconsin, and there on the table were deviled eggs. My sons accused me of bringing them all the way from South Dakota just so I could get rid of a few more dozen of those prolific eggs. I am so glad that my parents taught me perseverance, hard work, self-sufficiency, and faith in a loving and merciful God. Ya know, next year I'm gonna . . . .

Marilyn Mendenhall, Huron

A Debt

Twenty-one years young and free, I puttered out of Sioux Falls with a rust-colored Horizon—the car, not the romantic intersection of sky and earth—intent on filling in some of the terra incognita in my brain's map of my home state. I'd lived in Europe a year, and the Europeans had taught me to be more fascinated by the mysterious land of Dakota.

My ignorance of my home and its people, previously tolerable, now ached like the open sores of Hugh Glass. To resolve this, I would auto-trek around the state, penniless though I was.

The car was something of an inheritance from my gramps, a first generation German-American who had welded sheet metal in nuclear silos decades earlier. It had been his fishing car and still smelled that way, but my faith in it was complete. Faith, of course, always lets you down, so it can be reborn more seriously. The car died on a back road twenty miles west of Pierre, and the next village was at least that far ahead. It looked like I was in for a lousy afternoon.

Sunburn, exhaustion, and dehydration were the fears I wasn't even considering, and hope of fixing a car is generally out of the question for bookworms. My frontal lobe was fretting more on: What did the breakdown mean to the trek? and What dangerous people inhabited the West River wilderness around me?

I knew I was in or near Indian lands. As a wasicu, like it or not, I was a born representative of many histories with ugly parts. I came in peace, but who could tell? And who was I to come at all? That was the side of the romantic that my pals back in Europe, and often back East River, didn't quite get.

I hadn't walked a hundred feet before a pickup came along. Optimism kept me from hiding in the ditch. The driver had a hat and dark glasses (for the merciless sun—I had neither) and could have passed for a cowboy, an Indian, or both. He also had a mustache. A lot of West River guys have mustaches—a matter of style, or machismo, or maybe just something to twitch when they clue an East River boy like me in on the elementary distinction between, say, farmers and ranchers.

He asked about the trouble with the car, and I gave a verbal shrug. "Well, let's see," he said with a mustache-twitch.

The whole thing took less than five minutes. He was under the little car—no mean feat for the big guy he was—then slowly, gracefully, back into his pickup, digging for some crucial tool. He came out and showed me a Band-Aid, then slid back under the car. "Try it," he called, and I did. The dead Horizon re-awoke with the strongest growl it could give. "Just had to tape a wire," the man said, punctuating with another mustache-twitch. "You should be good to get to a mechanic."

Clumsily I thanked him. Gratitude had humbled me so, and I said I wished I could do something in return, though, of course, there was nothing. He became almost bashful, good gentleman that he was, and requested only that I lend a Band-Aid to somebody else someday, if ever the need should arise.

Jay Bethke, Sioux Falls

By Tom Dempster. Used with permission of Tom Dempster.

"Mni Sose (Missouri River), Big Bend Dam, Lower Brule. By Nick Estes. Used with permission of Nick Estes.

Dreaming South Dakota

a late February snow is falling
wet and sticking to the window
and I am peering out
of the screen
breathing in the crispness
the chill on my face
awaking me from a dream

I've been dreaming South Dakota
from way down in my soul
and it is passion gushing
through my heart the way the river flows

it winds its way across north to south
muddy churning currents
underneath placid waves
flowing gently into eddies at the waters edge
"quite the metaphor" I say
funny how the picture is the same
looking up from beneath the waves
at the sky so vast and serene
who could guess from either angle
the multifarious action
taking place in between

I've been dreaming South Dakota
from way down in my soul
and it is passion gushing
through my heart the way the river flows

my eyes are closed against the chill reaching in
I breath in just as a gust swirls
white against the screen
I can feel the flakes on my skin
stinging frosty freckles on my cheeks
and it takes all I can muster
to keep from crying
that this river is my home
its all I ever knew

I've been dreaming South Dakota
from way down in my soul
and it is passion gushing
through my heart the way the river flows

It was I who was submerged
pulled in by the murky undertow
and now I am surfacing
to plant my feet solid
on the shores of this valley
I've been made strong by dark currents
life turning events
as extreme as our seasons
and the river that has claimed so many
is also the water that heals and restores
just look at me now

I've been dreaming South Dakota
from way down in my soul
and it is passion gushing
through my heart the way the river flows

I am breathing and seeing
that what I have been told
is no longer what people say out loud
I can speak Mni Sose
and almost everyone knows
it is an older name for the Missouri

before the dams
before the towns and
before the fenced off boundaries

I've been dreaming South Dakota
from way down in my soul
and it is passion gushing
through my heart the way the river flows

and in this late February snow
that is falling and sticking
like ill informed ideas
that get put down as history
I know the river is freezing over
as the temperature drops
and come morning
everything will be covered and slick
I will awake again ready
ready this time
to cry out the words
alive on my tongue
Mni Sose you are my home
and it is I, I am South Dakota
born on these banks
made visible by truth

I've been dreaming South Dakota
from way down in my soul
and it is passion gushing
through my heart the way the river flows

Mabel Picotte, Chamberlain

Photo Courtesy of the State Archives of the South Dakota State Historical Society

Saving the Bank

Upon my grandmother's death in 1972, the local banker told my father, Albert Postulka, that his mother/my grandmother, Josephine Pistulka, had entered the Burke Bank on the very day it was to close during the Depression and purchased the neighboring farm to hers for a total of $2,100. This saved the bank from closing. Grandma was a very frugal woman and believed in the security of investing in the land, a trait that which would be passed on to future generations.

Judy Wika, Watertown

✿

Sparkling Country Gems

For some reason, unbeknownst to man, the darndest things happen in cold, blizzardy weather. And in South Dakota we have come to expect the unexpected. For example, sometimes cows calve when you least expect it, and then you look back at the calendar and say, "Oh, ya, that's when the bull got out." Sound familiar? Of course it does. Even the best managed operation has the unexpected happen, and when it does, the oft familiar S.O.C. (Save Our Calf) goes into operation.

Within minutes of a farmer finding a half-frozen bundle, the farm house becomes a safe haven emergency ward. The presiding nurse (alias country gal) spreads some blankets, warms the colostrum, finds the feeding tube, and administers her life support, loving care. And with patient efforts, many prayers, and a little time, Voile! She accomplishes a miracle—another bovine saved for the pasture.

Is it any wonder then, that I call the country woman a sparkling gem? If you think about it, the country matron's life-saving efforts involve a great deal of hard work and a tremendous cleanup effort. Yes, she saved the calf, but with bringing it back to life, she also precipitated nature to kick back into action. And you all know what I'm talking about? Right! Where there's life, there is also do-do—all over the place. As one country gal related to me about a calf left in her entryway overnight, "Whew! My house smelled just like a cow barn." But wasn't she a jewel to accomplish such a wonderful life-saving feat? Hmmm? And that thought brings to mind some other precious, life-saving moments.

Whoever invented the snow blower was a genius. It must have been a country person, and I am so thankful to have such an apparatus on our farm. Some years, we hardly use it, but with this past year's abundant snowfall, we would have been in a world of hurt without it. And that reminds me of the year that the snow blower proved its worth, and why we wouldn't be without one. As I recall, the snow began falling late one afternoon and soon turned into a severe raging blizzard that lasted for several days. At one point, conditions became so hazardous that even the main roads were blocked and impassable. And then, as luck would have it, a young couple with a new infant found themselves in a dire predicament. Their little one required a special formula, and their supply was running low, and they had no way to get to town. Never fear, the local farmers were here. Upon hearing of the dire situation, the local farmers with their trusty snow-blowing machines opened the roads and saved the day. What gems!

So now you have an inkling as to why I contend that South Dakotans are sparkling gems. The daily friction of trying to keep equipment working and livestock fed besides keeping the home fires burning during a cold South Dakota winter makes us sparkling country gems and hardy folk. If truth be told, I think South Dakotans are downright priceless!

Jane Green, Clark

My Dreamscapes

At the age of six, I began to lucid dream, meaning that I am sometimes conscious of dreaming. Over the years, I gain greater control over objects and occurrences in my dreams. I cannot make desired things simply appear before me, but I develop tricks for manipulating my dream world. If I am running from a menacing figure, I can say to myself, "When you turn that corner, there will be a door. You can lock it behind you and get away." And then it happens just as I say.

Lucid dreaming also brings pleasure—opportunities to appreciate the brain's creative expansiveness. It may be that dreamscapes are not entirely my own doing, that I encounter actual beings or other worlds there. But I want to take some credit for the creation of these intricate spaces. I once found myself walking through a university courtyard with ornate metalwork gates. There were trees all about and a dancing summer breeze.

My feet were bare. I wore a white nightgown. Becoming suddenly conscious of dreaming I reminded myself not to care that I was in public and barely dressed—that I should look around, take in the details. I looked down and saw the quivering shadows of branches and shimmering sunlight on my feet. I felt joy and amazement. In another dream, I walked wakeful and completely alone down Shop Street through the city of Galway in Ireland. I had not been there in the waking world for ten years. The night was still. I looked down at each cobble stone unevenly worn, at the glossy and colorfully painted pub fronts, the shop windows, and took in thousands of details greedily, like I would breathe in the sweetest sweet grass smoke. I was so grateful for that trip back to Galway, across time and space, to have that beautiful city to myself for a few moments.

I have lived and traveled in many places since leaving Flandreau, South Dakota, as a teenager. Yet the tree-dotted, big sky, river-run topography of eastern South Dakota continues to colonize my dreamscape. When I lived on Java, I once dreamed of walking through a dense, lush forest—a landscape as different from the northern plains as is any place on the planet. Suddenly the *hutan*[1], teeming with birds and palm-sized spiders atop artful webs, opened to a lively, shop-filled, 1970s Flandreau Main Street. As a child, I ran errands on my bike for my grandmother there. Looking to spend the pocket money she gave me, I poked around shops, sometimes for hours, followed by shop owners who suspected an Indian child might steal. After 9/11, in one night's dream I found myself walking through a café in Baghdad. To my horror, I wore a short dress, tight and made of an American flag! Fear turned to confusion. Crowding the tables on the café patio were big, blonde people, the German-descended types that populate the town of my childhood. The sky arching over our heads was vast and blue with big balls of white clouds. Surrounding us as far as I could see were golden fields.

I cannot exorcise the plains and main streets of eastern South Dakota from the places in which I come closest to being God, where I cultivate magical powers. I am Dorothy Gale's inverse image. Magical shoes and her desire for the plains of the waking world pulled her back from the Emerald City of her dreamscape. This place is formative. Unaided by sparkly shoes, it pulls me back from the Emerald Cities of my waking world. In my next dream, I may conjure red shoes to transport me elsewhere when the South Dakota plains rise before me like a great gold moon.

Kim Tall Bear, Berkeley, Calif.

[1]"forest" in Indonesian language.

Speaking South Dakotan

To be counted as a certified South Dakotan, you have to speak the language. Sounds easy if it were simply a matter of pronunciation or timbre or tone, but it's not. For the newcomer, unfortunately, it's much more subtle than that. You almost have to have grown up in South Dakota, so as to be inculcated from an early age with all the subtleties of the language.

I say language, but language is only the tip of the iceberg. Think of a play. Think of timing, and eyes averted, and far off stares. Think of people interrupting each other, and not really listening, and talking at the same time, and repeating things over and over. Talking South Dakotan is a theatrical exercise of the highest order. It wouldn't play very well on Broadway, because it's a method of communication which circumnavigates high above the narrow confines of Broadway.

South Dakota people don't talk to each other just to exchange information. If they merely wanted to communicate, they'd resort to phone or e-mail. Face-to-face conversation among people from South Dakota is similar to sending a satellite into orbit. Each speaker orbits around the person they're speaking to. This orbit is nothing but a fact-finding mission. South Dakota people are planets unto themselves. They each have their own atmospheres, in other words, with varying degrees of penetrability and impenetrability.

It's something that you have to have grown up speaking. You overheard it in the womb, then you eavesdropped your way through life. South Dakotans, by the way, are master eavesdroppers. Go in any café at noontime and witness for yourself the number of people listening in on several conversations at once, while all the while conducting their own conversation with the person sitting right next to them. It's a marvel to behold, really, and a miracle of multi-listening besides. Even the hard of hearing are not immune from this ability innate to people from South Dakota. It must be something in the stirrup, anvil, or hammer— and their various interconnections to the brain—but these considerations, no matter how interesting and deserving of further exploration, are beyond the scope of this piece.

South Dakotans have given themselves a further advantage, simply by passing down through all their succeeding generations the distinct ability to speak in code. Certainly the most famous example of this is the newsman Tom Brokaw. During his days as a news anchor in New York, Brokaw, while seemingly speaking of a deadlock in Congress, or of a human interest story where the human, against all odds, overcomes the barrier, would also at the same time be giving out detailed information concerning his dinner the night before in a swanky restaurant where he was on a first name basis with every one of the servers. You could find out what kind of fish he had—red snapper or salmon or walleye—just by listening to his news broadcast, but you had to be from South Dakota to pick out the subtleties. Otherwise, like everyone else in America, you were just listening to what he was saying. Unable to read between the lines, you were at the mercy of some news gatherer with no connections whatsoever to South Dakota. Oh, maybe he had an aunt who married a man from Winner, but the attachment was too dissipated by the time he fed the newsworthy stuff to Tom, who took it all with a wink and a grain of salt. The impartiality of tenor in Tom's tomes was actually what speaking South Dakotan is all about. I rest my case and bite my tongue. I'm not a native.

Chuck Holmes

_\(\)_

The Guyshed: A South Dakota Institution

Since South Dakota's earliest days there has been The Guyshed. It used to be painted red, filled with cattle, and provided the cover of appearing work-related. As South Dakota became less agrarian, the modern South Dakota guy had to find some way and place to bond—outside of the confines of a well-cleaned home. Claiming to need a barn and wanting three token cows probably wasn't going to cut it for the average South Dakota guy on a half-acre. He had to be innovative.

He needed to educate on the role of the guyshed as the modern monastery. It is a place where guys go to think, to pray, to ponder the great questions of the day. As guyshed dwellers can attest to, the guyshed dialogue is very cerebral. It may range from the meaning of life, touch on quantum physics, and rest at whether the Twins really have five good arms in the rotation this season.

On the half section where we live there are twenty-seven clearly discernible guysheds, and a couple of lesser temples (garages pretending to be guysheds). In fact, more properties HAVE guysheds than don't.

In South Dakota, getting the guyshed is pretty much a prereq-uisite for getting your mancard punched. It's sort of a shedmitzvah.

Guysheds come in many functional designs. Some are equipped with tools and power saws, but those remain optional. The problem with loading up on Black and Decker is that somebody up at the house is going to expect the guy to use his time in the shed building something. These chores would be fine if they were limited to that part of February between the Super Bowl and when pitchers and catchers report, but the other gender may find those dates too confining.

Above-average guysheds need a couple of things. Insulated walls—sprayed foam preferably—are a must. A guy has got to be able to get cerebral during those six months when the temper-atures are hovering below freezing, and an insulated guyshed facilitates that activity.

Cement floors are something the frugal guy has to include.

The contractor (a loyal and dependable guy-voucher) will explain to the Mrs. that if you add cement later, it takes a cement pump and a lot more labor costs. Therefore, to save the family money by incurring this seemingly not insubstantial cost during the initial construction, the dedicated guy will relent and accept a cement floor.

If a guy is going to spend a lot of time thinking and working in the guyshed, the Mrs. is not going to want him tracking into the house to use those nice facilities. Since the place is insulated and has a drain field and all anyway—obvious components of a simple guyshed should be running water and a bathroom.

Every guyshed has electricity—I think it is required in the guyshed code the county adopted a few years ago. It's also not a bad idea to include a padlock on the fridge—just to keep the kids from getting at the fruit drinks when dad isn't around.

Personally, I didn't get my guyshed until after twenty years of marriage. When we built our house we faced the moral and economic dilemma of a guyshed, versus finishing the kids' bedrooms in the lower level. The answer seemed obvious to me, but apparently I was a little too guy-cerebral in the whole analysis. Anyway, the kids liked their new bedrooms, even if it deprived them of my suggested bonding experience of sharing a wide open, cement floor basement as a bedroom through their teen years.

Some guysheds are purely for cleaning game, and you can admire that meat gathering motive. Other guys are bigger-picture thinkers. My friend Scott is kind of the Mother Teresa of guysheds. He built one that can take in and provide shelter and nourishment for the shedless guys in the neighborhood.

Finally, a little personal advice for the new guyshed owner. I would suggest against (unless you have very good major medical insurance) asking the Mrs. to clean up after the buddies in the guyshed. Besides, if you buy a powerful enough leaf blower, it doesn't take that long to dust anyway.

Lee Schoenbeck, Watertown

_ϨϨ_

Proud to Be a South Dakotan

I'm very proud to be an American, but I am also very proud to be a South Dakotan. South Dakotans are known across the nation for their work ethic, honesty, frankness, and willingness to stand up for what is right. In fact, I've heard stories about people getting hired strictly on the fact that they were from South Dakota. That speaks volumes about how the nation views us. Growing up in rural South Dakota and working on a farm/ranch my whole life has instilled in me not only many morals and values but has also taught me a way of life—the South Dakota lifestyle. What is this "lifestyle?" To us, it is our whole way of life: It is a strong sense of family unity and community togetherness. It is a strong work ethic, the attitude that "we can do anything we put our minds to"; the attitude that "hard work does not scare us." We can do what it takes to get the job done, and even if we don't necessarily like the exact work that we are doing, we will still have a good attitude and positive outlook. The attitude, "No matter how many times you knock us down, we will get up smiling and go again." The strong trust and faith in God, the realization that we are not in control. He is. The willingness to drop everything and help a neighbor in need, to put others' needs before our own. The attitude, not "What can this world give me and what can I take," but rather "What can I give of myself, and how can I better the world God gives us through my everyday work." The humble gratefulness for things as small as a beautiful sunset or a July thunder shower. The geographic location to be in the heart of God's beautiful creation, to be able to see open spaces, to witness the life cycle, to see the stars at night, to breathe fresh air, and to be so in unison with mother nature that what we do every day is directed by the weather. To work at occupations that are so fulfilling, even in tough years, because we know that what we do feeds the world. These are just a few of the many great parts of our lifestyle. I am very grateful to live in South Dakota—the best place in the world to live with the best people.

Andy Rausch, Hoven

Courtesy of SDSU Archives & Special Collections, Hilton M. Briggs Library, South Dakota State University, Brookings, S.D.

Dust to Dust

In my home hangs a portrait of two of my great-grandparents, Christian and Katherine Gross. I think it's a wedding picture. Christian had recently emigrated from Russia. Katherine was born here, the only one of my great-grandparents who could make that claim. They look young and strong, though they're not smiling. They married in the late 1880s. By age thirty-nine, Katherine was dead of diphtheria, having lost six of her twelve children to the ravages of what were, at the time, untreatable diseases. I don't know what Martin died of in the 1890s, but the five youngest children all died of scarlet fever in the winter of 1907. One after the next, Christian and Katherine's babies died. My grandmother, Helen Gross Huber, also contracted scarlet fever that winter, which then developed into rheumatic fever. But she survived. She turned thirteen that year, apparently old enough and strong enough to withstand the assault. In 1908, the youngest child was born. In 1909, Katherine died. How could she not have? Six dead children would leave any mother weak in body and soul and vulnerable to whatever vicious illness came along next.

Last summer I visited my grandparents' hometown, Bowdle, which was celebrating its 125th anniversary. At the municipal cemetery, my sister and I and our husbands visited the graves of many of our family members. We reminded each other of stories about them. Aunt Barbra was always so grumpy; we were scared of her. Lenora was a saint. Grandma's stepmother wasn't very nice to her, and she missed her mother, Katherine, until the day she died. "I can see her face just like it was yesterday," my grandma told me one day in 1989, eighty years after her mother's death.

That June day last year, a million dragonflies hovered over the cemetery, as if my family was saying, "It's us. We're here. Our being lives in this place," This is what makes me a South Dakotan. It's not because of my politics or my birthplace or the way I speak. I'm a South Dakotan because my family endured unspeakable hardship here, buried their children here, worked and toiled, fought frostbite and grasshoppers, blizzards and drought, and didn't leave. This was their home. My family is in the soil of South Dakota—their bodies, their sweat, their tears. My DNA runs through the roots and water and fields of South Dakota. I am here.

Randee Huber, Sioux Falls

Why South Dakotans Are Stubborn

Why are we so stubborn you say,
Because we don't live some place warm by a bay.

We have to fight with the cold,
That's why we are so bold.

Even during the coldest part of the day,
We still go outside to run and play.

Living in South Dakota is amazing,
Seeing all of the animals grazing.

The view of the horizon is great.
South Dakota is my State.

The space around with so many fields.
This can give people many great and happy deals.

With us putting up with this weather,
You can't expect us to act any better!

This is South Dakota, My State!

Shaye Jungwirth, Hoven

The True South Dakotan

Man, woman, or child.
Nothing in South Dakota is mild.

The winters are rough,
But, the people, Oh, they are tough!

The farmers are here,
And the rest of the world is out there.

South Dakota is a place filled with kind and considerate people,
And if folks doubt it, I challenge them to come see for
themselves.

South Dakota is my home.
It is the place to be, even though it is not close to an ocean or a
sea.

With the kindness of people all around,
The dedication, attitude of respect, and dignity floating
everywhere.

So no matter what, even through dust and grime,
All South Dakotans are true and divine.

Brayden Vogel, Hoven High School

The People of South Dakota

People in small towns
That everyone knows
That's what makes a South Dakotan

People who want to hunt
And people who want to fish most days
That's what makes a South Dakotan

People who go to school
And people who work hard
That's what makes a South Dakotan

People who like farming
And people that enjoy being in the country
That's what makes a South Dakotan

When you talk to people
And they argue over what tractor is better
That's what makes a South Dakotan

People loyal to their country
And people that enjoy what they do
That's what makes a South Dakotan

Joey Glodt, Hoven High School

To Be a South Dakotan

To the extent the fragility and the resilience of being human are not acknowledged . . . well . . . then one cannot be "from" South Dakota.

We are a state proud of our agricultural heritage. Our South Dakota farmers know the fragility of life and the resilience of character. Those who work the land, its farms, and its ranches are the barometers of community health. South Dakota farmers live in hope to be sure, but more than that, they personify the faith we have in each other.

Farmers persevere in ways many of us can only admire but not completely replicate. Farmers know mud, rain, heat, cold, snow, and wind better than anyone. They make their living from the elements. A "good or bad" year usually depends upon the elements . . . their frequency or lack thereof.

Farmers probably know more about life and death than we can comprehend.

These men and women of the land know fragility every day. In every corner of our state are cemeteries sharing the plot of a church whose days of active service are gone. Upon closer inspection, these cemeteries are well-kept and trimmed. Flowers give proof of a recent visit by a family member who may bear the beams of generational memories. Perhaps a child who died in stillbirth, a son or daughter who left the farm to defend our country, a family member who died from simple hard work, or grandparents who dared the elements years ago to make a living and a life.

These plots equally speak of the character the history of this agrarian culture has given South Dakota. There is comfort like a favorite blanket that wraps around me when I come home from far-flung zip codes of the past thirty-plus years. This deep DNA of character given to us by those who were stewards of the land is what we try to describe when someone asks us "where are you from?"

I can think of no better way to have grown up than having had a shovel in my hand, a John Deere Model B under my butt, a memory of hard work, the smell of freshly cut corn and rain-washed air. This was the golden age to be a child.

Fragility and resilience? Ask a farmer.

Steven Rasmussen, Nashville, Tenn.

By Chad Coppess. Used with permission of Chad Coppess.

We Are from South Dakota

We are from South Dakota,
"Where is that?" you might ask.
Well, it is a place like no other.

We are from South Dakota,
we are friendly people
and proud of our history.

We are from South Dakota,
we are farmers and ranchers,
John Deere is all we do.

We are from South Dakota,
we are hunters and fishers,
it is how we keep ourselves busy in our free time.

We are from South Dakota,
we are spiritual people,
half our population is Native American.

We are from South Dakota,
we can handle anything nature throws at us
because of our freezing winters and brutally hot summers.

We are from South Dakota,
we all think that South Dakota is awesome!

Scott Glodt, Hoven High School

DIVERSITY

Ogle Luta (Red Shirt), Red Shirt Table in the Badlands. By Nick Estes. Used with permission of Nick Estes.

~V~

Trading Encomienda for Tiospaye

They came from their own indigenous landscape filled with cactus, pinons, lizards, heat, family, friends, and the confinement of the *encomiendas* where Spanish landowners lived and enslaved local populations. The travels of these men from Mexico (who would be slaves) had taken months to drive the herds of longhorn cattle far to the north. The drive, once done, now offered up a choice to return home or to stay. Would they return to their homeland or would they be moved to settle in a place on the southeastern edge of the Badlands of the Dakota Territory? Would the end of their long days' work and a choice to relocate be a new beginning? These men began to settle in the area known commonly as *pejuta haka* or Medicine Root and colonially as Kyle, South Dakota. In what appears to be a movement *en masse* (perhaps over several years), the *encomienda* was traded for family and community-based *tiospaye*. One way of life was being exchanged for another, beginning with location and language.

Skin shades may have been similar, but where did belief systems meet? With all the land between Mexico and *pejuta haka*, what was it about the people who were "in place" that made men want to exchange the comfort of warm, dry winters for the discomforts of 30-mile-per-hour wind with driving snow? Was it the lull of rolling hills, creeks, and the utilitarianism of the wildlife? Was it a visceral attraction between the people of the Plains and the indigenous look-alikes whose mutually exotic languages issued forth in rushes of unmistakable emotion? What was it about these men who were clearly hard workers? Did the women see the advantages of not having to search for men not related to them? Had their men been given over to fighting in wars that too often took the strongest and smartest prospects for mates?

Whatever the motives for these cattlemen from Mexico, in moving from one landscape to the other, adopting and being adopted by the Lakota, they were now a part of a community created within the existing *tiospaye*. They became Lakota but by virtue of their surnames would be easily identifiable as Martinez,

Vocu, Gallego, and Hernandez. Their heirs today are sure to recognize the duality of their heritage and may be interested enough to investigate and claim their Hispanic status. But satisfaction must be found in knowing that their grandfathers and great-grandfathers, in choosing their grandmothers and great-grandmothers, chose the life and landscape of the Lakota.

These men of hard-fought ancestry and determination were now obligated to accept all the responsibility of being a member of the geographical area and culture that simultaneously nurtured and demanded strength of character and strength of spirit. They were bound to enrich the amalgam of possibility when describing what it is to be a South Dakotan.

Ronya Hoblit, Mandan, N. Dak.

By Chad Coppess. Used with permission of Chad Coppess.

Osha Adam, Washington High School Student, with the Koran. Photograph by Tom Dempster. © 2012 South Dakota State Historical Society Press. Used with permission.

Sioux Falls, South Dakota: In the Middle of Everywhere!

If we look at the makeup of the Sioux Falls school district, we see that over the last few decades, we have become surprisingly diverse. In 1980, there were 91 English language learners here. By 2005, there were 1,425, and by 2008 there were 1,612. Currently there are 1,932.

As recently as 1991, the district was 94.4 percent Caucasian. By 2001, the figure was 86.3 percent, and in 2011 it was 72 percent! We are changing rapidly!

And the number of "first languages" has grown drastically. If you move to Sioux Falls speaking one of the following languages, someone else in the city will also speak it: English, Spanish, Nepali, Swahili, Kunama, Amharic, Krahn, Somali, French, Kirundi, Tigrinya, Maimai, Vietnamese, Dinka, Orono, Ikrainian, Kayah, Myanmasa, Serbo-Croatian, Croatian, Russian, Laotian, Kurdish, Lakota, Neur, Anwak, Cambodian, Chinese, Dakota, Sudanese, Afar, Albanian, Kinyarwanda, Urdu, Bagla, Bulgarian, Persian, Romanian, Samoan, Srpski, Bhutani, Chomoran, Hindi, Italian, Japanese, Kazakh, Kenya, Lithuanian, Pacific Islander, Pashto, Tagalog, Telugu, Turkish, Wolof, Ethiopian, German, Greek, Haitian Creole, Hayeran, Hmong, Korean, Mandarin, Maori, Ogoni, or Shona.

At the beginning of 2012, there are fifty-seven languages plus thirteen dialects represented in the Sioux Falls school district. These are South Dakotans!

Ed Nesselhuf, Vermillion

A Window to the World

When people think of South Dakota, among the last things that come to mind are boundaries; most think of the wide-open spaces, where one can see for miles in all directions. That may be true in the physical sense, but until recently, South Dakota was a bound state, limited by its lack of diversity. The population consisted mainly of white people and Native Americans, with little contact from those in the outside world. This seems to have changed with the advancement of technology. Now that we can communicate so effortlessly with people from around the world and travel to distant places so easily, human interaction has profoundly changed. South Dakota is much more a part of the world.

As a member of the next generation in our state, I've witnessed diversity increase with each passing year. In the early days of elementary school, being able to communicate with someone of a different nationality was a rare occurrence, even in a university town. Today, my fellow students have come from a variety of backgrounds and countries, such as India, Russia, China, Germany, and Taiwan. They learn our ways, but, equally important, we learn their ways. Of course, immigration is only one of the contributors to cultural interaction; people are also reaching out to the world through technology. My generation is able to communicate with people from many different countries, and this encourages us to learn about their nations and customs.

I've lived in South Dakota for most of my fourteen years. My family enjoys traveling, but most of our lives are spent in our modest little town of Vermillion. This is where the ability to talk to almost anyone in the world comes in handy. I've made friends with people all over the United States, Europe, and even some in more remote places, like Thailand, Bermuda, and the Philippines. I'm not the only one, either; many teenagers are now connecting with other cultures through the Internet. So long as people are careful with what they reveal about themselves, they have the chance to safely communicate with thousands of diverse individuals. I've encountered so many different personalities, and, as a result, feel as though I have become a much more tolerant and open person. With technology constantly changing and advancing, our state will continue to be exposed to an incredible array of cultures and people. South Dakota is no longer simply part of the United States of America, but part of a much larger world.

Erika Lynn Moen, 14 years, Vermillion

∿

What Doesn't, What Does, and Vermillion

What makes a South Dakotan? I'm not sure yet. But I do know what doesn't, and it sure doesn't fit into what those who live outside of this great northern Middle think. We're flyover. We're dumb and racist and poor and white and straight and conservative. We like the Sweetheart Polka and denim and AM radio. We don't like people whose skin isn't white or whose food isn't red meat or whose beer isn't canned and cheap. Never mind that when I step into my classroom, I hear global accents: Jamaican, Polish, Iraqi, Brazilian, Sudanese, Ethiopian, Taiwanese, Russian, Italian, Lakota. Never mind that my students and I are too busy writing poetry, playing music, raising kids, studying to be nurses, helping our neighbors, voting, dancing, reading, loving, thinking, and learning to pay attention to the stereotype of who we are supposed to be.

What makes a South Dakotan, then, is indifference. Perhaps. We are indifferent to the nation's insistence that we be typical Red Staters, because we are too busy living the way we want to. Right now, we could not possibly care less if Holly and Jessica down the street are in love. Right now, we are heading down to Lalibela's on 12th Street in Sioux Falls, because we are hungry for a delicious, spicy berbere stew mopped up with sour injera bread. Right now, we are sitting with people we love in a long, tin-ceilinged bar, drinking cabernet or red beers, and talking about health care. Right now, we are reading Edna St. Vincent Millay, Wislawa Szymborska, and Junot Diaz. Right now, we are signing up for the annual AIDS Walk. Right now, we are sitting in a progressive, inclusive church that sings about God's love for every single, worthy one of us. Right now, we are warmth and goodness and intelligence and significance. This is what makes a South Dakotan. That, and a deep, lasting love for the Sweetheart Polka and denim and AM radio. I mean, we still are only human.

Lindy Obach, Sioux Falls

Mahpiyato (Sky nation) during the construction of tipis on Pine Ridge Reservation, Porcupine. The tipi represents a connection, not only as an earthly dwelling, but also with the celestial realms.

Integrating the Two Halves of Myself

East River/West River; city/country; tribal/white; reservations' preservation of heritage/the rest of South Dakota's blending of cultures. My own ethnicity—Ihanktonwanna/German. In my South Dakota heritage, these dichotomies manifested themselves in a black or white mentality. When I left South Dakota to go to college, that mentality was so strongly imbedded in me that I wasn't even aware of it. Years later, that dual mentality became physical as the disease of Multiple Sclerosis split my body in two—left side normal, right side weak.

As I began to make changes in my life to keep my body as strong as possible, the realization began to dawn that seeing and judging the world and myself in this either/or way can kill the spirit. I began to integrate the two halves of myself. I began to pay attention to my

The main tipi pole points north to Polarie, representing the connection. The saying is "What is in the heavens, is also here on earth." By Nick Estes. Used with permission of Nick Estes.

father and learn more about my tribal background, of which I had always been proud, but of which I knew very little. I enrolled at Crow Creek. I eased up on being critical. In me it was a trait that was more inherently German—the ancestry that had always prevailed.

Trips back to South Dakota became more frequent as my parents' health started to deteriorate. Upon moving back here, I felt my either/or worldview flaring up as I viewed myself as an outsider. My need to be right crept back and started to be as pervasive as when I left. Fortunately, I have started to recover.

Five years back in South Dakota, my mentality, like my hair, keeps getting grayer as I continue to learn from *mitakuyape*—all my relatives—be they blood or not.

My viewpoint keeps expanding. I continue trying to integrate my native/white elements that I separated for so long. I continue to work on my destructive perfectionism. Acceptance and integration are this South Dakotan's watchwords. I aspire to set a good imperfect example.

Karen Pratt, Sioux Falls

A Norwegian grandma with her lefsa, Sinai farm. By Adrienne DeBoer. Used with permission of Adrienne DeBoer .

Lessons from the Mulberry Patch

At the end of the long, straight driveway, past the white farm house and creek on the right, and the massive cottonwood tree and the red barn on the left, was the mulberry patch. My great-

great-uncle, Edward Linde, had constructed a make-shift fence out of old boards and chicken wire to house a grouping of mulberry trees. Inside the mulberry patch stood an old woman with a weathered face, my Auntie Emma Linde, who was my great-great-aunt. She held a large bucket, and after wrapping her arms around me in a tender embrace, she handed me a bucket, too. Together we picked and ate mulberries, our hands black from the dark purplish berries she would later use for jams, jellies, and pies. As we worked, Auntie Emma told me stories of her immigrant parents who had come from Norway to settle on this—their homestead land. As if a part of the family, every story came back to the land.

Ma had had three babies named Louisa. The first two had died during childbirth. The third Louisa was successfully delivered in the cornfield as Ma worked alongside Pa. "Ma," Auntie Emma told me, "squatted to the ground to birth her child," with the earth absorbing her blood, amniotic fluids, and afterbirth. "Then Ma wrapped the baby in a shawl, lay the infant down between the corn rows, and continued working beside Pa."

She told me that her brother, Edwin, my great-great-uncle, had frozen to death during a blizzard when he was seventeen, after having taken shelter among haystacks. Their family had stayed up all night banging pans together on the back steps in the hopes that he would hear them and follow the noise home, but the blizzard of 1888 was too horrific. Days later, his body was discovered a quarter mile from home. The horses, still hitched to the wagon, stood over his body.

Auntie Emma and Uncle Ed were unable to have children, so in their hearts, they adopted me and my brothers as their children. They were God-loving people who were kindly towards their neighbors and well-loved in the rural community south of Canton. This rural community was made up of descendants of immigrants who had come from Europe with the dream of one day owning 160 acres of Dakota Territory in what is now South Dakota. My aunt and uncle had donated a precious two acres of their land for the Romsdal Lutheran Church, which was named after their homeland in Norway. It remains an active congregation to this day.

As a fifth-generation descendant, I, too, grew up on this land, but for me, it was a source of trials.

My father was determined to teach us that living off the land meant we ate what we grew. We ate not only the sweet corn and other vegetables from the garden but also the animals—from the sea of bobbing, yellow chicks, which I cuddled in the hen house; to the grown, white chickens, which were beheaded prior to being plucked and readied for the oven; to the cattle we fed and to whom I sang the "Star Spangled Banner" while standing on hay bales; and to the sheep, which, in spite of my father's caution, became my pets. I learned not to name my food.

I can still taste the exotic mulberries and hear my Auntie Emma saying, "Do whatever you have to do to keep the land in the family. Take care of the land, and it will take care of you."

Kristin Linde Gedstad, Brookings

A South Dakotan's Success Story

It was 1910. A lad of ten disembarked from a German liner, the Bremen (steerage class), with his parents and six siblings. They had traveled from Selz, Odessa District (county), Ukraine, and then South Russia. The lad, George Kessler, would live the last fifty years of his life in Aberdeen, South Dakota. His ancestors included one of the Selz founders (1809), who had emigrated from Germany as a refugee from the German Alsace/Palatinate area to escape the looting, displacement, and conscription of sons by French and Germans engaged in the Napoleonic wars.

The liberal policies granted George and his wife's German ancestors by Empress Catherine's grandson, Czar Alexander I, were all threatened by succeeding czars. George's parents decided to leave before their children lost their German-language schools or before their sons were forced into the Russian military and to avoid the impending Bolshevik (Russian) Revolution.

George had had only two years of elementary education in Russia and two years in the new St. Mary's School in Aberdeen after their arrival in 1911. At age twelve, to help supplement his family's finances, George had to take work as a delivery boy first, then later as an adult meat cutter in grocery store businesses.

One December day in 1940 George entered his home on Aberdeen's Lloyd Street and announced to his astonished wife, Elizabeth (Sahli), and to Bob and Ann, that they were now the staff of a corner grocery business he had acquired after leasing the site with $600 in savings and a loan from a local wholesale business. After new construction, expansion, and remodeling, and fifty years after George's death, that small store and staff would become a supermarket with a staff of 300 managed by his son, Bob, then his grandson, Tim, and presently, his great-grandson, Reed Kessler.

Tim and Reed were graduates of Roncalli High School, where, months before his death, George, a fourth grade "drop out," completed chairing the fund-raising efforts needed for Roncalli's construction. For this and other reasons he became (posthumously) the first inductee into Roncalli's Hall of Fame.

He valued education and financed his sons' post-secondary educations. His son Bob succeeded him as CEO in the business he had established, and his son Ken graduated from Minnesota's St. John's University. His daughter, Ann, who had joined the Yankton Benedictine nuns' community in 1945, earned a Ph.D. degree from Notre Dame University and a subsequent professorship at Yankton's Mount Marty College. George and Elizabeth financed her world-wide research for her dissertation and a history book she authored.

What makes a South Dakotan like George Kessler? Who, upon his arrival in Aberdeen, could never have dreamed that one day he could afford a Mina Lake cabin and a sailboat (from which he fell and drowned at age 62). If he could be asked, he would credit his love of South Dakota for the equality of opportunity here. He would mention the acceptance of the German-Russian minority in Aberdeen and elsewhere in the state. He would describe South Dakota as a miniature democratic meritocracy where a son of a poorly educated family of immigrants could achieve the American Dream if he were willing to take risks, work hard, and return to the community what he could give. South Dakota's people make good South Dakotans.

Sister Ann Kessler, Yankton

❦

Waiting for Respect and Acceptance

My ancestors were already living here when South Dakota officially became a state on November 2, 1889. Since my family was established here prior to this area being recognized as a state, it seems logical that my ancestors would automatically be considered South Dakotans by some imaginary, unwritten grandfather clause. Right?

However, my late grandparents were not considered United States citizens until 1924. So, does that mean the ancestors I never met who were born, lived, and died here were not South Dakotans? It's very confusing.

I am Sicangu Lakota. The federal and state governments recognize me as a member of the Rosebud Sioux Tribe. I grew up in Todd County, South Dakota, which is all that remains of the Rosebud Indian Reservation—an area which once encompassed most of this region.

I live here because it is my home. I have personal ties to the land. This is the land my ancestors conducted ancient ceremonies upon—ceremonies which we have kept alive for thousands of years. The Lakota people are not going to go away. Yet, there are times when I feel unwelcome in this land where the license plates read "Great Faces. Great Places."

When I venture off the reservation, I am sometimes discriminated against by my fellow South Dakotans. I wonder why I am treated with obvious disdain, since many of the people who are openly unkind to me are strangers.

Still, it no longer matters to me how I am treated by many who also call South Dakota their home. During my personal evolution as a human being, I have come to terms with my own issues of discrimination, racism, and disrespect. So, just because someone chooses to treat me unfairly doesn't mean I have to take it personally. I do not seek to purposely antagonize other human beings. Why should the unhealed emotional issues of other human beings offend me? After all, it is their problem, not mine.

Sometimes I wonder how long it will be before all of the people who live in South Dakota get along and view one another as human beings instead of judging one another by race or skin color. I want my descendants to feel comfortable and truly accepted as South Dakotans. I pray that my grandchildren will live to see the day when the discrimination, racism, and disrespect displayed by many modern day South Dakotans fade away.

Vi Waln, Parmalee

Forever Smiling

Dakota (də ko' tə) def: 1. Ally, friend 2. Forever smiling. How many of us knew that we were thus defined? A title and legacy borrowed from our brothers, the Lakota. A title and legacy carrying a message of immense hope and optimism for those who settled the land . . . if only we had known. For those who were displaced, the meaning became empty . . . along with so many promises. We carried our pain and prayers across the prairie to build our dreams, blindly destroying dreams that already existed. Relying on the only heritage we knew. Hardy stock with a Puritan work ethic. Competition replacing cooperation—creating not allies or friends, but adversaries. Gaining vast resources and expanses of land but losing its sacred soul. Creating a trail of tears, forever crying. Red and White, White and Red . . . allies? Friends? A new dream we can strive to build with our brothers, the Lakota. A new era in which we live out the true meaning of Dakota on the land we share. Together looking toward a future as broad as the Dakota horizon and as limitless as the array of stars in our night sky. Looking toward a future for all—the kind of people we hope to be: Friends. Allies.

Paula Vogel, Aberdeen

BIOGRAPHY

By Chad Coppess. Used with permission of Chad Coppess.

◦§◦

The Red Tractor

It happened shortly after one of the worst dust storms to hit our farm that summer. It was a massive, menacing dark cloud that crept across the land, sucking up the loose soil as it moved across the fields, leaving everyone bewildered and in despair. I was playing in the dust banks left by the storm, making roads and trails in it with a long stick.

A black car drove into the yard, and a man in a dark suit got out. "Is your father here?" he called across the yard. "I'll go get him," I replied and ran to the barn where I knew he was working. The two men met in the middle of the yard and briefly shook hands. I waited in the shade of the barn. Suit-Man started waving his arms around, pointing in different directions and occasionally gesturing at the tractor in our yard. My Dad just stood looking at the ground with his hands stuffed deep in his pockets.

I could see his fists were clenched tight. Suit-Man stopped pointing, took out a bundle of papers from his inside jacket pocket, and handed dad one. Just then, a huge truck rolled into the yard, bringing with it a long tail of black dust. Suit-Man waved the men in it over to the red tractor, and they began to load it onto the truck. Suit-Man walked over to his car and watched them loading the tractor. Dad just stood and watched the loading. As soon as the tractor was loaded on the truck, the two men climbed into the cab and left the yard, causing another great cloud of dust. When some of the dust settled, Suit-Man drove away.

Anger rippled through me. I wanted to run at all three of them and bite and kick and scream. They had taken our farm tractor! How would we farm without a tractor? I ran to my father and threw my arms around him. Tears filled his eyes. He took a soiled handkerchief from his pocket and blew his nose loudly.

"But Dad," I started to protest, "they took . . . ." "Don't worry, Buster (He sometimes called me that even though I was a girl), we'll make it," he reassured me. He rumpled my hair and took my hand and we walked to the house where my mother, brothers, and sisters waited. Some years later, when the drought had diminished, he some way was able to buy a quarter of land, and the next year another quarter. In the following years, two more quarters were added to his operation. Best of all, a new red tractor always sat in our yard.

Optimistic and steadfast—my father was a typical South Dakota farmer. Hope for a better crop next year, better yields, higher prices, maybe some new equipment—these were what drove him on. He always had a deep concern for the land he farmed and for his family.

Geneva Hogue, Brookings

Hello, This is Betty B.

A sixty-something lady with a pink baseball cap was not the person I expected to meet in a downtown Midas on a sizzling July afternoon. I was in the Rapid City area for a class, and my car was not running properly. A colleague had recommended her local Midas. The shop was closed, but the technician and the clerk were there. That was how I met Betty B.

Her full name is Betty Bowers, but when answering the Midas or her home phone, it's Betty B. Her signature title dates back to when she started teaching, and there were two Betty's on staff— Betty S. and Betty B. Since then, she's known by all as Betty B. She volunteers at her son's Midas, where she answers phones, supports the mechanics' diagnoses, and extends a South Dakotan welcome to everyone. However, her story didn't start in South Dakota.

Betty B. grew up on a farm near O'Neill, Nebraska, with her parents and seven siblings. She attended a country school and had one of Nebraska's finest for a teacher—her sister. After country school, Betty B. attended St. Mary's Academy, a private Catholic school. She helped pay her tuition by raising chickens and sweet corn and by cleaning. After being a nun for two and a half years, she went to Wayne State College to earn her elementary degree.

Her first year teaching was rough, and by Thanksgiving, she was ready to turn her back on education. It was the advice of her two sisters, both teachers, which convinced her to stick with it. They told her, "You can't please everyone, so you decide what to do in your classroom so that each child can learn." Armed with new confidence, she launched a successful career in education.

From teaching in a self-contained classroom to helping start a middle school in Nebraska; from teaching ceramics to being an administrator in the Douglas School System; from being South Dakota's Director of Teacher Education and Certification to being the acting Dean and Director of Field Services at Dakota State University; Betty B. has been involved in all levels of education. She was an adjunct professor for South Dakota State University and Black Hills State University, served on National Council for Accreditation of Teacher Education review teams, and was active in many educational organizations.

She earned many awards and credits her staff for them. She says, "You can be an outstanding teacher without an outstanding administrator, but you cannot be an outstanding administrator without outstanding teachers." The award she holds most dear is the National Association of Effective Schools' Outstanding Elementary Principal of the Year award. As part of this award, she had lunch with President Reagan.

How does an accomplished educator and administrator go from dining with the president to answering phones at Midas? In 2000, Betty B. and her husband, Bob, were traveling to Pierre for the first Digital Dakota Network presentation and were in a car accident which dramatically changed their lives. Bob suffered a traumatic brain injury, and Betty B. became his caretaker and began to volunteer at her son's Midas.

She approaches each task with the same dedication and focus that distinguished her as an educator. She still encourages individuals to continue their educations to better themselves. "What makes a South Dakotan is the genuine support that South Dakotans give to each other—by taking people under their wings and by being sensitive to their needs," says Betty B.

Ruth Buchmann, Emery

Laura and I by the Shores of Silver Lake

I used to live about ten miles from DeSmet, and when I was little, I would go and play at a playground there. DeSmet is a small town in South Dakota where Laura Ingalls Wilder, author of the _Little House_ books, lived. I would go and look at the house that Laura used to live in. Laura and her family were pioneers—some of the first settlers in South Dakota. Her house was white with shingles. I often wondered what it would be like to live in a little house like Laura's.

Because I liked Laura's stories so much, friends of mine gave me a dress, which looked much like what Laura wore, and a doll to go with it. The doll was a sock doll with black-button eyes, a bonnet, dress, socks, and shoes for a complete prairie girl outfit. I would put on my dress and play with the doll, just like Laura played with her doll.

When I was six, I listened to the _Little House_ series audio books. Again and again, I would listen to Laura's adventures on the prairie and in town. I listened to the book _The Long Winter_ during the winter. It made me very thankful for the modern conveniences that I used to take for granted.

Now and then, I'll play with Lincoln Logs and make houses and other things. Soon a little prairie town is formed. I'll put toy horses, farmyard animals, and people around the buildings I make. My brother and I have fun with them. He'll make a certain figure walk around and talk, and I'll do the same thing.

In _By the Shores of Silver Lake_, I like Chapter 6, "The Black Ponies." Laura liked horses, and so do I. Laura had a dog named Jack, and I have a dog of my own, too.

Laura's books inspired me, and I learned a lot about pioneer life in South Dakota from the books that Laura wrote about herself. Like Laura, I like writing stories.

I think that Laura Ingalls Wilder is a great example of a true South Dakotan. That's my connection with Laura "in two shakes of a lamb's tail" as Pa (Laura's father) would say.

Jane Ardry, Brookings

A South Dakota Grower

Eleanor Toyne, eighty-eight years of age, is as ordinary and as unusual as any South Dakotan. She chose plants and people as her life's work. "I was third of five children and the first girl. I started college near home at Southern Normal in Springfield and then transferred to South Dakota State College during World War II. With two of my brothers in the service, I had to stay out a quarter to help with the farm."

Eleanor distinguished herself. "I graduated the summer of 1946 and was the first woman to graduate with a horticulture degree from what is now South Dakota State University. I really wanted to be a farmer, but women weren't farmers in that day. My father had an orchard of several acres and thought I could help him. I really didn't want to do that."

She traveled as far as Detroit on her way to a plant nursery job in Canada before she learned it was for Canadians only. She then took a bus to Kansas in response to a trade ad. "The nursery was run by an older man who lived with his mother. He met me at the bus. I found out what he was looking for was a wife."

Her job search ended when a nursery in Waterloo, Iowa, hired her. She started in the office, but began to work with plants when others were busy and duties were available. She also met Merle in Waterloo. "We married the day after Thanksgiving in 1955. Merle wanted to farm, but land was expensive. We rented a farm north of Springfield for a year and paid 'cash rent.' My father gave us a cow, and our other livestock was a dog." Years later, they bought her uncle's farm nearby.

Their family grew when they adopted two Korean children in 1962. About 140 Korean children arrived on two flights about a month apart in Portland, Oregon. "We supplied clothes so that we could recognize our children by their clothes. Our daughter was three years old and knew no English except for singing 'Twinkle, Twinkle, Little Star.' Our son was sixteen months and didn't speak at first. I knew two Korean words for bathroom needs. By fall, our daughter could speak English."

Eleanor continued working as seasonal help for Gurney Seed and Nursery Company. "We had plant questions from all fifty states! A common question was 'Why did this plant die?'"

Today Eleanor and Merle live in the country with a large garden near Springfield. "I didn't want close neighbors, and we have a twelve-year-old outdoor dog, Forbes. We didn't think Forbes would be happy in town."

Their three grandchildren, who are also South Dakotans, have been educated beyond high school. "It's a good thing they are doing what they like."

Eleanor enjoys growing food. "We should make our vegetable garden smaller, but how? We always have more than we can use. We don't sell it. Some goes to Dakota Senior Meals or others." Eleanor says Derby beans and Serendipity bicolor sweet corn from Jung Seed are the best. She enjoys bountiful harvest traditions.

Eleanor wants to be helpful to others. "That's why I volunteer in the Alternatives to Violence Project at the Springfield prison." Eleanor was unsure about the position, but others encouraged her. She also serves as a master gardener at Yankton Community Gardens and sings in her church choir. She enjoys living and gardening here and assisting others.

Eleanor concludes, "There are a lot of people in this region. If we'd all just get along, this would be a better world."

Brenda K. Johnson, Yankton

Breaking Codes, Repairing People

Raised on a family farm near Irene, but sitting in a small hut in the Aleutian Island chain during World War II, U.S. Army Sergeant Joe Anderson listened to the endless Japanese radio transmissions. Steady chatter was designed to bore or misdirect, and Sergeant Anderson and his colleagues had to stay alert for the smallest clue. As cryptographers, their success in breaking codes and intercepting the genuine Japanese military messages could save hundreds of

American lives in the Pacific theatre.

For several days in 1945, unusually quiet airwaves unnerved the small-town kid so far from home. What followed was a stunning message from General Douglas MacArthur, Supreme Commander of the Allied Forces. In the aftermath of atomic bombs falling on Hiroshima and Nagasaki, MacArthur's teletype message laid out the process by which the Japanese were to surrender unconditionally. Uncertain who was in charge after the bombs dropped, MacArthur addressed the message simultaneously to the Japanese Emperor, the Imperial Government, and Imperial General Headquarters. After sending the teletype from MacArthur to the Japanese, Sergeant Anderson quietly slipped the paper document into his pocket.

When he died years later, it came out of his closet folded up and into the possession of his younger sister, Verona. Like most veterans of his era, Sergeant Anderson said little about his activities in World War II. He said even less about his activities after he quit farming in Irene in order to travel the world for Gilfillan, a California company specializing in high-security radar. He deflected his family's questions about that missing decade of his life. When he returned to South Dakota to live permanently, he took a job far below his skill set, as a slow-paced television salesman and repairman at Midwest TV, on the corner of 23rd and Minnesota Avenue in Sioux Falls. He replaced cathode ray tubes in television sets and talked customers into upgrading from black-and-white to color sets, or to television consoles with built-in radios. Unfortunately, he drank heavily for many of those years, cementing his existence as a lonely bachelor. Often irascible, he seemed tormented by what he had seen or what he had done during his globetrotting years. When he died, his siblings thought his funeral would be a small family gathering. Instead, Miller Funeral Home in Sioux Falls was filled with dozens and dozens of completely unfamiliar people, many claiming that Joe was responsible for saving their lives.

Turns out that after quitting the bottle himself, he had for years quietly served as a one-man emergency hotline to people battling alcohol addiction. As with so many small-town South Dakota kids of past and current generations, my uncle's life was marked by quiet achievement. One might even say his greatest accomplishments flew under the radar.

Matthew C. Moen, Vermillion

Courtesy of SDSU Archives & Special Collections, Hilton M. Briggs Library, South Dakota State University, Brookings, S.D.

Bill Timmins: A Great South Dakotan

When I moved to Mitchell in 1983 to begin my teaching career, I quickly came to admire and become friends with Bill Timmins. Bill was older than I, but we were fellow teachers and he became a mentor to me. Bill passed away in 2003, but he left a wonderful legacy, not only to Mitchell, but to the state of South Dakota. The poet Yeats wrote, "Count where man's glory most begins and ends, and say my glory was I had such friends." Bill's glory in life certainly was his many friendships and his love and dedication to the state of South Dakota.

Bill was a great teacher, whom students absolutely loved. He always chose to see the best in his students and the good in people. The secret of his teaching success was simply that he loved teaching and he loved kids. For nineteen years, it was my privilege to have him come into my social studies classes and talk to my students about his experiences in World War II. Bill could captivate the students with his stories and have them on the edge of their seats for the entire class period. They loved his speech and they loved him. Over those nineteen years, he talked to over six thousand students at Mitchell Senior High School. Six thousand students today have a better understanding of World War II and what love of country truly means, thanks to Bill Timmins.

A few days after he gave one of his speeches, I would have the students write "Thank You" notes to Bill. The notes that the students wrote him were incredible. They expressed how much they admired him, how much they appreciated his service and sacrifice to our nation, and how much they had learned from him. I know that my writing this would embarrass him, but Bill Timmins was the best teacher I have ever known.

Bill loved the Corn Palace, Corn Palace Week, and everything about Mitchell. He always told my students that when he was overseas during the war, he didn't miss Christmas, birthdays, or any other holidays. He missed Corn Palace Week. While other soldiers hoped to be home by Christmas, Buck Sgt. William M. Timmins hoped to be home by Corn Palace Week!

Bill always ended his speech to my students by telling them about his only regret in life. In 1942, following basic training, He got a ten-day furlough. He came home to Mitchell and because he had to travel by train from his military base in California, he only had four days in Mitchell. His dad was living at the time in Geddes. Bill told the kids he was so busy having fun that he didn't take the time to go see his dad in Geddes. He called him on the phone instead. While Bill was overseas, he got word that his dad had passed away. Bill's dad never got to see him in his country's uniform. Bill would then tell the kids that if he had one wish in life, it wouldn't be for money or fame. His wish would be that he could see his dad one more time, give him a big hug, tell him that he loved him, and say he was sorry for not going to see him before going overseas. He would then end his talk by encouraging students to go home and give their moms and dads, their grandmas and grandpas, and any brothers and sisters a big hug and tell them that they loved them. He told the students that they would never regret doing this.

In 1945, when the war was over, he came home to South Dakota and never left the state he loved. Bill Timmins is one of South Dakota's greatest treasures.

John Solberg, Mitchell

$$\text{\textasciitilde}\sqrt{\text{l}}\text{\textasciitilde}$$

Robert Davies Lusk and Civic Leadership

Robert Lusk was one of the state's great civic leaders. An outstanding example of the South Dakota spirit, he was a graduate of the University of the Missouri School of Journalism. He wrote for the United Features Syndicate, the United Press, and *The Saturday Evening Post*, once declining an offer to become a correspondent in China. Although his life in New York, living in Greenwich Village during the Roaring Twenties, was exciting and the investigative and influential journalists he met there and in Washington challenged him intellectually, he had been taught to write about what he knew. And that was South Dakota. Born into a family of journalists, he returned home to join his father and brothers with newspapers in Yankton, Rapid City, and Huron, the family purchasing the *Huronite* in 1936.

Lusk experienced the Dirty Thirties, and although philosoph-ically conservative and politically independent, he supported Franklin D. Roosevelt's efforts to help the farmers through a variety of New Deal agricultural agencies. Robert Haeder remembers Lusk sitting on the concrete steps with his dad having long, in-depth conversations about how to save their farm near

Wolsey. Haeder's father was fond of Lusk as a human being and told his son that Lusk was a gentleman of great understanding and deep conviction. Lusk himself filmed with a 16 mm camera the damage that Depression era wind and dirt had done. His 1938 article in *The Saturday Evening Post* was about reclaiming this land. That film is on file in the South Dakota State University journalism department, as are two volumes of Lusk's newspaper columns.

During the 1950s, Lusk, who was well known in statewide political circles, worked with his legislative friends to try to re-route the unbuilt east-west Interstate highway in South Dakota. Both Senators Francis Case of Custer, the ranking Republican on the upper house's transportation committee, and Karl Mundt of Madison were personal friends of his. Pierre and Huron wanted the road to be built along the route of Federal Highway 14 rather than along 16, a prospect that would have pleased Brookings, too. Stronger interests prevailed, however.

George Manolis once said, "Lusk was the strongest publisher in the state in his day, and if he had lived, we would have had the entire Oahe project built in South Dakota. It would have provided water for irrigation and water supplies for cities for years to come."

Robert Osborn of Huron added, "Bob Lusk knew a lot of people, but died so young that he failed to collect his chips. If he had lived, Huron would be a different place than it is today. In Bob's day, Huron had the Army Corps of Engineers, the Railroad, Standard Oil Headquarters, and the Bureau of Reclamation. Returning to Huron in 1926, in 1928 Bob personally funded a survey to determine how Huron could ensure a prosperous future." He recalled Lusk picking up the phone, and within a short time a general from Omaha flew his jet in to speak to the Rotary Club about completing the Oahe Project in its entirety.

Lusk is also remembered as:

generous with pension and hospitalization plans, sick leave, and vacation time for his employees at the *Daily Plainsman* before benefits were common;

a giant in town, a mover and a shaker; with a great sense of humor; he never put on airs; he provided seed money to various projects, such as the swimming pool and the YMCA;

planner and promoter of projects that would enrich the lives of his neighbors: boards of Huron College, St. John's Hospital, Salvation Army, Chamber of Commerce, creation of jobs through irrigation, first chairman of Newspaper Association, director of National Reclamation Association, South Dakota State Planning Board, and Lusk Lecture at South Dakota State University.

A visionary, Lusk promoted Huron and South Dakota throughout his life. At his funeral in 1962, attendance was by invitation; the Episcopal Church was not large enough to seat all of his many friends. His library was donated to the South Dakota Art Museum. He continues to enrich South Dakota through the continuing philanthropy of the Christen, Hohm, Lusk Foundation.

Judith Carr Danielsen, Bruce

By Eric Landwehr. Used with permission of Eric Landwehr.

~~~~~

LOVED, ADMIRED AND RESPECTED

April 22, 1993. Following the memorial service in the rotunda of the South Dakota state capitol, eight state troopers carried the flag-draped casket of the late Governor George S. Mickelson down the front steps of the capitol, paused during a 21-gun salute, and then placed the casket in a hearse for the late governor's final trip from Pierre to his adopted hometown of Brookings. The caravan was led by a trooper's patrol car with lights flashing; followed by the hearse; then the blue Mickelson family sedan bearing license number 1, containing the governor's widow and their three children; next was a bus containing family members plus some members of the governor's staff; and, finally, a string of mourners in thirty-one private vehicles. The caravan proceeded out of the circular drive of the capitol past the governor's mansion, where the late governor first lived as a five-year-old when his father was governor of South Dakota. The caravan then turned eastward onto Highway 14.

At numerous rural intersections on Highway 14 between Pierre and Brookings, people stood at attention, with their hats off, their hands over their hearts, and some with American flags. Some people stood quietly in their front yards with their heads bowed or right hands over their heart. One man held his flag at half-staff with his Black Labrador hunting dog at his side, acknowledging the late governor's love of hunting. Hundreds of people lined the streets in the towns of Highmore, Miller, St. Lawrence, Wolsey, Cavour, Iroquois, Lake Preston, Arlington, and Volga. Some waved weakly, some held their hands over their hearts, but all stood quietly in tribute to their beloved governor. On both sides of Highway 14, which extends about one mile through the town of DeSmet, local men and women stood at intervals, holding one hundred American flags to pay tribute to the governor as the caravan passed through this prairie town of grieving South Dakota citizens and mourners.

Mourning friends and admiring citizens of the Brookings community lined the streets as the caravan approached the local funeral home. The first person I saw alight from the bus was Tom Adam, a Pierre attorney, married to Patricia, the late governor's youngest sister. Tom proceeded to tell me that this trip to Brookings was the most incredible of all the times he had traveled Highway 14 in eastern South Dakota. He reported that, as the caravan passed through the rural eastern South Dakota countryside on this sunny day in April, farmer after farmer after farmer paused, stopped and dismounted their tractors, stood at attention, removed and held their hats over their hearts as the state trooper, the hearse and the trailing vehicles passed their farms.

April 23, 1993. The bitter, sweet celebration of life, the funeral service, for the late governor was held at the over-flowing First United Methodist Church. Following the service, the funeral cortege proceeded to Main Avenue, then southward through the business district of Brookings where mourners stood in silence on the sidewalks and streets, many with their hands over their hearts. The elongated cortege continued toward Greenwood Cemetery past Southside Park, where Brookings Middle School students waved flags and watched history unfold in the display of love, admiration, and respect for the first governor of South Dakota to die while in office.

George Speaker Mickelson was a governor who desired and worked diligently to provide opportunities for young people to remain in his beloved state.

He was truly a South Dakotan.

Lewayne Erickson, Brookings

Senator George McGovern with Farmer's Union delegation. By SDSU Archives. Used with permission of SDSU.

What Makes a South Dakotan—Politically?

Today South Dakota is a Red state (conservative Republican), but it was not always so. During the Great Depression, rancher Tom Berry was elected as Democratic governor in 1932. My great-uncle, Ed Schneider of Yankton County, was a member of the Democratic majority in the state legislature in the early 1930s. During the next few years, however, the situation changed drastically. By 1947, there were only four Democrats in the entire body. In the early 1950s, I was called the only Democrat in Beresford. The party made a comeback in later years, but the political mix of the state is perplexing.

According to a recent book, *American Nations* by historian and journalist Colin Woodard, South Dakota contains three of the eleven "nations" that comprise North America. The extreme eastern part of the state north of Minnehaha County to the North Dakota border is part of what he calls "Yankeedom." As the name implies, Yankeedom originated in Massachusetts, spread across New York State and the northern Midwest to Minnesota, from whence it was brought to South Dakota.

Coming up the Missouri River from Iowa and Nebraska was "The Midlands," which originated in Pennsylvania. Several tiers of counties to the west of "Yankeedom" and east of the Missouri River constitute that portion of South Dakota. The western half of the state is part of "The Far West." Because of the importance of ranching and mining, western South Dakota has more in common with Northern Arizona than it does with the crop-raising "East River." Woodard seems to be suggesting that inheritance is more significant than environment in creating South Dakota's political culture.

However voting habits are acquired, who should we consider as a typical South Dakotan? Would it be George McGovern, born in Avon, raised in Mitchell, and educated at Dakota Wesleyan University? During World War II, he piloted B-24 bombers over Germany. After receiving a Ph.D. degree in history from Northwestern University, he returned to DWU as a professor. In 1954, he accepted the job of executive secretary of the state Democratic Party, taking on the task of rejuvenating the moribund organization. Following his election to Congress two years later and then his elevation to the U. S. Senate, he ran for the presidency in 1972. There were rumors in South Dakota that McGovern was a Communist, which he was not. But he was very liberal, and that did not sit well with many people. In the 1990s, Republican Speaker of the House, Newt Gingrich, blamed "McGovernites" for all that was wrong in this country.

In sharp contrast for the honor of typical South Dakotan is conservative Republican Karl Mundt. As in the case of McGovern, he was an academician. Born in Humboldt, educated at Carleton College and Columbia University, he became a professor of speech at Eastern State Normal School in Madison. Mundt was elected to Congress in 1938 and eventually became South Dakota's only four-term U. S. Senator. In the 1950s he joined Senators Joseph McCarthy and Richard Nixon in an effort to save the nation from Communism. As an advisor to presidential candidate Dwight D. Eisenhower in 1952, he devised the formula "K1, C2" (Korea, Communism, Corruption) with which to lambaste the Democrats. A state that can produce two such diverse individuals must have a split personality.

So who was more typical, McGovern or Mundt? Perhaps they represented the extremes and most South Dakotans fall somewhere in between. A person's political affiliation does not constitute that person's entire being. Yet politics is important, and one's ideology is determined to a large extent by one's culture (religion, education, family heritage). Where our ancestors came from and what they experienced has a profound bearing on our *Weltanschauung*.

Carl M. Frank, Mesa, Ariz.

Senator Karl Mundt receives visitors in his Washington, D.C. office. By SDSU Archives. Used with permission of SDSU.

PEOPLE

Tsiyon Girmay and sister Hawan Girmay. Their father, a U.S. citizen, immigrated from Ethiopia 16 years ago. By Tom Dempster. Used with Permission of Tom Dempster.

South Dakota as I Know It

Some people say we South Dakotans are different. I agree. Some folks call us tough because of the harsh, cold winters. I'm not a fan of winter, but I've got a long list of people who are. I've been here mostly all my life. I am always happy here because I never know what Mother Nature is planning that day. We could have it below zero one day and fifty-five another day.

I'm young, but I do know a thing or two about this place. I know that every summer I can walk outside and see green. Green everywhere. And in the winter, I can walk outside and see white. I remember all the days I'd run outside and play in the frosty, winter snow.

I can always count on there being something to do in South Dakota. There was never a time when I didn't have anything to do.

All of the people out here are so nice. I have always had the sweetest neighbors and friends. Whenever someone new moves into South Dakota, I ask, "Do you like South Dakota?"

Linnea Kervin, 9 years, Brookings

Grandpa the Man – A Proud South Dakota Volunteer

My father, Lester Verley, was the third generation of a South Dakota family whose first member landed in New York in 1736. The family migrated to Massachusetts and New Hampshire, then to Wisconsin with their furniture-making factory. After fighting in the Civil War, George Verley moved his family to South Dakota.

Les graduated from Hurley High School in 1933 in the middle of the Depression. These were trying times when helping others survive shaped people, including him. He served others as a well driller and a public servant, including being mayor of a small rural town. In those days it was called helping; today it has a fancier name—volunteering.

The winter of 2010-2011 brought my 97-year-old father's volunteerism to a close. The ice was too treacherous to venture out to Avera McKennan Hospital, where he had volunteered since 1996, when he moved to Sioux Falls from our home in Centerville.

Grandpa the man (my son's childhood name for him; my mother was Grandpa the lady) loved being a volunteer at Avera McKennan. It made him feel good to be able to help others. He also loved meeting and talking with people from all over South Dakota who came to Sioux Falls for care. So many interesting people and their stories are now a part of him.

My father maintained he was able to volunteer so long because of the care and help of his son and daughter-in-law, Darryl and Jeanne, and their children, and the fact that "his legs were good." This doesn't take into account all the reasons why he should not have been able to volunteer: losing his right hand Christmas Eve my senior year in college, colon cancer, kidney cancer (one removed), stroke, macular degeneration, back fracture, broken ribs, shingles, on-going gall bladder problems which require surgery every five to six weeks, plus multiple old-age-related problems. He just kept truckin' because as he says, "If you stop, you're dead."

He accumulated 8,000 hours on the volunteer wall. He said it was probably more than that since the last couple of years he couldn't see well enough to punch in on the new computer. When he was honored for his volunteer work, he said all he wanted was the "O-O Award"—oldest and orneriest. He sorely misses his volunteering, seeing his friends, and being needed.

Now in his 98th year, his legs are failing, and continuing to live on his own is becoming more difficult and lonely for him. He has reluctantly agreed to go into a nursing home, although I'm sure he'll find a way to be helpful there—if only in sharing his stories of South Dakota.

To me, my father epitomizes a South Dakotan, from pioneer sodbusters onward. Helping is in the genes, volunteering being the new genre.

Peg Bailey, Sioux Falls

~❧~

Grandpa was a Cowboy and an Indian

Grandpa was a cowboy and an Indian
And he would often be confused,
'Cause he didn't look like either one,
A fact he often mused.
His pa was a white freighter
Who drove mule-pulled wagon trains.
His ma, a Lakota maid,
A nomad of the plains.
Grandpa did a fancy jig
While his fiddle played along,
Or he'd croon the long, sad verses
To old-time cowboy songs.
Still, he sang Lakota chants
O proud lost warrior days,
Stepped high in bells and moccasins
To the beat of Indian ways.
Grandpa wrangled for white ranchers
From the Keyapaha to the Jim,
'Til he wed a Santee maiden
Then on his allotment, his own spread did begin.
Grandpa raised horses and cattle
That thrived on prairie grass.
Nine children grew strong and healthy
Working at the ranch's tasks.
He struggled, but never prospered,
Watching the years and children go,
'Til the ranch died with the cattle
And the Keyapaha ceased to flow.
Grandpa was still an Indian
When his cowboy days were done,
Then he rode the range of memories
Of ways forever gone.
Tiyospaye mourned his passing
And the drum beat at his wake,

While gospel hymns were harmonized,
Beseeching God his soul to take.
Grandpa's a cowboy and an Indian
In God's eternal band
Where he'll ride forever
In heaven's prairie land.

> *Virginia Driving Hawk Sneve's contribution to this book is an excerpt from a story first published in Grandpa was a Cowboy and an Indian and Other Stories, Lincoln: University of Nebraska Press, 2000.*

South Dakotans Persevere

On May 25, 2011, there were rumblings of a potential flooding situation for the cities of Pierre and Ft. Pierre. Many of us who were born and raised in Pierre and Ft. Pierre laughed off these rumors as nonsense. After all, we had the Oahe Dam to keep the water under control. Less than twenty-four hours later, the flood waters were creeping in at an alarming rate, and it became evident to everyone that flooding was imminent. During this time, mass chaos descended on both cities. Everyone in the flood zone had to face the fact that the danger of losing their homes to the waters of the Missouri River was a very real possibility.

As the first wave of flood waters crept up my street the morning of May 27, I remember looking around in shock at the chaos on my street. People and vehicles surrounded every house, and everyone was frantically shoving their possessions into moving trucks and trailers as they tried to beat the flood waters now lapping at their doorsteps. Some people cried, and some hung their heads, but mostly they looked numb with disbelief that the homes they had raised their families in were going to succumb to the dirty waters of the Missouri River.

Memorial Day weekend brought an amazing turn-around in the response to the flooding situation. What began with only family and friends helping each other turned into a massive, city-wide effort. Companies were building levees, volunteers were diligently sandbagging, and strangers were offering their time and vehicles to assist people in evacuating their homes. All these efforts were being done as quickly as possible. Families who were not affected by the flooding offered their extra bedrooms and campers to those who had no place to go. Local businesses donated food to the displaced and now homeless people, as well as to the volunteers, who were working tirelessly to save homes.

The tasks were difficult, and everyone was working with little to no sleep, but, amazingly, no one gave up. Everyone continued doing what needed to be done. No complaints. No excuses.

The hundreds of men, women, and children who came forward to help their fellow community members in their time of need exemplified what caring citizens do. Each one was determined to help others even though many had sustained losses themselves, and they showed compassion to those who had lost everything.

The people of Pierre and Fort Pierre, who were affected by the flood, were amazingly resilient. They had just lost everything for which they had worked their entire lives, but they were determined to come back stronger than ever once the flood waters receded. And they did just that.

Though the flood was a devastating experience for everyone involved, it also provided an opportunity to see that South Dakota is made up of people who care enough to help others, who are resilient, and who persevere against all odds.

Lindsay Bruckner, Pierre

The Barnstormer

As the story goes, a tiny airplane, delicate as a dragonfly, lit on the late summer stubble of my grandfather's west forty. Let's say it was 1920—a very stylish year in my imagination. The pilot, a stranger known as a barnstormer, stretched his long legs towards the house. He flashed a carny's smile at the seven boys, who stood like stairsteps, all but the tallest in mended, hand-me-down overalls. Just like that, he knocked on grandma's rickety screen door. No one had ever knocked on that door. It sounded more like a rattle than a knock.

I'm sure the barnstormer had craggy, slightly handsome features and way more charm than was acceptable around these parts. He may have taken off his pilot's helmet, the one that looked just like Lindy's, to talk to grandma. Her name was Mary, and the boys could see that she wasn't one bit surprised to see this man at her door. She was a smart, tall Bohemian woman. She was the oldest of ten children and therefore the only one who wasn't sent away to college. She helped raise her siblings and then went off with a temperamental Irishman to rear seven of her own.

"Mrs. Cole," the barnstormer said, according to my father, the fourth step. "I wanna sell plane rides on your farm, but I need these boys to haul water for me." Why did the plane need so much water? Where was he getting fuel for the plane? This is a story told by an awestruck seven year old, and these details were not important.

"For your services, I will give a free plane ride to the person of your choosing." He swept his hand towards the boys. There was probably more to the agreement. Grandma was a gifted trader, but "plane ride" was the only word those little boys heard.

People crammed into Model Ts and jounced the four dusty miles in from Tyndall, happy to spend a dollar to see their homesteads and stores in an amazing new perspective.

The little boys hauled pump water in pails about as big as they were. It was hot, heavy work, and they loved it. They were working for a chance to fly away in an AIRPLANE. Whom would mother pick? The oldest claimed the advantage because he was, well, the oldest. The youngest claimed the advantage because the youngest is always the favorite. The five in the middle probably worked hardest because they had to win by merit, or in the case of Nester, charm.

When the sky burned purple and gold, true to his word, the barnstormer rattled that door again. "Now, which one of the boys will ride in the plane?" The boys knew better than to speak out, but they glistened with hope.

My grandmother didn't say a word. She took off her apron,

shook out a cloud of flour, and folded it. She slammed her Sunday hat on her head and tied a scarf around it. She stepped out of the kitchen door into the little plane and flew away from them all. They had never ever imagined that their mother could fly. When you think about it, what else could she have done?

Every one of those handsome boys, except the youngest, flew terrifying missions for years in the Great War and some again, in Korea. Every one of them came back alive, but none came back to that farm. Their sons flew in different wars, and now their grandsons, and amazingly, their granddaughters, are flying in scary wars right this minute.

They all got their plane rides, and they never stopped flying.

Kathryn Cole Quinones, Brookings

Pioneer Spirit

During World War II my mother, Elizabeth Taylor, was working in Chicago. Yes, she shared a name with a famous woman, but couldn't have been more different than the actress. Mom shared an apartment with Jean Peterson, a woman she met at a Methodist rooming house for "girls." Occasionally Jean's brother came through the city on a troop train, and during one visit Jean introduced her roommate to him. As soon as the war ended, he asked her to marry him.

Betty had grown up in a lovely Wisconsin town, and had never been more than 200 miles away from home. But her mother died when she was a child, and she learned to be self-sufficient at a young age. So she didn't hesitate accepting the proposal; she knew he came from a good family and was a person of character. Just one hitch; they would be moving to South Dakota, 600 miles from her family. The Interstate highway system was only a dream; if her father wanted to come for a visit, he would have to take the train to Huron, which was still 160 miles from Winner, their new home.

William T. "Dub" Peterson and Betty Taylor were married on June 11, 1947, in Baraboo, Wisconsin. They set out for South Dakota to make a life together, sight unseen for her. In these days it's hard to imagine not going to visit the new location where you would be living, but travel was much different in those days. What must my mother have thought when they arrived in Winner, a small town on the prairie, where the wind blew most of the time? In her writings Mom commented on how laid back the people were and speculated, "Perhaps it was because you can't rush cattle." Their first home, and mine, was an apartment above the gas station my father purchased. We lived there until I was two, when we moved into the only house my parents ever owned. Dad died in that house when he was seventy-six years old. The next year Mom sold the house and moved to Sioux Falls to be near me, her only child.

The Prairie is My Garden by Harvey Dunn is one of my favorite paintings. A woman bends to pick flowers on the prairie, a sod house in the background. The woman has always reminded me of my mother—the same lean woman, working outside in a dress, a look of determination on her face, and not afraid to try anything. Making the best of her surroundings. What gives some people the courage to be pioneers? To pull up stakes in a safe, comfortable place and go to an unknown land? Reading the *Little House* books, I always wondered if I could be one of those people. They must be willing to risk leaving comfort behind in search of a better life. My mother was one of those who took the risk and became a South Dakotan.

Jean Peterson Nicholson, named after my Aunt Jean, the matchmaker in the story. I grew up in Winner, and now live in Sioux Falls.

Jean Nicholson, Sioux Falls

By John Banasiak. Used with permission of John Banasiak.

Vanilla Bug Spray

Grandpa smells like a cookie
each day when he steps out.
He sprays on some vanilla
if there are gnats about.
It's better than most bug sprays;
I really think it's true.
He doesn't stink like Cutter's,
as most outdoorsmen do.
There's only just one problem

that I can really see.
Whenever I go near him,
it makes me crave cookies!

Marie Cleveland, Aberdeen

The Pickerel Lake Pontoon-Riding Ladies

Kate's cabin is the bashful gray one,
peeling white shutters, wide porch, concealed
under an awning of ash groves.

We chase each other in a convoy of cars
on knobby gravel roads, past year-round glass homes,
reflecting sport courts and wave runners,
to wooden steps outside her screen door
where we reach for sustenance and familiarity.

We've been doing it for years, wedging trips
between commitments, obligations, even dilemmas,
the amicable divorces and the sour ones,

trading flip-flop heels for white canvas mules and
preferring weight gain over any maladies after fifty-five.

Janie picked the day this year to coincide
with her "best time" between treatments. Our Janie
whose weakness has not smothered her laugh lines
as we took turns with her wig, then insisted we count

the red-headed cranes who were stopping late
in their flyaway north and "be sure and walk to the bend,
and watch purple loosestrife scrambling up stone shored walls. . . ."

rallying us with each intimation, each incredibility of life and
breath,

as Kate leads the way, single-file down the dock,
another rhythmic pilgrimage, Neptune's fresh water nymphs,
plump and not so—gray and dyed—shy and bold, wrapped
in crayon colors of windbreakers on a pontoon piloted
by an ex-Navy man, Pete, who tags along
and grins at the loose conversations
of seven ladies who don't embarrass easily.

And as we settle on white vinyl cushions around Janie
like star-shaped ivory petals surrounding
the delicate stamens of a water lily,
we begin to hover on old glacial waves, trying to make sense
of losing suppleness, vitality, and each other

while the sandhill cranes dance and trumpet with us
and tip their red hats compassionately before they depart,
for they know what it means to return
year after year and they know what it means
that no one be left to stagger alone

as we mimic their migrations back and forth
to our floating asylum in blue-green water.

Sue Rose, Aberdeen

꒰꒱

South Pacific South Dakotan: At the End of the Day, A Budget Shopper

Sephora: Grand Mecca Of All Things Purrtty—And Worthwhile.

I first stepped into the "Mother Ship" last summer 2011 along the Champs Elysees in Paris, France—Oglala Lakota College LIT students in tow (on an international study abroad) who were already long-time "card carrying members" of *the* beauty central: Sephora. I've frolicked obsessively, blissfully with that store since (online especially).

And who do I have to thank? South Dakota Tribal College Native gals, of course. Urban Decay, NARS, MAC, Benefit—these are just a few brands that manufacture those delectable goodies that enhance local indigenous beauty. Thank you, maske! I have seen the light and am making an "effort" again applying pretty face paint more regularly.

No, I don't have terse, political writings about comparing United States Native spaces between home (American Samoa/ Hawaii) and South Dakota Oglalas here (later, dude).

No, I don't offer up the compare/contrast rhetoric between Native Pacific Ocean thought and philosophy frameworks vs. that of Native Lakota here (at least not for this essay).

No, I don't care to spin feminist critiques bred initially in Western sensationalism of gender role theories and imposed on United States indigenous women here (for another day, 'kay?).

And no, I have no offerings of housing discrepancies of the Pine Ridge Indian Reservation HUD (not here, but elsewhere I do).

Instead, let's allow this essay to express more urgent issues: make up and cosmetics. Sugar Pill brand remains at the top of my list. May I recommend the Burning Heart Quad Pressed Palette? And I just ordered a cream liner palette from Smashbox dot com at half off. Haters, read no further.

Foolish is he/she who cannot get past their limited assumptions of who South Dakota's First People are. Lakotas not only publish heavy weight indigenous sovereignty intellectualism; dance in eagle feathers and jingle dresses at powwow gatherings; hold sacred ceremonies that still mystify, intrigue mainstream America (because that's what "outsider" weirdos sentimentally look for); and have revitalization processes in Lakota language— many also wear make-up. Really good make-up. Really good make-up from Sephora (and from Ulta, Allure, Macy's, Neiman Marcus).

If you enter into my own Native neck of the woods (er, umm, my own Native neck of the Pacific Island jungles), one will not only

discover our Samoan people dancing, singing, ceremony-ing, culture ing, Native-ing, language-ing, publish-ing, elocution-ing wildly of historical/political disparagements—immediately and unapologetically, an onlooker can testify that we Island chicks love a good, creamy lipstick. Sometimes it comes as an applicator wand.

I'm pretty sure Sacajawea or Queen Lili'uokalani enjoyed a really great moisturizer—local style. Can't we talk about that, too? No shame in revealing how we await the next Hello, Kitty line of mascara or nail polish. Ya oughtta see us in our French tips!

We are more than just our politics. Face it.

Native gals are simply enhancing ancestral beauty, ancestral identity (this phrase is for those ridiculously desperate to confirm their own limitations on mysterious Pocahontas-like Indians that live on the Great Plains and need to read—or hear, or speak—the word "ancestral" since it makes them feel more "Indian," or something).

It's okay to enjoy being pretty, girlfriends. I do not downplay how that is a way to reclaim, revitalize, renaissance all things "NDN," all aesthetics of previous centuries. If you can get a mail-in rebate for blush, more power to you.

In other publications, a reader of this essay will discover my writings can regularly lean toward aesthetics, art, literature, theory, politics, philosophy, and Native language immersion of high academics.

This time around, I am happy to disappoint.

Kiri Close, Kyle

Battle Hymn of the Prairie

She opens her eyes to a glorious morn
On the farm in Dakota where hubby was born.
The sun's fingers slip between blinds that are tasteful
And name brand. Albeit, to him, a bit wasteful

On this tightfisted prairie. 'Tis a battle she picks
To be "Martha Stewart" living on a farm in the sticks.

Breathing in country air, she throws back the covers,
Admiring percale in the air as it hovers
So crisp, so cottony-smooth and sought after
By women of substance, refined; prone to laughter

On this uncultured prairie. 'Tis a battle she picks
To be "Martha Stewart" living on a farm in the sticks.

Her bare feet touch carpet, denying a pebble
Brought into her lair by the Philistine devil
Who ignores echoed pleas to leave boots at the door!
Ten years now this topic has nagged at her core

112

On this base, earthen prairie. 'Tis a battle she picks
To be "Martha Stewart" living on a farm in the sticks.

She flicks off the rock, and with it, her beef.
To the bathroom she limps now, and jungle motif:
Snakeskin shower curtain and framed leopard print
Hanging over the biffy. The walls: sagey-mint

On this artless old prairie. 'Tis a battle she picks
To be "Martha Stewart" living on a farm in the sticks.

Refreshed, she is ready to conquer the day.
Toward Pampered Chef kitchen she goes now to play.
Past leather sofa, eggplant pillows and throw,
There's something amiss. What's this? Oh no! No!

There are cows at the window! Calves in her yard!
They smashed up the flower pots she worked on so hard!
The one patch of smooth, weed-free grass on the place
Is top-dressed in cow pies from rogue black-white-face!

She shricks for some backup, her spouse now awake
From unmerited rest. "Grab the gun, for Pete's sake!"
Startled bovines run bawling from island of grass
Between earsplitting yelps that skin hides and bend glass

On this miserable prairie! 'Tis a battle she picks
To be "Martha Stewart" living on a farm in the sticks.

Is anyone else here unhinged by these wenches;
These renegade cows who find holes in the fences?
Apparently not! And least of all, he
Because time and again those cows work themselves free

On this "come what may" prairie! 'Tis a battle she picks
To be "Martha Stewart" living on a farm in the sticks.

Fencing tools, steel posts and barbed wire abound
In the shop, on wood pallets left lying around

By this cowboy who hurried, and then ran to town,
Forgetting to go back and bolt panels down

On this unfinished prairie. 'Tis a battle she picks
To be "Martha Stewart" living on a farm in the sticks.

Matching burdens with others' is risky at best.
But in one case she did, and came out of it blessed.
When she told neighbor Angie 'bout cows getting out
Ang shared stories of scrotum sacks lying about!

On this unscripted prairie. 'Tis a battle she picks
To be "Martha Stewart" living on a farm in the sticks.

She left a quaint house with a sun porch in town
And moved thirteen miles to be near his farm ground.
God, grant her the wisdom to change what she can.
But as you know, Lord, it will not be her man

On this wild, untamed prairie. 'Tis a battle she picks
To be "Martha Stewart" living on a farm in the sticks.

No paved roads bring traffic, no street lamp she sees.
It's the silence she loves, living free as the breeze.
Out here she found romance, while some gal's still hopin'
To find her own farmer in spaces wide open.

On this big windswept prairie. 'Tis a battle she picks
To be "Martha Stewart" living on a farm in the sticks.

It's not for the weak, the unyielding, nor helpless
To be a farm bride—she's got to be selfless!
'Cuz tasteful accouterments don't pay land rents.
Love rides a shrewd horse, and it's called Fixin' Fence

On this practical prairie. 'Tis a battle she picks
To be "Martha Stewart" living on a farm in the sticks.

Paula Ness Northrup, Letcher

Photo Courtesy of the State Archives of the South Dakota State Historical Society.

Postmarked in South Dakota

Almost twenty-four years ago, I walked into the tiny Centerville, SD, post office with my five-month-old daughter in my arms. When I asked to buy stamps to mail some letters, the postmaster asked me if I needed a weight.

"No, thanks," I said. "Just the stamps."

"I mean the baby," he said kindly. "Do you want me to weigh your baby?"

Being new to motherhood—and new to the Centerville area—I wasn't sure what to make of this. But sure enough, I found myself handing my daughter across the counter and into his outstretched hands. He placed her gently on the metal scale.

"Eighteen pounds, nine ounces!"

He was delighted, and so was I.

My children are now grown, and I live in Mitchell (where as far as I know, they don't weigh babies at the post office). But ironically, the post office is where I talk with other empty-nesters. We catch up on news about our kids and hold packages with out-of-state addresses. Catherine (the post office baby) is in graduate school in Indiana—with no plans to return.

Perhaps it all started in Centerville, I say. And I laugh.

Yet I think of a commercial that aired a few years ago, warning South Dakotans that young people are our state's greatest export. I suppose it's true. We educate them well, instill a sound work ethic, and send them away.

It's a haunting statement.

Last fall, I found myself looking out of Catherine's upstairs bedroom window. I looked onto the scraggly yard, over the tops of the outbuildings, beyond the barn with the sagging roof to the horse pen, the stock dam, the brown fields and wide gray skies.

The random thoughts entered. Would she have stayed if the yard had been nicer, the roof less saggy, if there had been more to do? And what about the other young people in our state? Will they be more likely to stay in South Dakota if the salaries are higher? The economy better? The jobs more enticing? Maybe. But maybe not.

Certainly, we must do everything we can to strengthen our economy for the young people who want to stay in South Dakota and for those who would like to move back to the state. But I think we must also recognize that the urge to fly away is characteristic of many South Dakotans. In fact, it's part of our heritage.

I remember a bittersweet scene from Laura Ingalls Wilder's *By the Shores of Silver Lake*. Throughout the golden autumn days, Pa and Laura hear the sound of wings. Both are struck by the urge to go, to fly, to push west, beyond the Dakota horizons.

In the book, Ma's determination to settle in De Smet ultimately wins. But "Ma" doesn't have to win in every story. Our state has young people who feel the urge to fly as deeply as Pa and Laura. For these young people, there is no need for us to wring our hands or devise new ways to entice them to stay. Rather, we must offer them the opportunity and the permission to leave.

Perhaps they'll remember their return addresses and come back home. But maybe they'll keep flying, confidently postmarked as South Dakotans. To these young people, let us also give our support and blessing.

Jean L.S. Patrick, Mitchell

ON THE HIGHWAY

Maps in my car
Maps at home
Is this a map in my purse
My mind is on the highway
across the plains
over the badlands

I don't have much money
That doesn't worry me
My little Toyota is my pal
not much gas or oil
no matter how long the trip

I yearn to be on the highway
a new adventure
friends
strangers
so many people to meet

SUNDANCERS

Eagles fly.
Whistles blow.

The dancers dance day after day
gazing upward, following the sun.
They give of their bodies
and of everything that is spiritual.
They pray. They pray. They pray.
We join them as best we can.
    We pray.
    We dance,
our feet lightly touching Mother Earth
    in unison. I pray to Grandfather.
    I pray to God.
I pray to the dancers
giving so much of themselves
that we will be strong
    in body,
    in spirit.
I dance by my relatives
old and young,
sick and strong.
Sharing the pain.
Sharing the happiness.
Holding tight to our beliefs
    This is our strength.
Prayers move over the land,
    traveling with the breeze
On and on
Settling like dust on
    our relatives
    the four legged
    the two legged
our feathered friends.
Over our Mother Earth.
Touching all lightly.
We return each year to this
    our Sacred Land.
    We pray.
    We Dance

THE BEAUTY OF LIFE

Take the time.
Look around.
So much beauty in this life.
The baby with the smile of an angel.
The melting snow. Spears of grass
    pushing through the earth.
An old car falling apart
    still reaches the end of the rainbow.
Many have lost loved ones
    who moved on to make room
    for another on earth.
Don't be blind to the homeless
    and the suffering.
Offer them a hand.
Offer them a prayer.
Help just one.
Someone will help another.
The politicians may not be the best.
They may be the worst.
But we have the freedom to be happy
    or sad.
That wonderful freedom.
Pain in the back. Strength diminishing.
Oh, we have all our limbs.
Arms to embrace.
Legs to carry us over the earth.
Yes, there is beauty in the world.
Look around at everything that lives.
The smallest insect. All are relatives.
We share this land, the blue sky.
So many wonders of nature.
Oh, such beauty in this life.

Marilyn Pourier, Kyle

What's In Our Hearts

What connects us to the scent of rain on the earth,
to the last sight of geese in the fall,
to the first sight of geese in the spring,
to the first gasping breath of the newborn calf,
to the warmth of our homes when winter winds blow?
We are the sum of our senses and more;
we who grow a living from the land
cannot live without being connected
to this sky and to this earth,
needing to feel the soft rustling of long green corn leaves
brushing against our legs and bare arms,
to feel life in our very steps as we stride through our days.
Still, we lie awake at night
worrying whether ends will meet,
whether the path we have taken will work out,
whether the rain will come,
whether the sun will shine,
whether our will and physical core
shall weaken or stay the course.
We have found the good, while dealing with the bad.
We have stayed, when others have left.
Such is the power
of our land's beating heart.

Visions

Does the spirit of the first settler
forever plow his first straight furrow
again and again,
turning over virgin sod, planting
the purple petals of pasque flowers
upside-down in black earth,
the plow being pulled by the same work horse

that brought his wagon to his claim?
Do herds of shaggy buffalo
roil dust clouds high up
to a blue, sunned sky
while fast, paint ponies carry saddleless riders
with bows and arrows closer and closer,
as even more ancient men,
the mammoth hunters, surround
their prey, showing courage as naked
as their will to survive to thrust their spears
into the huge beast at close quarters
again and again?
Visions cross and criss-cross each other in the great
twilight of eternity in an ageless dance, joined continuously
by all those who have breathed the same open sky I breathe.

On Any Clear Night

Standing outside in my houseyard,
living as I do away from all light
that people make,
the ground on which I stand fades outward --
dark, flat, and formless --
until the night sky sweeps upward
in a blaze of white, yellow, and red --
star sprinkles --
a solid, curving wall -- an infinity of suns --
from this darkened earth.
I fall skyward,
heaven bound.

Mac

He rode the rails with the tramps
in his younger days,
which might explain why
he never wore his wealth.

121

Occasionally I would see him at farm auctions,
looking nondescript,
wearing baggy, striped coveralls.
He usually stood over to the side of the sale ring,
not much of an expression on his face
except for his eyes that showed
he wasn't missing a bid,
or who was talking to whom.
Strangers paid him no attention, but
the locals knew what land he had,
and he had more than most.
He was a lot like other older men
I knew who were large land-holders –
most you couldn't pick out of a crowd
by the way they acted or held themselves.
Mac, like these others,
looked like a perfect fit behind the wheel
of his older faded work pickup
as he drove away down the dusty gravel road
to where he lived.
Still, I couldn't help but marvel at the man
who had had the insight
to buy and hold Coca-Cola stock
during the depths of The Great Depression
and never saw the need to cash it in.

Bruce Roseland, Seneca

Kylie and Jared, students. By Kim Smiley, teacher. Used with permission of students and Kim Smiley.

Who are you and what about you makes you a South Dakotan?

We aren't just talking the state you live in. We are talking what characteristics, values, talents do you have that make you, what you consider to be "South Dakotan?" Or, what makes you a part of South Dakota's "new generation?"

These students from Enning - Union Center answered these questions with the pictured "Hey, I am a South Dakotan!" symbolic self-portraits after learning about people from past generations, cultures and backgrounds during a SD History Adventure Field Trip conducted by the SD Discovery Center, supported by a SD Humanities Council grant.

Interviews with People in Aberdeen and Watertown on "What Makes a South Dakotan?"

Points made about the characteristics of South Dakota and South Dakotans in several dozen interviews conducted by Lawrence Diggs of Roslyn in Watertown and Aberdeen during early 2012.

** = point receiving special emphasis from a number of people
= point made by a few people

CHARACTERISTICS OF DEMOGRAPHY, GEOGRAPHY, THE LAND, AND THE WEATHER
** Wide-open spaces, openness of the land
Small population of the state; smallness of the cities and the towns
Flatness of the land
"Big sky" country
Diversity of the weather
Many people don't like cold winters
Smell of cow manure
Desolation of countryside

HISTORY, SOCIAL STRUCTURE, AND INSTITUTIONS
The state is a result of its deep agricultural or pioneer roots
In little towns, everyone knows everybody else
Social divisions exist in the towns (there is a "pecking order")
South Dakota is a diverse state

CHARACTERISTICS OF THE PEOPLE

** People are (very) friendly (Most-often mentioned characteristic)
** People don't communicate very well or at least very deeply
People do communicate deeply (especially if you know them well)
Drivers acknowledge other drivers with a "steering-wheel" (or "windshield") wave
People are hard workers
People are religious
When you're new in town, the second thing people ask is, "What church do you go to?"
A popular table prayer starts, "Come, Lord Jesus; Be our guest . . . ."
People are reserved
People avoid talking politics
People will say, "It's not my problem."
People avoid conflict; they are not good at conflict resolution
People are cliquish; it is hard to break into established groups
Inertia is common. People often say, "We've never done it that way before."
A lot of people don't appreciate music and art
People accept things as they are
People are traditional or are blinded by tradition
People possess strong values
People are busy
There is a lot of volunteerism
People enjoy it here; they like being in the state
Ethnicity (especially German and Scandinavian) is important
(Latino newcomers): We feel like we belong here

ACTIVITIES, ATTITUDES, AND PROCLIVITIES OF THE PEOPLE

People enjoy socializing at coffee shops, bars, and other places
People enjoy big meals with family at Christmas and other times
Sports play a large role in local communities
Hunting is a major activity (mainly of men)
Gender segregation, while declining, remains more prominent than in some other states
Ballroom dancing (was) popular
South Dakota is an automobile-oriented society
Young people are heavily into texting, twittering, and using

cell- and smart-phones
Young people, especially, complain that "there is not enough to do in town"
A lack of public transportation limits some people's mobility
People enjoy a variety of foods
There are special peculiarities of the language used by South Dakotans, e.g. "Pierre"
People feel safe; many do not lock their doors or install alarm systems in their houses
There is a strong strain of independent thinking and anti-government attitudes

Lawrence Diggs, Roslyn

RELATIONSHIPS

Lois and Delbert Aulner. By Tom Dempster. Used with Permission of Tom Dempster.

By Lisa Borja. Used with permission of Lisa Borja.

Bending Only Slightly When a Strong Wind Blows

"I am you," it revealed as I drove past once again. The tree stands rooted to a slight slope of land on the far South Dakota end of my drive between where I live in St. Paul, Minnesota, and where I grew up in Brookings. Since I began making this drive when I moved to St. Paul in 2004, I have seen it many times, and it has whispered to me in every season. For some reason, this time in late autumn, I finally heard what it had to say.

128

The tree is hidden from both directions in a rare hilly area in the predictable flatness of these Great Plains. At first when I came to it, it popped out like some paranormal anomaly—not a "Big Foot" but definitely a "Big Tree" of the prairie. Though it doesn't surprise me anymore, it still stands out. It hides behind its hilly knoll, and when I come to the hilltop and the land drops and rolls down around me, there it is, dwarfed alone among the vast grassland. It is a sprig of hope that survives in a place where, one surmises, other trees surely used to stand once upon a harvest moon.

I distinctly remember how I felt when I first saw cows crowding underneath the tree's branches. There is a herd of black angus in the area, but I had never seen them near the tree. On the day I saw them gathered around it, I laughed. I did not smile, but rather laughed with a burst of joy at the thought that this lone tree, which I had seen so many times on my lone drives, was never really alone.

It dawned on me that this tree might even prefer its particular lifestyle: its spacious environment, limelight location, and occasional visitor. It might enjoy a simple purpose in shading that particular piece of ground, just as the cows might enjoy shuffling across the field in summer to find that cool patch and catch some relief. And it may—just may—be aware of my admiration of it and enjoy that, too.

"I am you," I answered when I saw the tree and finally heard its revelation. Unlike the tree, I have the freedom to drive by and prove that I am not as rooted as it is—as I sometimes feel. Some days it feels good being rooted—grounded, stable, among the familiar. Lately, however, it feels more like being stuck, bored, and half-buried in routine. I feel a narrow purpose, like a cog in a wheel in a machine in a factory. In a recession. Layoffs impending. Like the tree, I am hardened on the outside, wrinkled, chipping, and bending only slightly when a strong wind blows.

While it seems lonely, this tree only looks alone. When I stopped the car and listened to what it had to say, it urged me to look around at the grass, cows, fields, farmhouses, roads, and towns that shared the same sun, sky, stars, rain, wind, and snow. I could not see anyone, but I knew it was surrounded, too, by people. And it was repeatedly sought out, admired, and appreciated, at least by one in particular.

Like me, a born-and-raised South Dakotan, this tree is on the border between states, poised beside a dependably straight road. It seems to know its unique place in this vast expanse that visibly reaches out and holds all life and things and people together. Like me, it is sometimes between seasons and sometimes between homes, surviving simply and apparently for no reason other than to reflect the passage of time. Like life, it is constant and ever-changing, belonging to no one person yet belonging to everyone under the sun.

Even the cows.

Lisa Borja, St. Paul, Minn.

Photo By Christian Begeman, Buffalo Ridge, SD. Used with permission of Christian Begeman.

~~✿~~

Tornado Tuesday

It was a dark and stormy Tuesday night throughout the whole state of South Dakota. Off an old dirt road in rural Hartford, my family sat in our living room watching the evening news. Suddenly all the electricity went out, and the sky began to turn greenish. The world seemed to stand still.

My mother suggested that we all move to the basement. As my mother, brothers, and I ran toward the basement door, my father ran to his bedroom for a flashlight. None of us made it to the basement before our house was lifted off of its foundation and set back down in the backyard. My oldest brother and I were on the stairs when they collapsed beneath our feet. He held me close and sheltered me from everything flying around us. My mother and youngest brother had fallen directly to the ground because their first step was not there, and my father was thrown out of his bedroom. As we all made our way to each other, my mother had to help my father into the basement. We found a ladder and climbed out of our eight foot basement and began running to my mother's brother's house, which was right next door. The tornado was behind us, so it seemed that every three or four steps we took, we were pulled back another step. We were brought into my aunt and uncle's house and were given warm blankets, and they helped my mother and father clean up. When the storm had passed, the ambulance came and took my parents to the hospital. My aunt and uncle took care of us until they came back. The following day friends and family came to help clean up what used to be our house. We moved out what we could and put it into a moving truck which was parked in our yard.

We lived with my aunt and uncle for several months before moving into a hotel and then a rental house. Throughout the whole process of moving and cleaning, our friends and family were there with us through it all. That is what I think it means to be a South Dakotan—to help as much as possible and to be there when your neighbor need.

Danielle Eldredge, Hartford

The Gift of Generosity

It's in our most vulnerable moments that we learn the most about ourselves and others. In 2009, I spent nearly two months in a Sioux Falls hospital recovering from same-day surgery. Everything that could go wrong, did. After returning home, the recovery was long and discouraging at times. South Dakotans surrounded me and carried me when I didn't have the strength to do anything for myself. South Dakotans brought food to our home three or four times a week for several weeks. South Dakotans cleaned up our yard for winter. South Dakotans took personal days from work to sit at my side when my husband couldn't. South Dakotans sent gift cards for gas and food. South Dakotans volunteered to complete construction jobs my husband had started before my hospitalization. South Dakotans painted our home and refused payment. South Dakotans prayed with me and for me. South Dakotans sent e-mails to the hospital every day for weeks. South Dakotans worked hard as nurses and doctors to restore me to health. What makes South Dakotans? People who unselfishly give of themselves to others in need. I'm so proud and thankful to be called a lifelong South Dakotan myself.

Nancy Weber, Watertown

My Ten Grandmothers

"Now, students, think about who your grandparents are. Who has a grandmother?"

I raised my hand. Most of us fourth-graders had a hand up in the air.

"Okay. Now, how many of you have two grandmothers?"

132

Again, up went my hand. Again, up went some other hands. "How many of you have three grandmothers? That would be two of your regular grandmothers and maybe one of your grandmother's mothers, or maybe your grandfather's mother. Three grandmothers? Anyone?"

I didn't quite understand that part about grandmother's mother or grandfather's mother, but I sure had grandmothers and grandfathers. Up went my hand again. Only a few of the other kids had a hand up.

"Alright, does anyone have four grandmothers? Okay, just a few of you."

I put my hand down.

"Now, let's see who has a grandfather. Raise your hand if you have a grandfather. Wait, yes, Deanna, what is it?"

"I have ten grandmothers."

"What? Ten? No, that's not possible. Grandfather. Anyone have a grandfather? Raise your hand if you have a grandfather. Wait. What is it, Deanna?"

"I do, too, have ten grandmothers." I took a deep breath and started to say all their names as fast as I could go, "I have Grandma Mabel, Grandma Vick, Grandma Milk, Grandma Eva, Grandma Lucy, Grandma Bessie. . . ."

"Stop! You cannot have ten grandmothers, Deanna, that's just not possible. Okay, let's move on and we need to get this done before it's time to go home. Grandfather. Raise your hand if you have a grandfather."

I raised my hand as other kids did, too. And I knew I had only four grandfathers, but why did the teacher say I could only have four grandmothers?

I wondered about it all the way home. I asked Mom why the teacher thought I could only have four. All Mom said was, "She doesn't know." I left it at that for many, many years.

I taught my first four years at a school where I had many relatives.

"Hey, Auntie, hi, how are you?"

"Hi, good to see you! Tell your mom and dad I said hi, okay?"

"Yeah, okay. Toksa."

I started another teaching stint at another school where I had many relatives.

"Hi, Auntie!" turned into "Hi, Grandma!" over the years. Then, I began to hear echoes of the past.

"That's your grandson? How could that be? Your daughter's just a junior in high school!"

"Yep, he's my grandson. Just go with the flow."

"But I don't understand it. Your daughter must have had him when she was what, ten? That's impossible!"

"Hey, he's my grandson. Okay? He's my grandson."

"Did you adopt him as your grandson?"

"Nope, he is just my grandson, period. I have to get to my classroom. Have a great day!"

It was not until the last ten years that some inkling of understanding has crept into some people's brains. Take tonight, for instance. A teacher was standing with her charge after the concert, waiting for the parents to come claim their son. My sister asked the boy if he needed a ride because she could take him. Confusion began to cloud the teacher's eyes. She is a very kind teacher, and she is beginning to understand some of the ways.

I spoke up. "Sure, come on, takoja. Grandma Nadine will take you home."

"Okay, Michael, go with Mrs. Stands."

"Michael, Grandma Nadine will take you home. You sang good tonight. Tell Mom hi when you get home. Night, everyone."

"Okay, Nadine will take you, Michael. Thanks, Nadine, and goodnight, Deanna."

Ahh, goodnight.

Deanna Stands, Wagner

Turtles

When my grandfather was a little boy, he fished in the Cheyenne River and would catch catfish, rainbow trout, and a lot of other fish. We didn't know that my grandfather fished there until this past summer when Dayton, Wade, Donavon, and I went swimming. We all wore goggles, and when we looked under the water, we saw a rock. It was big, about the size of a laptop, so we all swam to it. We picked it up, and it started to fall to pieces. We tried to be careful with it and put it on the bank. It was tan, oval-shaped, and slimy from the mud and moss. It looked like a turtle, but at first we thought it was a dinosaur egg.

We carried the rock to my house and showed it to my grandpa. He said that it was a fossil and that it was probably that old turtle that he and his friends would try to catch. He told my friends, my brothers and sister, and me about this turtle that lived in the Cheyenne River. He and his friends would try to catch it with their fishing poles, but he said it was a smart one. It was fast and would always swim away.

They gave up because the turtle was too hard to catch. They called it Beast Boy. Grandfather named his car after this turtle and called it Beasty Boy.

Grandpa said seeing this fossil reminded him of his childhood, so we gave it to him. He kept it for a while until it fell off the table and broke. We picked up the pieces and put them in a cardboard box which we put in front of his shed. It's still there.

Now when I fish in the same river as my grandfather did, I think about the kind of fun he had. I still have that same kind of fun in the same place that he did.

Ray Fast Wolf

A South Dakotan Childhood

Long before I would have awakened, my father, and often my mother, would be out in the barn milking our cows on our grade-A dairy farm near Sylvan Lake. My father would come in for breakfast with frozen tears on his face from feeding the cows and horses in the harsh 1950s winters. After the milking, there was the separating of cream from the milk and pouring the milk into cleansed cans for transportation to the pasteurizing site in town.

If Mother was not already gone to her job teaching school to supplement the family's dairy-farm income, she would be helping to apply the electric milking machines to the cows after they were placed in their stanchions. Like a lot of small farmers, both Mother and Dad worked off the farm to supplement our income, Dad doing carpentry and mining and Mother teaching at a country school.

Having a dairy farm meant that we had to be home both morning and evening to milk the cows. Evenings I remember my mother chopping wood to fuel the wood-burning stove while Dad did the milking. My job was to cook dinner, which I did pretty well for an eight-year-old, unless I was too immersed in the Nancy Drew book I was reading and let something burn.

Like the other South Dakotans I knew, my parents were honest, hard-working, and always ready to help a friend or neighbor. Being raised on a dairy farm was limiting, in that we were unable to be gone for days, but liberating in the exploration of the granite rocks, catching crawdads in the creek going through our farm, riding horses in the meadows, picking raspberries, having gooseberry-eating contests, ice skating on the frozen creek in winter, and teaching our pets to perform on the wood Dad was cutting.

It wasn't all play; my sister and I also helped in the family vegetable garden and cleaned the chickens my mother would behead. My childhood served me well in teaching me to be resilient, self-reliant, honoring of the environment, and appreciative of food grown naturally. My childhood, like that of other rural children, provided me opportunity to use my imagination and to develop a good work ethic. I would not trade my childhood experience for anything. While others live among soaring towers of steel, South Dakotans live in the expansiveness of nature, learn to cooperate with Mother Nature, and know the truth of our interconnectedness with our environment.

Judith Kennedy, Lead

⚜

The Milk Check Paid the Bills

When Duane and I were married in 1954, his parents moved off the farm, and we moved in. We were the third generation on the farm, which had been established by Grandpa Albert A. Bohn in 1898. For us, it was a typical farm. Eighteen milk cows, farrow-to-finish hogs, chickens, acres for corn, alfalfa, oats, wheat, and maybe some flax or sunflowers. Duane milked with a hanging Surge bucket and poured the milk through a strainer into a ten-gallon can. He manhandled those cans into a wooden cooler, where running well water cooled the milk to insure quality until the milk hauler from the cheese factory picked it up. The hauler returned the emptied cans filled with whey, which Duane fed to the pigs. My job was to wash the cans and the buckets before the next milking. It was the milk check that paid the bills.

Technology hit when Duane purchased a milk tank cooled by electricity. The dairy went from Holstein bull-in-the pasture to artificial insemination. The pasture-fed cows rotated between small sections by way of an electric fence. A silo unloader and a gutter cleaner eased the physical labor. The Dairy Herd Improvement Association tested the milk of individual cows for butter fat content which led to "scientific" culling of the low producing cows. Duane purchased the first of the registered Holsteins for our son's 4-H projects, and this was the beginning of the show-quality milking herd.

The Dubo Holstein herd became our hobby and obsession as well as income producer, and 4-H Achievement Days and the State Fair were our family's vacations. Duane's service as delegate to the National Holstein meetings took us to Philadelphia, Milwaukee, and other interesting places.

When our son Harlan graduated from South Dakota State University with a dairy production degree, he joined the farming operation. Through the years, these dairymen began using embryo transplants and computer analysis of not only the milking herd (hogs and chickens went by the wayside), but the crop land as well. The Harvester silo for wet corn or haylage added to the carefully managed feeding of an individual cow's production and breeding. It was a good, challenging life.

When grandson Greg came home with a degree in dairy production and an urge to milk cows for a living, it worked for a while. Expansion costs prevented the necessary additions and improvements, and even with three off-farm incomes, the milking herd had to be sold. Today dairy remains on this farm. There are still calves and heifers, but the dairy industry, especially here in the I-29 corridor, has changed dramatically.

The dairy industry has gone from "small" herds of 100 or so to the huge dairies (not farms), where cows are counted by the thousands. The milking is done by trained milkers, in 8-hour shifts, 24-hours a day. Feeding and breeding is controlled by computer-based technology which lets the herd manager maintain attention to individual cows. Raising the calves, breeding the mature heifers, and calving have become specialized activities done by contracted professionals at other sites.

The five generations of dairymen who built our Dubo Holstein brand are typical South Dakotans. We are proud to be rooted in the pioneers who settled in this part of the country. Our generation on this five-generation farm has had our time, and as much as we would like things to stay the same, they do not. We hopefully chose the best, ignored the unworkable, and trusted we have made the right decisions for the following generations.

Marjorie Bohn, Milbank

Daughter-Father Relationship

The sun is warm on my legs as I skip down the dusty gravel road. One of my hands clutches a lunch bucket while I gather a few interesting rocks with the other, anticipating what lies ahead. It's my turn to take lunch to dad as he works in the field! The soft summer breeze is sweet and with it comes a unique popping sound. A moment more, and the old green tractor comes into sight, churning up dust as it comes down the row of corn. Dad sees me and lifts a lean, brown arm in a welcoming wave. In a swirl of fine black dust and a few intermittent pops, the tractor stops and dad jumps down. We sit down together in the warm dirt with our backs against the hard tread of the tractor tire. Dad opens his lunch box and pours a cup of coffee from the thermos. He shares a cookie with me. The air is fragrant with the mixed aromas of coffee, earth, and sweat. The sound of my dad's voice mingles with the whispering of the corn leaves. I'm enveloped in warmth . . . the ground below, the sun above, my dad beside me. This is true beauty. This is South Dakota.

Ramona Bloodgood, Mitchell

From Caviar to Cows

They say everyone has a story in them. Here is mine. Did it start the day at Culver's when I realized that all cows were not boys and girls? Or the day I was told that Rocky Mountain Oysters were not from the sea? Or the day we drove to Huron (one syllable) and my son exclaimed, "What enormous goats they have in South Dakota!" (They were a herd of Charolais cows.) Or the eagerly anticipated radio "stock market" report, with me hoping that the NASDAQ was up?

No, I know when it began. Eighth floor, William Beamount Hospital. Detroit, Michigan. June 1, 3:13 p.m. The doctor—I don't remember his name—looked me in the eye and said, "Your husband has eleven weeks to live."

Widow. Widow at forty. Widow at forty, with a six-year-old. Widow at forty, with a six-year-old, who needs to get in the elevator (not a grain elevator), press the button, and find her new life.

But which one? I wish there was a great big store with flashing lights titled "The Life Store—BUY*SELL*TRADE—Returns Welcomed!" Kind of a cross between Walmart and a thrift store. I could stand in the aisles with captions like: Entertainment, Business, Culture, Sports and pick something fitting. Would I have gone down the agriculture aisle? I would have rather gotten my teeth drilled, or so I thought.

Dating with wrinkles, age spots, and lunch-lady arms (you know, arms that waggle when reached across to put peas on your plate) was a trip! But I embraced it head-on. A little too much.

I had the age spots on my face and neck frozen off. The doctor told me they would naturally fall off in two weeks.

Well, two weeks later, on a date with a lovely man and an even lovelier glass of chardonnay . . . "PLUNK" . . . age spot in my chardonnay! God has an incredible sense of humor. Hey, he made giraffes with blue tongues! Well, on the next date, with an even lovelier gentleman, and beer, he casually mentions he is moving to South Dakota to help with his family's hunting and fishing lodge.

The closest I've come to hunting and fishing is hunting for bargains at Macy's and goldfish crackers. I said goodbye (no kiss at the door) and found Mitchell, South Dakota, after looking in the vicinity of Greenland and Antarctica. It happened to be the same latitude of Farmington, Michigan (where I lived), so I accepted a second date.

One year later, my now husband and I packed up our three kids (my son and his two daughters), one cat, and two dogs into our 200,000-plus mileage Grey Suburban and headed west to a home we bought on the Internet.

Here I sit today at Ruby Tuesday, overlooking I-90, reflecting on my story, and laughing. I'm thinking about the first time I saw big bales of hay, and my son said they looked like cinnamon rolls. And about putting lipstick on in the car and realizing it was frozen. Or noticing that an entire town could smell like cow. And about the first time I saw a Christmas tree in a school and said a prayer at a public meeting. Or about the first time I realized that the entire state had the same area code. Or how beautiful the horizon looks during a thunderstorm, and I never even got wet!

Does God have a sense of humor? Absolutely! And what does it take to be a South Dakotan? Faith. And lots and lots of luck! Okay, and a few age spots in your chardonnay!

Laurie Yeo, Mitchell

Taking Time for Retirement

South Dakotans are known as hard workers. Even after retirement, most men who farmed return to the fields to help out the relative who now farms what was once his land. Or, if they're city workers, they may decide to start sacking groceries at the store or volunteer at the hospital. Women never know when to quit either. They keep busy with housework after they've retired from teaching, nursing, or holding an office job. They may even decide to take up quilting or gardening.

But a group of my friends and I have finally learned how to retire, at least for a little while each day. We gather for coffee and conversation in the cafe area of the local grocery store every afternoon from three to four o'clock. We bring our own mugs, purchased from the store, so we have to pay only the refill price for our coffee. And we fill our mugs ourselves at the big coffee urns sitting on the counter along the wall, opposite the big windows. We move two or three tables together so we can all sit around one long space. The women sit at one end, the men at the other. That way, the conversations can be geared to the interests of the group. Sometimes, though, we all talk about the weather or politics together. If someone has a birthday, we celebrate it right there. The birthday person provides a cake and ice cream purchased in the store. Usually, they bring plastic forks and paper plates from home to serve the treat. We all sing the "Happy Birthday" song before we begin to eat. I often wonder what shoppers in the rest of the store wonder when they hear that song being belted out. Winter or summer, we take the time to gather and share an hour of our lives. The rest of the day may be busy, but that specific time is for relaxing, visiting, and doing absolutely nothing but being retired!

Marilyn Kratz, Yankton

Photo by Greg Latza. Used with permission of Greg Latza.

South Dakota's Horse-powered Epochs

I'm honored to breakfast daily with an interesting amalgam of South Dakotans ranging from long-eared curmudgeons to middle-aged guys who remember Oleo, and a few youngsters who stumble in wearing stylish, sleeveless vests for coats and think Oleo was a store-bought cookie. They gather before dawn at the local café to predict the weather, kid and kibitz about one another's imagined frailties, and enjoy eggs of the sunny-side variety. They

142

also talk shop.

As the interloper of the group who writes but doesn't know beans from buckshot about hoses, tractors, or cars, I've discovered that my breakfast friends represent South Dakota's three distinct horse-powered epochs beginning with dirt paths that morphed to gravel roads that blossomed into tarred highways snaking like wagon wheel spokes out from the state's dozen or so major trading hubs. They cover the horsepower waterfront on this sea of grass we call home. The older guys grew up astride horses or harnessing placid pairs of polite Belgians on cold mornings in dark barns. The Oleo mixers fondly remember sitting on springy tractor seats and keeping time to the rhythmic intonations spewing from the upright exhaust pipes. The youngsters in padded vests recall double-clutching their way through high school in two-tone Chevys with padded dashes.

They all can lay claim to being world-class experts on horsepower. Believe me, they know their business. If I had a horse with a hitch in its get-along, a vintage tractor with a bad cough, or a car with a cantankerous clutch, these are the virtuosos I'd call for help. Fortunately for all of us, similar masses of prairie polymaths are common in South Dakota.

Wherever they are gathered, their conversation is akin to a college-level course on the common measurement of energy equivalency, otherwise known as horsepower. They know the subject backwards and forwards.

The oldest in our crowd grew up with horses. They can spot a splay-footed sesamoid a mile away. They remember with sad eyes the faithful horses that were part of their lives, with names like Bluebird, Bessy, Big Jim, and Prince.

Then there are the vintage tractor enthusiasts at our morning klatch. They can recite the horsepower of B. F. Avery's ponderous steam traction engine or the 1915 Mogel 8-16, which could duplicate the heavy lifting of eight draft horses with hooves big as pie tins. They own neckties and logoed caps the exact color as the handsome Massey-Harris Junior Model 101 or one of the other makes and models. They know that industrial yellow was the official color of the nearly five-ton Minneapolis-Moline Model 706 and may throw in its horsepower on the drawbar without being asked.

Heck, I'm a city guy. I don't even know what a drawbar is.

Then there are a few younger coffee sippers who occasionally mumble something that sounds like "mocha" and grumble because the coffee isn't served as it should be with whipped cream dusted with cinnamon on top. They probably wouldn't know a horse's pastern from a hole in the ground, but give these youngsters a screwdriver and a pair of pliers, and they'll overhaul a '56 Golden Hawk Studebaker blindfolded. Don't even ask them about door windlaces, headlight bezels, or latch knuckles. But if you need a bezel or fender skirts for a '47 Hudson Commodore, stop by a South Dakota café some early morning before sunrise. They'll tell you where to look.

Those warm, friendly, early morning South Dakota places are havens for horsepower mavens.

Chuck Cecil, Brookings

Buddha Overhears a Conversation at a High School Basketball Game in Rural South Dakota

It's funny how friendship lives
all the days and nights where it is

I'm hoping your youngest makes the three
you're hoping my oldest is still free

Frank Pommersheim, Vermillion

Two Degrees of Separation

South Dakota is the only state I have called home. I've lived in Sioux Falls, Vermillion, Pierre, Belle Fourche, and Lead, all within the four corners of this state, and it is all I know. In South Dakota, we can forget West River versus East River, and we can forget big city versus small town; because if we live in South Dakota, we invariably know someone who knows someone who knows us. When we talk to a new acquaintance and discover where in South Dakota they live, our next question is: "Do you know so and so who lives there?"

Is this an almost daily occurrence in our lives? Yes. It's routine because of the size of this state and because of the intimacy that exists here. My husband's sister made that abundantly clear when my children and I flew into Washington, D.C., to visit her the day after the 4th of July in 1985. As we drove past the Lincoln Memorial, she said, "Yesterday 700,000 people celebrated Independence Day on the Mall between the capitol and the Lincoln Memorial—that's more than the number of people who live in South Dakota."

For me, the small world of South Dakota started fifty years ago when I started dating Bob, my husband. My mom asked if his dad was from Colton, near where she grew up. I asked, and sure enough, he was. My mom remembered Bob's dad as a little boy selling newspapers for the *Colton Courier*, which his dad owned. Who would have thought?

Because South Dakota is as friendly as it is, we think we know everyone. It's as simple as the county license plates, which tend to be conversation starters in our "Great Faces, Great Places" state. When I notice the license plate county number of any town in which we've lived, especially the smaller towns, I immediately think I should know the person in that car.

People moving into South Dakota, like my son-in-law, Kris, soon learn the proverbial six degrees of separation just doesn't apply in South Dakota. Kris grew up in Minneapolis, where anonymity is possible. After living in Sioux Falls for only two

145

weeks, he remarked, "Two degrees of separation. That's it!"

We were celebrating our son Scott's birthday at a local restaurant. Earlier that day, Kris had a meeting with a business representative named John. When Kris arrived for the birthday party that evening, John walked in the door of the restaurant. Scott said "Hi" to John.

Kris asked, "You know John?"

Scott replied, "Yep, his daughter played basketball at Lincoln High School, where I coach." Kris just shook his head.

Two years later a similar coincidence happened. While eating at another restaurant, my daughter noticed her high school chemistry teacher sitting at a table with his family. Amy eagerly conversed with Mr. Erickson and introduced her baby. Then Kris walked up and said "Hi" to Mr. Erickson's son.

This time Amy's jaw dropped as she said, "How do you know each other?"

Kris said, "We're both doctors at the same hospital."

Small world. No. Small South Dakota. These examples are a testament to the fact that even with a growing population, two degrees of separation is not the exception but the rule. People born outside of South Dakota must think we South Dakotans speak a foreign language with our two degrees of separation conversations. But for natives, it's part of the charm of living in South Dakota—the state we love.

Katherine Amundson, Sioux Falls

A Network of Intertwined Lines

Imagine the people in the cities, towns, and farms dotted over the prairies, the Black Hills, and the Lakes regions of South Dakota, all joined in a network of intertwined lines. What makes a South Dakotan is embodied in this picture, because we who live here seem to find connections no matter where we go.

Take my case as an example. I have recently moved into a retirement community where I did not know anyone. Yet people have extended their friendship in the true spirit of South Dakota cordiality, and it didn't take long to discover connections. The CEO of the community is the son-in-law of a couple that I have known since the early 1950s. A lovely woman, originally a resident of Lennox, knew my sister, a caretaker for the children of her niece. Although years past the age of retirement, an admirable couple living here still maintain a business in Martin. I know their daughter, a successful music and drama teacher in Plankinton, and their granddaughter, equally talented, who is an administrator and teacher in Stickney. While serving as a volunteer on the library committee, I met an outstanding lady whose daughter was my son's freshman English teacher. A retired pastor, whose apartment is near mine, once preached in the same Methodist church in Beresford which I had attended when I was young.

Two connections to one person: A woman who worked for the state of South Dakota through several governorships knows a former student of mine who was a close associate of the late Governor Janklow. The other link: Her son owns a painting of a landmark in Midland, a garage and repair shop owned and operated by my uncle years ago.

After joining the Writers' Club, I met a wonderful lady, originally from Artesian, who is a mutual friend of a woman from Draper, a retired member of the U.S. State Department Diplomatic Corps. Then I met another lady, herself a retired member of the same organization, who also knows my friend. Several apartment residents are my fellow-alumni from Dakota Wesleyan University in Mitchell. DWU people seem to have instant camaraderie and mutual friends. Very recently, a gracious lady from White River came here to live. As it happens, her late husband attended high school in Beresford during the same time that my brother, sister, and I did. He grew up on a farm in the same area as the farm where I was born and raised.

These experiences are not at all unusual. This is what makes a South Dakotan. We even know by name and in many cases, by personal contact, our U.S. senators, representative, and governor. People who come from more heavily populated areas are amazed at this as well as how easily we relate to each other. Even if the connections are not direct, everyone seems to have a mutual friend, relative, or acquaintance in common.

We, who are fortunate enough to live in this great state, realize that a meaningful life means caring for and appreciating other people, both from the past and the present, who have made South Dakota the friendly, wonderful place that it is.

Ethel L Hughes, Rapid City

What It Means to be a South Dakotan

I was writing a Valentine's Day card to a good South Dakota friend—"your friendship is good for my heart and soul"—and I thought to myself, so is South Dakota.

South Dakota truly is a state with, and of, heart, mind, and soul. I've lived in Pierre, Webster, Virginia, Washington, D.C., Webster (again), Vermillion, Redfield, Brookings, and now Michigan. Although Michigan is where my house "stuff" is located, South Dakota is still my home of the heart.

Growing up as the daughter of former Governor Sigurd and First Lady Vivian Anderson was a very special life. No matter where we lived or traveled, South Dakota was always a big part of our lives.

In Washington D.C., we always attended the South Dakota picnics and political gatherings, and we welcomed visitors to our home. Although I was young, and usually the youngest, at most of these gatherings, hearing people reminisce about "good ol'" South Dakota wasn't lost on me.

When I moved to Michigan to further my education and to find a position at Michigan State University (MSU), I was delighted to discover that one of my co-workers and her husband had gone to school at Black Hills State College and that he had worked at Ellsworth Air Force Base. A huge painting of Sylvan Lake hung over their fireplace—a grand reminder of their time in South

Dakota.

A former MSU co-worker now resides in Brookings. For years I kept telling him how wonderful South Dakota is, and after a month of living there, he told me I was right. He could see how special life is there.

South Dakota will always be known for its beautiful scenery, weather, agriculture, tourism, hunting, fishing, and the Midwest work ethic, but for me, it's the people.

Nowhere will you find more caring, kind, and considerate folks. I think the people are the state's biggest asset. When you tell people where you're from, their eyes light up as they begin to relate their favorite trip to, or through, South Dakota. It sparks conversations about fond memories of youth or college life.

People will comment, "I have a co-worker from South Dakota," and then express how impressed they are with their co-worker's commitment, dedication, and integrity—hey, it's who we are and what we do, and it's how we South Dakotans live our lives.

Most of my friendships are with people in South Dakota. As I grow older, I realize how much more those friendships mean to me. I find myself checking the state's weather forecast as much as our local weather. With family members, I share diverse happenings in the state to keep them informed as to what's happening "back home."

Being a South Dakotan means having pride in your state, its people, and its heritage. It means supporting its growth and innovations and sharing love for home with those you meet. Although health reasons preclude me from traveling, I cherish the visits to South Dakota I have been able to make in recent years. I value the friendships I have, and the memories I have made. I know my parents would agree with me!

Kristin K. Anderson, Okemos, Mich.

⟟

We're Not in South Dakota Any More

Sure, the sandstone buttes that lay before me touched a sky of robin's egg blue, creating a landscape that was overwhelmingly beautiful. But I didn't need to double-check the road map or look at a sign along the road to know that I wasn't in South Dakota's Badlands. Rather, it was the people I encountered who convinced me that I was a long way from South Dakota.

The open-air vehicle in which I was riding on the scenic drive through Monument Valley Navajo Tribal Park in Arizona was encountering similar vehicles. Not one of the people riding in those vehicles was smiling or waving at me and my family. South Dakotans, I reflected, wave at other motorists. If they are driving down the highway and encounter another vehicle, a quick raising of the index finger off the steering wheel is what etiquette requires. Those they know are given a wave with their whole hand.

South Dakotans do more than wave at other motorists. We look for people from the same county when we travel in South Dakota beyond the borders of our home county. When we journey outside the borders of South Dakota, we scan parking lots for vehicles bearing the familiar license plate with Mount Rushmore on it.

Why? Because the thought of meeting these fellow South Dakotans makes our hearts race faster than a rabbit in coyote country. Chances are, we know the person, or we know someone they know. We want to find out who it is. I thought about a gathering I was at where two women from Centerville were also in attendance. Did they know each other? They did not, but they met and talked. Did Susan know the chiropractor in Beresford? Yes, she did. Well, that is Laura's daughter-in-law. Susan and Laura talked some more. They discovered they had both attended high school in Pierre although several years apart. This sort of thing happens to South Dakotans all the time. A South Dakotan is one who knows we are all connected to each other.

As the vehicle in which I was riding traveled down the road at Monument Valley, I thought about the other people touring the arca. I smiled broadly and waved to them as our vehicles passed by each other. It's what a South Dakotan does.

Dorinda Daniel, Pierre

Photo by Greg Latza. Used with permission of Greg Latza.

Homecoming

Even though I lived in the Twin Cities for thirty-five years, I still consider myself a true South Dakotan. At age eighteen, I could hardly wait to shake the dirt off my shoes and leave South

Dakota forever, but I soon learned it wasn't quite so easy to take South Dakota out of my heart! Being surrounded by trees in Minnesota made me claustrophobic, and I yearned for the wide-open spaces of South Dakota. I missed the beautiful sunrises and sunsets, the rolling prairie with the contrasting flatness, the ever present wind, and the stillness of a summer evening.

I married another South Dakotan, but our careers kept us away from "home" until we reached a point where we were finally able to return to our roots. It was a bittersweet homecoming, because my husband passed away six months later. That's when I experienced the generosity and compassion of South Dakotans, along with their willingness to help others during tough times. That's one of the hallmarks of South Dakotans—if a farmer passes away during the growing season, his neighbors show up and finish the harvest. Helping our neighbors is what we do.

South Dakotans are friendly. When I first returned, I wondered why everyone I met on the highway waved at me. I thought it was because I drove a bright yellow Mustang and it caught everyone's eye, but when I switched to a more practical SUV, they still waved, and I realized they were just being friendly. It's what South Dakotans do!

I love the relaxed attitudes of South Dakotans. When you go to the grocery store on the weekend, don't plan on getting in and out in a hurry, because in every aisle you will encounter friends and neighbors visiting and catching up on the news. People just aren't in as much of a hurry here as they are in other parts of the country.

The weather in South Dakota can be a challenge, from droughts to floods, blizzards, and thunderstorms, and, yes, even tornados. But South Dakotans are tenacious and take the weather in stride, realizing that that's just part of life on the prairie!

Returning to South Dakota and the roots my grandfather planted when he homesteaded here 129 years ago was one of the best decisions I ever made. I love this land and the people who live here!

Lois Peterson, Huron

PLACE

Camels and cows roam freely near rural Sinai. The camels are used for the Nativity reenactment at Sinai Lutheran Church each Christmas. By Adrienne DeBoer. Used with permission of Adrienne DeBoer.

Before Burning the Homestead

He hasn't gone in lately because of his asthma.
The place reeks of rotting wood, moth balls, dampness, and must.
But one last time, as he shuffles from room to room,
he's transported to a place where
a family congregated around the now decaying organ
to sing hymns in German,
a tiny woman canned jars and jars of vegetables, fruit, meat
and designed dresses on a size four dress form,
a boy collected duck feathers to sell.

His children, novice antique hunters, have rescued chairs, bed
frames, dressers from the crumbling plaster and smell,
from the raccoons who've made a home in the attic walls.
He examines the leftovers - mangled mattresses, a rusting cream
separator,
shredded calendars, a cracked gravy boat.
He understands what's left can't be saved -
Time has crawled through the broken windows
Along with water, rodents, and dust.

Tonight after his sons finish milking,
If the wind's right,
This house will burn
To make room for a new generation that wants to forget that it
survived
Two tornadoes within two weeks in April of '62.

Coughing, he fumbles in his overalls pocket for his inhaler.
It's time to go, or he won't be able to breathe well for weeks.
He heads out, leaving that business behind,
And plans a trip into town to play checkers with Mel.

Anne Moege, Mitchell

154

By Christian Begeman. Used with permission of Christian Begeman.

Dakota Land

We are *am ha aretz,*
What the Hebrews called
People of the land
We are Dakotans
Keeping vigil here.

We are all temporaries,
And so are all our works.
The hills and plains, the rivers and
The Badlands sculpted by

The winds and rains and melting snows
Are more permanent than we.

We all came as visitors
Whether Lakota Sioux or Cheyenne,
Pawnee, Crow or Mandan;
Norwegians, Danes or Hutterites,
Germans, Finns or Mennonites,
Or Irish to the land.

The first visitors
Learned what most of us
Have yet to learn:
We do not own the land.
Our titles and our deeds
Make us caretakers for a while.

The Dakota land and skies
Those hills and plains and valleys,
Those flat lands and arroyos,
Those Badlands sculpted by
Winds and rains and summer sun
Have come to own us.

It leaves a longing in our hearts
When we move away,
Which we do not recognize until
We return to smell once more
The fragrance of the summer sage
Blowing in the wind.

Yes, Dakota Land, you own us.
We are but visitors and sojourners here,
Temporary caretakers and witnesses to
Your beauty and your grandeur.

Michael D. Ryan

156

The ReMember Center, Oglala. By David Michaud. Used with permission of David Michaud.

South Dakota: Through a Child's Eye

blue skies
        snow sledding
                animal tracks
nourishing rain
        sticky mud
                yipping foxes
bright sunshine
        horse riding
                singing birds
colorful sunsets
        leaf collecting
                deer in headlights

Shannity Robertson-Hare, 9 years, Vermillion

My Ancestral Homeland

To me South Dakota is more of a state of being rather than a state of location. More specifically, I think of the Sisseton Wahpeton Reservation, where I was born and grew up. There's an old saying that holds true and that goes, "You can take the Indian out of the reservation but you can't take the reservation out of the Indian." This used to have somewhat of a derogatory ring in my younger days, but now as I think about it, there's more truth to it than I had thought.

It has something to do with "belonging." South Dakota is a state of the nation and identified as a geographic location. I like the term "homeland," which just happens to be in South Dakota. As the homeland, it precedes statehood, and its roots go deeper than settlements, towns, counties, land demarcations, and ownership. When my feet touch the soil, it connects me to my ancestors and my mother earth, and I have a comforting feeling that someday I will rest in her bosom.

No matter where I go, I feel as though a part of the homeland goes with me. Yet I am not complete until I once again feel the soil and my beloved ancestors. This was true when I went to a government boarding school to become assimilated into the ideal American. Some think it so strange a young boy would prefer the starvation and desolation of reservation survival to a modern civilized life. The government created insane asylums for those who thought like this.

Where I felt this again was when I was in the military service overseas. The loneliness and desperation were so great that I thought it would never end. I felt that I didn't belong and how great it would be to be back in the world. I was overjoyed to view the skyline of San Francisco. It looked like what I imagined would be paradise. I realized that I wasn't yet home, even in South Dakota. It wasn't until I entered our house that I felt like I belonged.

Sometime later, I went back to San Francisco on BIA Relocation. The government believed all that was needed was to get the young Indians off the reservation and get them a job, and that's about all they did. After fifty years, I still have dreams or maybe nightmares about trying to get home. Sometimes it's easier to leave than it is to come back. I left on a good passenger train for the West Coast and returned to my homeland ten years later on a freight train. Now I'm living on my ancestral homeland that just happens to be in South Dakota.

Elden Lawrence, Peever

Varieties of Experience

Someone who has experienced the variety of our great state, who is familiar with how friendly the people are, who appreciates the "elbow room," who enjoys the magnificent scenery, and who wants to live here forever—that's a South Dakotan.

Spending my entire life of seventy-eight years right here in South Dakota, born in the same house my dad was, his father's homestead southeast of White Lake, I feel, makes me a true South Dakotan. I spent eight years attending a one-room country school three miles from our home there, then taught five years in that school.

Marrying a school administrator, I lived in different areas of the state, experiencing the enjoyment of wherever we lived. In time, we moved from the undulating prairies of the east to the granite spires of the west, giving me a taste of the variety of this great state.

Involved in the beginning of the conversion of the railroad into the 114-mile Mickelson Bicycle Trail, as well as riding it many times, and because of time I have spent on the Centennial Trail, I have witnessed the natural beauty of our Black Hills—the mysterious geologic formations, sudden weather changes, towering evergreens, grassy prairies, verdant meadows, and vistas that make you smile. Rustic barns and trendy restaurants, sophisticated art galleries, quaint attractions, bed and breakfasts, artists, Indians, cowboys, and business people are within distances to enjoy near the Mickelson Trail.

I have rested above the rustling creek, listened to the chorus of the variety of birds, and heard the wind whistling through the pine, while watching the graceful movements of wildlife grazing in the valley. By participating in cycling tours throughout the state, I am aware of the different types of scenic beauty. When you are on the seat of a bike or hiking, you don't just look at nature, you become part of it.

Spending many years at the Badlands KOA, which our family built on the Pine Ridge Reservation, I had the opportunity to be involved with many of the Lakota people. Travelers from all over the country constantly praised our great state. Most had never witnessed the stillness while looking up at a completely black sky, filled with bright stars, the elbow room, the magnificent scenery, and the friendliness of the people who live here. They, like I, loved the remote, unspoiled, and untamed portion of the historic Badlands. This wilderness of canyons, gullies, ridges, peaks, and spires is unforgettable.

Teaching mountain bike classes at the South Dakota Outdoor Woman's Workshop, held every two years at different ends of the state, again gives me the opportunity to enjoy our nature to the fullest.

Although many of my friends spend the winter in warmer climates, I have never left the Hills. I continue to enjoy our winters and the many activities that are available during the colder months here in our state. I truly enjoy the change of seasons. I don't want to miss any of them. I am a South Dakotan!

Jeanne Kirsch, Rapid City

※

Treeless in South Dakota

I was born and raised in New York, not the city, but 150 miles to the north, where there are people, hills with aspirations of mountainhood, and trees. And more trees. My middle son on a visit to the East Coast family noted that in New York the cities are in the trees while in South Dakota the trees are in the cities. A nuanced but significant distinction, in my opinion, and one that makes a South Dakotan.

The sum total of our geology, climate, and ecosystems makes us a mostly treeless state, except for pockets of urbanization, riparian corridors, and a relatively small hump in the lower left hand corner of our state map. This hump is named not for its striking geology but rather for the aspect given by the trees, in this case a relatively dark-needled spruce. I cannot help but think that had there been more trees on the prairie landscape, the spruces in the Black Hills would have been less striking and the area might have been called the Twisted Rock Hills or Red Path Hills or something equally poetic.

I love the treeless vistas of the prairie. I can breathe here, physically and emotionally. When you talk to a South Dakotan, whether born or transplanted, the wide-open spaces are a thing of beauty, a balm to the soul. The openness feels safe and welcoming. My brother, of the above mentioned East Coast family and firmly rooted in his urban tree landscape, finds the openness overwhelming.

On one visit, I took him out to the grasslands, where he whipped out his camera, set it on panoramic, and began snapping away. I've tried to describe this at home, he said. People don't understand that it looks like the ocean, but with grass.

I suppose there was a time in my life long ago when I would have not been able to envision a treeless landscape, that the only corollary I would have had for such an expanse would have been ocean. I now cannot fathom *not* knowing the prairie. This is my place. This is what makes me a South Dakotan.

Anne C. Lewis, Pierre

❧

South Dakota through New England Eyes

"There's just nothing to see out there—just nothing!" My senses are on alert as I hear someone complaining from the back of our bus traveling across the state. I had been basking in the scenery and jotting down glowing details on my yellow pad when the voice interrupted my reverie. "Nothing"?

I gazed at a rusty windmill by a weather-beaten ranch house, the barbed wire fence stretching as far as I could see, and horses trying to feast on dried grass. A cloud of dust dancing after a speeding vehicle disappears behind an oasis with a clump of trees tilted against the wind. "Pleasant Valley Road" winds out of sight. Not a thing blocks my vision. "Nothing to see"?

I grew up in Maine, but ended up in South Dakota in 1960. I left behind roads covered with canopies of trees and rocky shores lapped by the ocean. Here, in my adopted state, I have learned to love and embrace its far-reaching farmlands and mysterious, whispering prairies; the mighty Missouri and its brown, barren buttes; the concrete ribbon of I-90, slicing the landscape in two; and the Black Hills, steeped in history. I've loved every bit of it for over fifty years.

Every fall, I head out with snacks, a good book, yellow pad and pen, trusty camera, and that old, collapsible lawn chair. I'm ready to travel the countryside, scanning the farm fields with the monstrous machines grabbing the golden corn stalks or munching their way through a bean field.

I might travel down County Road 117 to Newton Hills State Park. I follow the winding, shaded road down to the lowest area of the park, find a picnic table, and park my lawn chair. I might see turkeys or deer. Nearby, Lake Lakota is also designed for quiet relaxation. A sign tells boaters that boats cannot exceed five miles per hour or produce a visible wake. From a rocky shoreline, I can see the pine trees across the small lake and the colorful, deciduous trees shading the swimming beach.

Another afternoon, I could end up at Union Grove State Park, with its cool, dense forest, where I can stand on 1,309-foot Parkview

Hill. I can hike a trail that descends through scented woods to the murky, muddy waters of Brule Creek with its gentle, rippling waters.

At Lake Vermillion State Park, I can take time to simply absorb the scene of a shimmering lake dotted with fishermen's boats. How many times has a walking trail with the soft crunch of pine needles reminded me of Maine? Benches on the bluff invite me to sit and gather in the panorama of farmlands, a farmstead with a silo, the lake below, and a grove of scrub brush dotted with maple trees glowing with the season's reds and yellows.

Local signage takes the reader back in time, referring to "a soft breeze," a "golden hue," and "rolling hills" while "bison move across the land at a slow pace" with "low grunts." A "meadowlark song keeps harmony with the insects' low trill." A "prairie dog's high pitched bark" warns "of danger nearby." The meadowlark still sings, the insects still buzz, but yesterday's tall grass has given way to fields of food; concrete covers the bison resting place. Yet, the "beauty and memory still live on."

I find it hard to explain all this to my friends back East (or to the voice in the bus!). They don't understand the silence and beauty of open spaces, the rich farmlands, the solace of parks, or the grandeur of the Black Hills. I just invite them to come and visit me, for I am a South Dakotan!

Priscilla Field Jorve, Sioux Falls

The Drive to Work

Each day I travel eighty-eight miles one way to work, and every trip reveals something new. The early morning sunrises, with their bright orange and blue colors, are the most beautiful. I post pictures on Facebook for others to enjoy.

Seeing an eagle sitting in a distant tree, flying overhead, or picking at roadkill alongside the road is exciting. In our Lakota culture, an eagle flying overhead means good luck or a blessing.

There are always cows and calves. I enjoy watching the calves romp and chase each other. I'd love to take a picture with one, but I'm sure I couldn't catch one, let alone take a picture.

The deer and antelope are an ever-present sight, but it's the deer that most frequently cross the road in front of cars. My son put deer alert whistles on the front bumper of my car—so far so good. Once on Scenic Table there were about twenty deer standing inside the fence. As I passed, I looked in my rearview mirror and saw them jumping the fence and crossing the road.

When we hit the rez line, the majestic, awe-inspiring Badlands (*maka sica*) come into view—a picturesque sight. I like taking pictures at this spot when snow is covering the formations or after a rainstorm when the color of the formations is vibrant and rich.

Near the White River, there are always turkeys standing, fluffing their plumage, or dancing alongside the road or standing in the middle of the road, and they won't move until you're right up on them.

When I round the bend near the Ranger Station, I know I'm close to work.

The little stop-in-the-road called Sharps can be either desolate looking or crowded with actual traffic jams. There are always dogs looking for hand-outs or kids on horses racing up and down the ditches with dogs in tow.

Around the corner from Sharps, there's a pond with lots of turtles—big ones and little ones—basking in the sun on the logs. Once a little turtle, about the size of a fifty-cent piece, was crossing the road, and I stopped and carried it across the road.

Only eight more miles and I'll be at my destination.

The drive home is so different. The prairie sunset is beautiful even when there's a storm on the horizon. The winds can be fierce with dust storms and an occasional flying trampoline from a roadside house. I've driven through blinding rainstorms where the windshield wipers couldn't keep up with the rain, and then I've driven out of them onto a dry highway.

There are stories of "ghost cars," which follow you across the Badlands, and of hitchhikers who disappear into the night when you let them off or who get into the backseat of your vehicle without your knowledge and push against the back of your seat.

You don't want to think about these when you drive home alone.

The deer are notorious at night, and you have to be ready to brake at any time. On clear nights, I love the bright, twinkling stars, the occasional falling star, and the full moon when it's bright and appears to touch the top of the Badlands.

On Scenic Table, the pinkish-orange glow of the city lights up the horizon; this is a comforting sight. There's also cell coverage. If I need to call someone, I do it then before I head toward the Cheyenne River Breaks.

The airport lights come into view, and the two-lane highway turns into four. I'll be home soon.

Gloria Eastman, Rapid City

By Terry Sohl. Used with permission of Terry Sohl.

Francis Case Lake overlooking Platte Creek, Missouri River. By Tom Dempster. Used with permission of Tom Dempster.

Becoming a South Dakotan

There is a sense in which the landscape makes us. I suppose that's true of everyone, everywhere, but perhaps we live a little closer to the landscape than people in more populous locations. I grew up elsewhere, and it took some time here for me to be transformed into a South Dakotan. I realized it had happened one summer when I spent several weeks at a seminar in Connecticut.

166

The meetings were excellent, I enjoyed the other participants, and it should have been a great experience, but something didn't feel right. On an afternoon walk, I finally knew what was wrong: it was the landscape. There were droopy trees everywhere, their branches hanging over the roads and paths. The sky was too small. I felt enclosed, trapped. I missed the open feel of South Dakota. We call ourselves "the land of infinite variety." That may be a slight exaggeration, but our landscape does offer great variety, from the glacial lakes of the northeast to the farms and ranches of the middle to the Black Hills and Badlands out west. There is something different every few miles, all of it sliced by the Missouri River into what we call "East River" and "West River."

South Dakotans tend to spend a lot of time outdoors, and maybe that's why we are psychologically shaped by the landscape. We like things that are a little wild, a little ornery. We enjoy changes that sweep in like our blizzards and tornadoes. Yet we can be patient, too, happy to drive a hundred miles for a cup of coffee with an old friend. We value independence, and yet know that there is much we can never control. The awareness of place that we South Dakotans carry can help us understand and accept the inevitable cycles of life and death. Every little town has its prairie cemetery, every old farm its collapsing barn or shed, and in the fall fields of sunflowers hang their blackened heads like mourners. We had a cabin in the Black Hills ghost town of Galena for many years, and that landscape gave me a meditation: "Bear Butte Creek, Galena, South Dakota." The banks seem taller this year. Flat rocks scoured smooth by centuries of ice water are suddenly exposed to sun and thin air. Rosy with age, gaping at the light, they will crumble away too long after I am out of time. Already I'm an inch shorter than I was in my teens. Newly old, I blunder through the gulch scattering dead cells, hairs, memories, words, the electricity of dreams. No need to carve my name on that fence. I have already happened to this place, and it to me. Inhabiting this world means being broken. Time carves us all like rocks shaped by rushing water as we dissolve into the universe. The borders grow thin. Years wear away all surfaces exposing what remains to one perfect June morning.

Nancy Veglahn, Sioux Falls

167

~\|2~

Tapping Ancestral Environmental Knowledge

My family homesite is in the rural South Dakota community of *Toka Nuwan*, or Enemy Swim, located on the Lake Traverse Reservation in South Dakota. It is an ancient and historical community and has been inhabited for thousands of years by *Dakota* ancestors. I am reminded of this fact by the *maka paha*, or burial mounds, that surround this community today. They are the sites of the final resting places of ancient *Dakota* relatives.

Enemy Swim was also mentioned in the journals of French mapmaker Joseph F. Nicollet. It is a beautiful home, surrounded by glacial lakes and prairie potholes that support abundant wildlife. The invading Euro American settlers also wanted the *Dakota* homeland as a resource to fuel the commerce and industry of their society. This unresolved history of violent conquest and conflict has kept many of the descendents of the Euro American settlers and tribal communities apart.

The *Dakota Oyate* or Nation has many ancient sacred ties to beloved prairie earth. I was introduced to this valuable heritage through my relationship with *Kunsi*, my maternal grandmother. During my childhood, my siblings, cousins, and I were fortunate to spend many hours with *Kunsi*. It was through her guidance that I learned to appreciate and respect the *Dakota* landscape as a relative and a vital part of creation. This belief in kinship is expressed by the phrase *Mitakuye Owasin* or "All my relatives." She taught me to honor the ancestral environmental principles of the *Dakota* people, and through her influence I developed a love for the land. This appreciation for the natural world and the conservation ethic the *Oyate* has for the *Dakota* homeland produced an environment that was beautiful, pristine, and rich with natural resources. If one has never had the experience of observing an eagle in flight in the vast blue prairie sky or heard its whistle carry across the landscape, how could one then mourn the loss of this impressive bird if it were to disappear? Those of us who live and work in the natural world understand how nature enhances our quality of life.

Today, experts in climatology and environmental engineers

have warned the global community that we are dangerously close to the tipping point where catastrophic climate events can and will occur. As there is only one human species, it would behoove the world community to invite dialogue and incorporate the ancestral environmental knowledge of tribal people in order to care for the earth by reviving damaged ecosystems caused by human activity. The challenge is to develop a new relationship between mainstream American society and tribal communities, even though difficulties shaped by scars from old wounds still remain. South Dakota is made up of many rural communities that depend upon the environment for their livelihood. The future of the seventh generation demands that modern society develop sound environmental management policies that also allow for economic development. If we fail to have these necessary discussions, we will do so at our own peril.

Gabrielle Wynde Tateyuskanskan, Waubay

By Christian Begeman. Used with permission of Christian Begeman.

By Chad Coppess/www.travelsd.com. Used with permission of Chad Coppess

I'm from South Dakota and Other Tall Tales

The social scientists and pop culture gurus who say we're heading for a homogenized global village have obviously never visited the Corn Palace. They're as wrong as a sun-struck prairie dog mistaking a badger hole for his home.

Place still matters and always will, a reality that misplaced prairie dog would soon have discovered in a very personal way.

South Dakotans are WhereYaFrom people, a trait that will be with them forever. If you've moved away or traveled much, you've seen it and felt it at every introduction.

"You're from South Dakota, huh? Wow, never met anyone from there."

Or, "Met someone from Fargo once."

At which point you have one of three choices:

You can smile and say nothing and chalk it up to an illiteracy of caricature one might call placism.

You can casually point out that the distance between Fargo and Sioux Falls is greater than the distance between New York and Boston. You might mention that you—born a small-town South Dakotan—have spent more time in New York or Boston than in Fargo. Not that there is anything wrong with Fargo.

Or, you can go the Big Mystery-Heroic route and describe landscapes so vast and nature so dominant that implicitly the message becomes only strong and stubborn and grounded people can survive. People who know that civilization does not necessarily mean city, that nothing comes easy, and that next year's rain is as important as the sunshine of the moment.

WhereYaFrom people are practiced in the fine art of place. I have not lived in South Dakota for thirty years, but if I met someone today from Woonsocket or Wall or Wolsey, I feel certain that we'd be in "do-ya-know" discussion about a mutual friend in no time at all.

Years ago I went to a large social gathering in Washington, D.C., where I overheard a woman introduce herself as a South Dakotan to another group of people. She spoke in that economical, matter-of-fact twang that turns "t" into "ch" and cuts "g" off at the pass right after the "n."

As in: "Doncha know farmin's a good wayda live?"

This woman did not know I was also from South Dakota when, later, I surprised her by walking up and saying, "I bet you are from Volga, South Dakota." She was amazed that I got it right until she learned I also was from South Dakota, and we laughed at the small-town-in-big-world moment. Actually, it wasn't that hard a guess. Her Dutch name narrowed her down to Volga or Platte, maybe New Holland. I knew she wasn't from my hometown of Castlewood, where the Dutch also settled. So even if she wasn't from one of those places, she'd have family there.

Lately I've been ramping up the Big Mystery routine whenever people ask me about South Dakota. It is a fortuitous antidote to the iPad spheres so many of us live in, where everything is supposed to be known and controlled to your whim and available instantaneously at your fingertips.

So I go big and I go mysterious in my South Dakota introductions, and I barely have to stretch the truth. I describe snow banks so large they have to put red flags on school buses so they can be seen in winter (memories from the winter of '69); sculptures carved from entire mountains; the majestic violence of thunderstorms laying siege to horizons; monstrous dams backing up prairie oceans; and a Badlands moonscape so stark and foreboding it makes the Bermuda Triangle look placid. I go macro in a microchip world.

And, of course, I always mention that special monument to grain in Mitchell. We may not be Bogie and Bacall, but no matter where we go or what we go through, we South Dakotans will always have the Corn Palace.

Chuck Raasch, Alexandria, Va.

Where the Creek Curves

Long before I arrived at the ranch house where I would be living, I knew I was home. The house was merely a shelter from the elements. Necessary, but still only a shelter. Home was all the land that stretched for miles and miles 360 degrees around me. Home was the rising and falling of the deceptively gentle prairie hills. Home was the sound of the water in the creek I had to cross to get to the house. Home was the herd of deer grazing in the field in the late afternoon, as I barreled onto the gravel road, going way too fast from too much highway driving. It was deer, who looked up in unison in the fluid movement of one being, communicating with their eyes, "We don't drive like that here." Home was the huge sky arching over me filled with stars and galaxies that I would be able to see without the light pollution of towns and cities. Home was the carefully tended road winding beneath me.

As it turned out, no humans were there to welcome me, which was my preference. It's easier for me to be aware of what is going on inside me and around me when I don't have to tend to the pleasantries so often expected in the human world. I stood a long while before entering the house. Corrals stood empty and a tottering old barn that once was vibrant with life leaned with the warmth and character of cows and horses and the people working with them, and of comings and goings. Wind stirred in the cottonwood in the yard. The sound of the artesian water steaming up from the ground was the final note that I was home. I breathed in the quiet silence. When I walked in the house, only the glass separated me from a golden eagle flying within a few yards of the window, blessing this journey, foretelling fecundity.

This particular place was situated down in a bowl, with the creek forming a horseshoe around it. I could trace the curve of the creek by the way the owls positioned themselves in the trees that grew in her bends and meanderings as I sat out and listened to them bringing the night to life.

"You're really weird for sleeping out in the pasture every night, leaving your bedroll out there for the snakes to crawl into," said a friend of mine.

"No," I said, quietly in that place inside me where it's safe to say things like this, "No, weird is to pass your life in a place as exquisitely beautiful as the prairie and not sleep out."

What? Miss the shooting stars, Northern Lights, the doe silhouetted against the pale dawn sky, the night hawks dipping sporadically barely above the tops of the grass? Miss the cold air that stirs without fail, announcing the sun's appearance? Never climb to the top of the hill and lie there in two-feet-tall grass, waiting for the moon to rise and spill liquid silver all over the prairie? Miss the coyotes howling in the dark? Miss the watery call of the Sandhill Cranes migrating ancient paths? Miss the honking of geese flying above you throughout the night? Never waken in the morning to find yourself in the middle of a herd of cows who've formed a perfect circle around you, breathing warmth toward you as they welcome you into their circle? Miss the bald eagle flying so low as to hear his wing brush the air? What? Miss knowing my home?

Sylvia Anne Marchetti, Kennebec

Home

I didn't realize how remote South Dakota is when I lived here, how far away it is from everything. It was just home, worn and comfortable. Now, I know I've arrived home when I walk out of the Rapid City Regional Airport and see the ethereal northern sunlight illuminating the big cottonwoods growing near the creek behind Highway 44 and the foothills beyond. This great, sprawling view of the Black Hills stretching before me after a flight is one of the most beautiful things I have ever seen. It means I have returned home.

Growing up, I had two places to call home, modest as they might have been: one in Rapid City and another up in the Hills near Sheridan Lake. On summer evenings in our neighborhood, the children on our block gathered to play games and run up and down the sidewalks and through each other's backyards until well after dark. Before bedtime, I sat on the driveway to watch the bright stars above. On weekends, however, my playmates were the water spiders and fire flies that lived along the small creek meandering toward the lake. In our little mountain lawn, I was amazed by the delicate small ferny plants and flowers that grew wild in the green. My sister and I climbed up and down the piney slope behind our trailer-cabin, sometimes reaching part of the Centennial Trail that ran along the spine of the mountain. There we would visit the "saddle tree," a ponderosa pine with an odd curve at the base of its trunk that was perfectly suited for children to sit on and pretend to be riding horses. Other times, I walked alone down to the lake early in the morning to sit on another stump that jutted out a few feet above the water. There I could find baby birds nesting in a hollow pine nearby, their tiny cheeping more fascinating than any textbook science lesson. I startled small herds of deer on my solitary childhood walks, watching their white tails disappear as they bounded away. As we grew, our excursions into the woods lengthened, and by the time I finished high school, the Hills felt so much like home to me that one chilly autumn day I surprised myself by feeling perfectly content to curl up and rest under a granite outcrop, so much like a woodland creature, while my dad hiked nearby. When our car died one very snowy night in downtown Rapid City, this same sense of being at home, even if not physically in my own house, struck me just as strongly. My sister and I just walked across the street to a restaurant where we found some friends and caught a ride home after having a cup of hot chocolate.

Through my years living away, this sense of South Dakota being my home has never left me. Often, people I've met when I lived in California and Texas have not understood my strong identity as a South Dakotan, my strong desire to return. I can only guess that it is because they have not known the magic of a childhood lived among the pine trees, roaming free under the stars. A woman from New England once asked me if I knew what the strange sound was that we were hearing in the forest. Astounded that someone could not know, I told her that it was the wind blowing through the pine trees, the quiet hush of my home.

Kristina Roth George, Rapid City

East River Meets West River

Differences between the two:

East River	West River
Corn fields	Prairie grass
Farmers plowing	Ranchers herding
Fishing	Rodeo
Seed caps	Cowboy hats
Liberal	Conservative
Town 5 miles away	Town 50 miles away
State Parks	Federal areas
Social	Independent
Corn Palace	Wall Drug
Boats	Horses
Pheasant season opener	Black Hills deer season opener
Bingo	Deadwood
Cottonwood trees	Spruce trees
Jackrabbits	Mountain lions
Friendly	Cautious
Wine	Beer
Twins	Rockies
State Fair	Central States Fair
Public radio	Country music
Ice fishing	Fly fishing
Golf carts	ATVs
Farm fests	Stock shows

Different, yes, but so very much the same.

High school sports	High school sports
Churches	Churches
Love of the land	Love of the land
Icy roads	Icy roads
Gardens	Gardens
Universities	Universities
Generous	Generous
Caring	Caring

Linda Sandness, Brookings and Colleen Langley, Nemo

On North Flintrock's Bend

Just seven miles north of Faith,
Down a wagon road that wends,
Was an ol' log house, pole corral, and stall,
On Flintrock, since 1910.

The place was small—Times were tough,
And hardships came a clutter,
But it was all we had, no chance of something better.
Just that ol' log house, pole corral, stall and us,

It sheltered tired and aching feet,
And honest, callused hands,
Poverty was plain to see, not hard to comprehend.
At the ol' log house, pole corral, and stall,
On North Flintrock's bend.

It was nothing to be proud of,
In the years "I knew it all."
Many times I felt like giving up
That ol' log house, pole corral, and weathered stall,
On North Flintrick's bend.

But now I'd like to have it at the corner of my lot.
In that ol' log house
I'd hang curtains, calendars, and key,
Maybe a picture—two or three
Of pole corral and stall on Flintrock's bend

I'd wrap my arms around it all,
And give it one big squeeze,
That ol' log house, pole corral, and stall,
And years of memories.

Memories are forever,
While yesteryears and yesterdays all end,
Like the ol' log house, pole corral, and weathered stall,
On North Flintrock's Bend.

Irean Clasen Jordan, Faith

⚜

What It Means to Be a South Dakotan through the Lens of a Lakota

From my perspective, South Dakotan defines a geographical area and how one fits into that place to bring meaning to one's self-identity of "Who am I?" I draw from the notion of South Dakotan in the context of identity. I think of inclusive versus exclusionary practices and how these sole forces impact and shape one's experiences as a Lakota. I often think of South Dakota and capture the deep essence of what were once the indigenous lands of what is known as South Dakota.

Who I am is first defined by my place within the boundaries of my Lakota reservation, all of which border the state of South Dakota and Nebraska. As a Lakota, my experiences were shaped looking from the inside of my reservation boundaries outward wondering about this place called South Dakota, which certainly did not capture my world view. I think of South Dakota as a place so external to "my place" which I identify as "my home"—the Pine Ridge Reservation. As I reflect, many thoughts emerge, one in particular, the uncomfortable(ness) of being among those different from who and what I identify as people like me. However, contrasting that thought is the notion of being among my own Lakota people within those indigenous Lakota lands (reservation borders) as a place of comfort; as a result I didn't feel the need to step into that space of South Dakota as a young girl. Today, I draw from the past experiences and convey that my identity lies not from being a South Dakotan, but rather a Lakota who had experiences drawn from South Dakota.

Maxine Brings Him Back-Janis, Oglala Lakota

Our Living River

In 1978, after moving into one of Vermillion's oldest houses, my husband, Jerry, and I learned from a neighbor that both our house and the one next door were built from lumber salvaged by its owner, Swede Swedeborg, from the Farmer's Home Hotel after the great flood of 1881. The Missouri River had lifted the hotel from its foundation and floated it downstream to Burbank. Mr. Swedeborg disassembled his old hotel, loaded it on a wagon, and hauled it to the new town being built on the bluff. A hundred years after that flood, we were introduced to the river's power by that house, which stands as a part of its legacy. In 1983, we moved out of that old house and built a house of our own design into a south-facing hill and faced toward the sun. On a clear day, from a second story window, we can see the Nebraska bluffs beyond the Missouri.

For more than thirty years, the river has been our main summer destination for recreation. We love to canoe and wade or float in the shallow water near a sandbar or island. We've seen shovel-nosed sturgeons, carp, beavers, cormorants, eagles, and herons—green and great blue. Life is abundant on our remaining fifty-nine-mile stretch of the wild and scenic Missouri. Together with friends who also love the Missouri, we work with the Living River Sierra Club Group to preserve the serenity and wildness of our river. During the great Missouri flood of 2011, caused by much larger than usual snow melt and rain in its upper basin, we were banned from the river for an entire summer because the waters rushing out of the Gavin's Point Dam and floating debris had made boating dangerous. In mid-summer, we joined others at a flooded farm near Wagner, helping to sandbag and save a new straw-bale house from the flood. Finally in late August, the water slowed down, and we were allowed to float the river. That glorious, sunny day, we met friends at High Line and pushed off in canoes and kayaks to discover what the river had done. A few stretches of shoreline were littered with concrete and rebar by landowners who'd built close to shore and had dumped the rubble to keep back the waters, but other areas were as natural as before. To our delight, we found the Missouri had created vast sandy beaches on Goat Island and numerous sand bars along the way to Clay County Park. We stopped to rest from rowing and celebrated the ways our river had re-shaped the land. Now it's a healthier habitat for the least terns, piping plovers, paddlefish, and paddling people like us for whom the river is essential to life.

Norma Wilson, Vermillion

South Dakota

To all who will listen, I'll gladly relate
Some interesting facts about the "Coyote State."
We proudly uphold her motto, "I lead,"
While forty-seven others graciously concede.
The beautiful Black Hills, her proudest possession.
For fame, name, and history, ask no concession.
There, boldly sculpted in stone atop Mount Rushmore,
Washington, Jefferson, Lincoln, Roosevelt (Theodore).
There's Harney Peak—over 7000 feet high.

The country's largest gold mine is at Lead nearby.
Production of crops is her main occupation
Which her land sends forth as if proud of creation.
Wyoming, Montana, as well as North Dakota,
Plus Nebraska, Iowa, and Minnesota
Hug closely round her borders all happy to know
That South Dakota being there adds to their glow.
She's flat and rolling with sparse population,
But to those who love her, the heart of our nation.

Thornton Whaling Westbrook, Brookings

Identifying the Prairie

These great plains are content to sprawl uncontained.
For us it's been enough that communal knowing
was inscribed in the directions of a countryside.
But space gets away from you here, gets away from an agency.
Something was not at ease with the cornered off geometry
of unnamed blacktop that we know as "the Jorgenson road."

Overnight like button weeds
institutional-green street signs appeared at crossings
naming them meaningless things like W St. and Avenue 462.
A Bureau of Something has seen a need to standardize and
quantify.
Likewise new blue numbers came up one morning
at the mouth of every lane
as if having sprouted from the ground to signal the growing
season.

Before, dirt roads were named for a knoll, a slough, a bluff, a
bend in the river,
irregularities enough to be noted in the flow of flatland
extending beyond the rim of vision.

Our most indelible placing came from the families of farmers
who plowed their names into soil like seed corn
and saw them set on in the regard of their neighbors.
Any man needing to travel these roads
knew them like storm warnings in a summer sky,
could read them like wind and name them for the home place
of settlers by which they'd been known to his father and his
father's father.

So what of the regimented squat poles holding anonymous
numbers?
These are different from our leaning, tight-lipped mailboxes,
(some held in the arms of Uncle Sam
or home-made into a branch of burled wood like a bird house)
all opening up to our dialogues with the world.

Do they serve a busy-body satellite
that would have the rural world on a shorter picket rope?
Who is it wants our lanes and field access, our county roads
labeled off and codified, and why?
Tracking numbers for the GPS or mapping software
that will tell the lost where thy are in relation to everywhere else?
Are we being issued license numbers that authorize us
to live where we have always lived?
Perhaps they're like name labels sewn in our camp clothes.

Who's keeping track of what
with these off-beat street signs at corners of bean fields,
as if "Burbank Road and 523rd Avenue"
could thus be annexed to an urban world?

I feel my vast expanse of prairie
reduced by blue numbers,
and labels, taller than corn,
shooting up at four corners.

Maureen Tolman Flannery, Evanston, Ill.

182

By Christian Begeman. Used with permission of Christian Begeman

Grain Elevator: Pukwana, South Dakota

I pulled myself up through a shaft of cornfed light.
It broke over my face and left
a floating transparency
of me intermingling with dust
stirred from the bottom of the pit.

The ladder extended beneath my feet
like stilts in concrete.

I stopped at the top,
let my arms extend, leaned
backwards from the steep rails

and imagined
diving to the first rung:

my hands freed from clutch,
air gliding past arms,
abandoned grains below to catch.

I surveyed the final step:
a reach across empty space

to a room where machines belts lived
like discarded shoelaces draped
over a nail in the back of a closest.

Fraying canvas laid on metal wheels
which connected cogs
unable to recall action.

The windows – portraits of open land –
revealed fields occupied
with itinerants: combiners
bringing in grain.

Flying above field dust,

sparrows dove and swelled
in sweeping arcs,
mixing into the endless contrast
of ground fading
to burnished sky.

Sara Stockholm, Chamberlain

TOWNS

Photo Courtesy of the State Archives of the South Dakota State Historical Society.

On Growing Up in a Small Town

I am from
　　the sleeping porch high up in my grandmother's house,
　　　　where tiny glass creatures on glass window shelves guarded my sleep
　　from the alley below rich with bright-colored hollyhocks
　　　　and rain-swollen rivulets that led to the fairgrounds across the street
I am from
　　a large front porch, whose screens kept at bay biting insects of evening
　　with large boulders of peeling mica that lined the steps at its feet
　　　　and fireflies that illuminated corners of the yard
I am from imagination and day dreams and long days of summer
　　from the sailing of great vessels of scrap wood nailed tenuously together
　　　　and led by a tether of string through backyard pools and rain-filled gutters
　　from the challenge of seeing how deep you could wade into puddles
　　　　before water spilled over the tops of your galoshes
　　　　and left the cold squishy feel of wet socks between your toes
　　from riding empty oil barrels in the sea of Leo Smith's flooded backyard
　　　　and waging war with other vessels in the flotilla
I am from the warm scent of homemade bread in my mother's kitchen
　　from a dislike of lima beans that swallowed whole made your stomach ache
　　from the strawberries that ripened in my mother's garden
I am from
　　summer sunburns that peeled skin from my brother's back and mine
　　from sand piles and mud pies and crab apple wars
　　from hugging my dog
　　from life that moved too fast as it didn't move at all

　　Laurie Bogue, Denver, Colo.

A State Made Up of Small Towns

Historians, being human, often find what they are looking for, just like everyone else. I am a historian and also a small-town boy from the Midwest who has lived now in Brookings for thirty-eight years. When I am talking to someone from out-of-state, I often mention that I live in the fourth largest "city" in the state, with a population of 22,056 in the 2010 census. I expect them to raise their eyebrows a bit or to shake their heads in disbelief, and it often works out that way.

In a nation where four-fifths of the population now lives in what are classified as metropolitan areas, to note that almost two-thirds of South Dakotans live in places of fewer than 20,000 people is to say something distinctive about the state. When Sioux Falls and Rapid City are subtracted from the equation, 88 percent of the rest of the state's residents live in places smaller than 20,000. As a longtime professor of history at South Dakota State University, I often remarked to my students that the history of the state is largely the story of its small towns (along with their rural hinterlands), writ large. As everywhere else on the globe, we are an increasingly urban society, but South Dakota retains more of its rural, agricultural heritage than do most other states in the Union. Apart from Sioux Falls and Rapid City, we are by definition a state of small-town residents, along with our farmers and ranchers.

Like many of our friends, my wife, Kathy, and I often find ourselves telling others that Brookings is "a great place to raise kids." That is a major reason why we enjoy living in the state so well and have remained here so long. Not that our community is a little Nirvana. It contains its foibles, peccadillos, and blind spots, just like every place else. Still, I think that people in our town and all around South Dakota—though affected by similar class and social divisions prevailing elsewhere—are generally more egalitarian and socially conscious, less ostentatious, and more self-effacing than people in other parts of the country tend to be. Our neighbors to the east have a reputation for "Minnesota niceness," but a similar quality is easily perceivable among the residents of this state, too.

We are naturally inclined to look out for our neighbors and to lend them a hand if we see that they need one. Local newspapers frequently run stories about spontaneous outpourings of neighborly solicitude and generosity for someone in the community who has been injured, fallen ill, or suffered a setback. Men mow the lawn or paint the shutters, while women bake casseroles or run errands for the unfortunate individual or family. South Dakotans are not unique in this type of behavior, but they are distinctive in their high degree of civic-mindedness and community spirit. South Dakota and North Dakota have been measured as possessing the nation's most elevated levels of "social capital," defined as participation in community affairs, organizational activities, and philanthropic ventures.

So when you think of a South Dakotan, yes, think of the Marlboro Man, the lone horse rider, the proud woman homesteader, the highly independent, freedom-loving individualist, and the don't-tread-on-me, self-sufficient resident of a carefully maintained castle. But also have in mind a community-oriented citizen, involved in local organizations and initiatives, voting in larger numbers than do people in most other states, and concerned for neighborhood, community, state, and national betterment. The two types exist side by side in permanent tension with—but not necessarily in contradiction to—each other.

John E. Miller, Brookings

By Tom Dempster. Used with Permission of Tom Dempster.

Dakota Town

The elevator stands watchman,
its windows claimed
by the stones hurled by
boys who have left.
Now there are tires moaning
over the highways bringing
wind gusts past the last gas pump
where an old man in overalls watches
headlights and taillights
all day.

189

The streets are just Dakota summer dust
where the rain sinks untouched
to the sewers that have stopped their
hissings through the pipes,
and the out-houses are filled to the brim.

A farmer has jerked his country school
from its roots among the uncut weeds,
and his haystack mover has taken it
to his home outside the town.
The church, the bar,
the hardware store, and the lumberyard
have been claimed
for fences and windbreaks.

The graveyard lies at the edge
of a cornfield by the edge of town,
along the highway ditch,
the tombstones among sunflowers nodding
at the moaning tires going by.

Doug Cockrell, Sioux Falls

Manchester, 1943-44

The school house was the largest building in the little town of
Manchester, South Dakota. This is where I started my education
in September 1943. My mother and her sisters had also attended
this school. At one time this school had had all eight grades and a
high school, but as the community and town became less
populated, the children who wanted a high school education had
to go to either DeSmet or Iroquois.

At age six, I'm sure I was very scared to go to school. There were only ten of us in the big building, which had a huge fire escape tube on the north side. When the teacher was away, sometimes the boys would sneak upstairs and slide down it. At recess time we played Ring around the Rosy or duck-duck-goose in the snow, or we played in the stable. One of the fondest memories of attending school there was Orlin Brown's birthday party. One afternoon we got out of school early (it was winter time) and went to his house, which was only a quarter of a mile away. We went sledding and afterwards had cake and hot chocolate. Orlin started school the same year I did.

It was wartime, and in the fall Mrs. Grotto, our teacher, would take us for nature walks to pick milk pods for the war effort. The cotton in the pods was used to make parachutes. During the winter, we "huddled" around the big wood burning stove for our lessons. When the weather was nice, we would walk to Blote's gas station and grocery store for candy.

Blote's gas station and Wallum's Corner were the gathering places for farmers when they brought their grain to the "big" elevators. The men would have beer, and the kids got bottles of pop. There wasn't a lot of money then, plus a lot of things were rationed, so this was a real treat.

Manchester used to be a bustling community with a bank, a creamery, and a mercantile store where my aunts had been employed when they were in their teens. The only things that I can recall being on Main Street were a garage, the Town Hall, the town pump, and the house where Tobermans lived that also housed the post office. All the meetings and social events, including dances, were held at the Town Hall. Our school's Christmas program was also held there. I remember we sang "Joy to the World," and whenever I sing that Christmas song today, I can still see myself on that stage singing with my schoolmates. There was also the Presbyterian Church, where my sister and I attended Bible school. We would bring our lunch (peanut butter sandwiches) in syrup pails and sit on the front steps of the church and eat.

My parents purchased the Waters's farm in DeSmet, and on March 1, 1944, I had to leave the Manchester school. I was sad to leave. The school gave me a scrapbook with the names of all the students who were attending the school at that time, and I still have it.

I was taught strong values by my parents, my teacher, grandparents, uncles, and aunts who had survived the hardship of the '30s in this area. Today all that stands in Manchester is a monument with the names of the people who lived in the Manchester area, a flag pole, and one building, but the memories are still there!

Ione Johnson, Flandreau

By Sandy Robertson. Used with permission of Sandy Robertson

Resilient

If I could choose a single word to describe a South Dakotan, it would be "resilient." The word resilient, according to *Webster's New World Dictionary*, is defined as "bouncing or springing back into shape, after being stretched, bent, or compressed."

Our ancestors, who came here in the late 1800s, certainly were stretched, bent, and compressed by dry, hot summers; cold, harsh winters; and long periods of isolation on the vast, unsettled prairie. Our grandparents faced World War I, the Great Depression, and the Dust Bowl years. Our parents, who were raised during the years of hope following the harsh 1930s, had their mettle tested by World War II, the Korean War, and the Cold War. My generation lived through the unanticipated challenges of the Vietnam War, antiwar protests, and Watergate, but we never forgot our South Dakota roots, where we were taught that right is right and hard work pays its own rewards.

Many of us grew up in small towns in South Dakota with names like Ola, Alpena, and Storla. We have fond memories of small-town swimming pools, Sunday afternoon baseball games, card games in the Legion Hall on cold winter nights, Wednesday night summer band concerts at the local bandstand, late summer carnivals on Main Street, horse races and rodeos, and class reunions. Some of us returned to these small towns only to find the brick school houses closed and only the playground's cottonwood trees and well-worn swing sets remaining.

Many of us moved to larger cities like Sioux Falls, Rapid City, Aberdeen, and Watertown, but our early memories linger in the small towns of South Dakota, where we had our beginnings and where we were stretched, bent, and compressed into the people we are today and hope our children and grandchildren will be one day. I am a South Dakotan because my ancestors were resilient, and life on the prairie taught them that life's challenges were lessons that they needed to learn and that someday their children and their grandchildren would need to learn. I am proud to be a South Dakotan.

Richard Jensen, Sioux Falls

How a Village Raised a Child

From my point of view, this little town of Centerville had and still has many "true South Dakotans." Here is why.

Residents of eastern cities during the late 1800s and early 1900s had an unusual and disturbing method of handling their orphans. When their numbers grew large and the children's homes began to overflow with older children, authorities put them on trains headed west. The trains stopped at all the small towns, and children were left with families who offered to provide them with food and shelter. No questions asked! The children were usually old enough to be of help to the persons who stepped forward to give them a home; they were taken more for their labor than for love. I can only imagine the trauma they must have experienced.

In 1896, a young boy was left in a neighboring town. He was treated so badly that the following year he jumped on a train and came to Centerville. Here he was met by kind-hearted people who treated him with respect. When officials came looking for him and others who had run away, our townspeople hid the wayward lad until he was safe.

He was small in stature, very thin, and always happy and childlike. Topped by a thick mop of reddish and usually unruly hair, he was given the name of Rusty. It turns out he had been born on May 7, 1881, and was admitted to the "Home of Destitute Catholic Children" in Boston at the age of twelve.

I remember Rusty as a middle-aged man, but he looked like a kid to me, partly because he was so small. He always seemed happy and carefree. There was a public water fountain in the center of town with steps on one side allowing a small child to climb up and drink. I often saw Rusty standing on the top step to quench his thirst. He was a kind-hearted, trustworthy lad who loved everyone. You could find him playing with children or helping an adult with a small task. He was truly a part of this town.

Rusty was mascot for the townsmen's baseball, football, and basketball teams. His ill-shaped feet made it impossible for him to participate, but he was issued a uniform, which he wore with pride. The people of the town wanted him to feel that this was his home. As he grew older, various business establishments hired him to sweep and clean. His wants were simple, yet he never had to worry about where he would sleep. He was always welcome at every business that he cleaned to stay the night. Winter or summer, he always had a roof over his head.

His given name was Joseph Crane. He died at age sixty-five and is buried in the Centerville Riverview cemetery.

He knew nothing of the finer things of life and could have cared less. But he knew more about the Golden Rule and practiced it more diligently than most folks whom we call great. He did not have to remember to practice this rule, because he did it instinctively without expecting anything in return. All these things he learned from the town folks who cared for him.

As far as I know, he never went to school. I never heard him utter a word, only make funny sounds. Since no one ever heard him speak, we assumed that he had no voice. If he had come to town today, I'm sure the circumstances would be very different for him. Today, these "South Dakotans" would not be able to give this lad the good life that he was able to experience several decades ago. He would probably be tested and analyzed and given over to the care of helping professionals that officials think would best be able to help him. Instead, he lived a happy life, free from worries, and was a delight to the people and the town.

Hillary Clinton once wrote, "It takes a village to raise a child." The people of Centerville proved that it took a loving, caring town to give this orphaned young man a full, happy life. That is why I refer to them as true "South Dakotans."

Millie Petersen, Centerville

The Only Life Worth Living

There are many reasons I am proud to be a South Dakotan—the state's amazing natural beauty, the independent spirit of the people, and the fantastic diversity of opportunity. But what makes my heart really swell is the generosity of the people. Take the fine folks of Wakonda, my hometown, as an example. In the last five years, the people of this community of 300 have given more than $200,000 out of their own pockets to fund community causes and to help area residents in need. The most recent benefit raised more than $60,000 for the Wakonda Volunteer Fire Department. On one beautiful February night in 2012, more than 575 people—some traveling long distances to attend—crowded into the local Legion hall, where there was standing room only and where they had run out of food for the free supper, to support the cause. Thanks to their generosity, the department paid off its loan on the new (used) pumper truck it had purchased and was able to make federally mandated upgrades to its equipment. Just eight months before that, in 2011, the community had given more than $25,000 to save the Wakonda swimming pool from closing. In early 2011, when community members heard the town might shut down its beloved outdoor pool due to the increasing costs of running it, volunteers not only raised money for the pool to keep it open in 2011 and beyond, but also worked at the pool for free to keep costs down. Before the pool effort, at least three benefits raised a combined total of more than $50,000 to help individuals in the community suffering from serious conditions like cancer and brain aneurysms. Before that, when the legion building burned to the ground, the community gave more than $70,000 to make up the gap between what insurance would pay and what the actual costs of a new building would be. Residents moved fast and were enjoying their new Legion hall just one year after a fire took the old one.

But it's not just through their pocketbooks that Wakonda residents have been generous. Through the years, people have given hundreds of hours of time and talent to keep the community going. Some do the heavy lifting, others share their personal equipment and supplies, and many donate their expertise in construction or painting or bookkeeping or baking, whatever is needed for the particular job. Some excel as communicators, making dozens of calls to get the word out. Others are simply there to support volunteers. Area residents know that, together, we can do just about anything. Such was the thought behind the Wakonda Community Café, which was built ten years ago when the privately operated café in town went out of business, leaving the town without a daytime eatery. First, community members gave more than $50,000 toward the project. Then, they donated their time and talents to build the building, which today is leased by a café operator. For ten months in 2010 and 2011, when there was no café operator for the first time since the building was constructed, the café became the Wakonda Volunteer Café. Two area residents served as volunteer managers. Others cooked, waitressed, washed dishes, and cleaned, all without being paid one cent for it. So, when I think about South Dakota, it is the big hearts of the people and the selflessness I see demonstrated regularly that impresses me. In Wakonda, like in so many other South Dakota towns, the people know that the only life worth living is a charitable one.

Riva Sharples, Wakonda

Now You See It, Now You Don't

In the autumn of 2011, my son Sam and I went antelope hunting in a dry place and got rained out by a rare two-day downpour that turned the dusty back roads of Fall River County into mud, frustrating the hunters and forcing most of the game under cover and out of sight. The rain blurred the line of the horizon and transformed the glowing, yellow-brown landscape into a circle of empty gray silence. The local pronghorn population vanished, as if a hidden hand had transported them magically to some unknown pastoral realm, where they could hunker down in sheltered draws or graze invisibly on uncut alfalfa, waiting out the rain, inaccessible and out of reach.

Adjacent to one of the deserted county roads stood an abandoned country schoolhouse, whose walls were mottled with swallow droppings and water stains, yet still bore the faded white paint and plaster of days gone by. The floors were unsafe, but from the doorway Sam and I could see that the gutter beneath the chalkboard was still intact, although the slate had long since been removed. On the east wall, there was a beautiful row of three large windows that bore nothing now but broken shards to greet the morning sunrise. Who were the children who attended this school? Where did they go? The faded slats gave no clue.

A few miles further, we plied our way forward to the deserted burg of Ardmore, a ghost town, whose water tower punctuates the South Dakota plains like a rusted exclamation point, about a mile north of the Nebraska line, less than twenty-five miles east of the Wyoming border, south of Hat Creek on the old Burlington route, and well west of the 98th meridian in God's country.

According to some of the locals, it's called God's country because He's the only one who lives there. But at one time someone did, including the notorious Western outlaw and horse thief, Doc Middleton, who made his residence Ardmore before drifting off to parts unknown, only to die later in a Wyoming jail cell of erysipelas. In 1927, President Calvin Coolidge once stopped in for a visit, and word has it the town survived the Great Depression without one single family going on the dole. In 2004, *National Geographic* even did a story about Ardmore. But since 1980, the last time Ardmore appeared on any official census, it has slept peacefully, like a silent memorial to the failure of Thomas Jefferson's agrarian dream, with nothing but deserted buildings and houses, faded signs, rusted machinery, and abandoned cars to people its empty streets.

Of the Great Plains, American novelist Wright Morris once said: In the dry places, men begin to dream. Where the rivers run sand, there is something in man that begins to flow. West of the 98th Meridian—where it sometimes rains and it sometimes doesn't— towns, like weeds, spring up when it rains, dry up when it stops. But in a dry climate, the husk of the plant remains. The stranger

might find, as if preserved in amber, something of the green life
that once lived there, and the ghosts of men who have gone on to a
better place. The withered towns are empty, but not uninhabited.
Faces sometimes peer out from the broken windows, or whisper
from the sagging balconies, as if this place, now that it is dead—
had come to life. As if empty it is forever occupied.
(*The Works of Love*).

One of these towns, so the story would have it, was Ardmore.

Rodney Rice, Rapid City

Abandoned House, Ardmore, SD. By Rodney Rice. Used with permission of Rodney Rice.

_✿_

Small-Town South Dakota

Do you have what it takes to live in rural South Dakota? Do you know all of your neighbors? Have you ever lived an hour and a half from a Walmart? Well, if you have ever lived in Hoven, you know what I mean. Hoven is pretty much in the middle of nowhere. In Hoven, there are a gas station, restaurant, post office, grocery store, cheese factory, co-op, repair shop, and drug store, and that is about it. There are about 500 people living in Hoven. A lot of the people have or work on a farm. My grandpa and dad have a farm about five miles out of town. I have been helping out there since as long as I can remember. In Hoven, everyone knows something about farming. You are not going to find someone who thinks chocolate milk comes from a black cow. Everyone works hard around here and knows you have to earn what you get. Farming is not easy, and it teaches you how to work hard. Nothing will be easy in life.

The bigger towns that are close to us are Aberdeen and Pierre. Each of them is eighty-five miles away. They are a lot bigger then Hoven but are nothing compared to Sioux Falls. Living in a small town means having a small class when you go to school, and in my opinion you learn more. My class has nine kids in it. Even though you learn more, you do not really get a choice on who your friends are. You learn to make friends with everyone. You also know who your neighbors are; I could tell you who almost everyone is in this town. Living in a small town teaches you a lot of things. It teaches you to work with what you've got. Your friends and neighbors are the people who you work for, work with, or work for you. Although you might be an hour and a half away from anything, you learn to keep yourself entertained with your friends and family. I like living in a small town, and I think you would, too.

Bailey Zweber, Hoven

WEATHER

Photo Courtesy of the State Archives of the South Dakota State Historical Society.

Wide-Open Spaces

Prairie Life: People often ask why I live on the cold, harsh prairie in the South Dakota winter when I've lived on a Caribbean island, in the mountains, in the desert, and in other, more hospitable places than northeast South Dakota. I tell them I choose to live on the wide-open prairie because here the sun and the earth touch each other twice a day, and I get to see that. The sunsets here are incredible, and I love that!

I love the wide-open spaces, where all the trees we have are here because someone took the time and effort to stick little sticks in the ground with the faith that they would one day provide shelter from the wind and stop the snow. Our ancestors were investing in little sticks for our future beautiful trees, and I love that, too.

In the spring, there is one day, I swear, when, almost overnight, the whole world comes back to life. It is indescribably beautiful! The dead brown grass and leafless trees disappear, and an incredible range of fresh green takes over our world—how can you not love that?! We get to watch summer storms roll across the prairie, building strength and sometimes even fury. There is a beauty in seeing that power build, grow, and nourish the earth.

While I may whine about the cold and the snow and the wind chill, I really do love life on the prairie. The world is beautiful and simple here. I feel closer to God where I live in the four distinct seasons and witness His creation. For me, life just doesn't get much better!

Ann Taecker, Watertown

A Memorable Experience

It was still dark when I left my car at the Black Hills State University property lot and found the assigned state car for my trip to Eagle Butte to supervise student teachers. Often, I would leave at sunrise and return at sunset. While traveling Highway 212, I remembered the bumper sticker that said, "Pray for me. I travel Highway 212."

I decided to stop at Faith to get a cup of coffee and a homemade caramel roll, which was still warm and was the best in the country. Morning seemed to be a time when the men in the community would gather and visit about basketball games, the weather, events of the day, and maybe even gossip.

After I left Faith, I passed Red Elm. Every time I saw the sign, I had to laugh. The first time I took the trip, I thought it said "Redeim." That set me thinking. "Faith," "Redeim": it all seemed logical in a Biblical sense. But on the way back, I saw that it was Red Elm. The "l" had a hole in it, making it look like an "i."

Finally I got to Eagle Butte. I would visit the student teachers three or four times during the semester to observe their progress. They would keep a portfolio in which they included pictures of their bulletin boards, samples of the assignments they gave, lesson plans, and unit plans, which would be helpful to set up their own classroom. Before I left, I gave the student teachers a copy of my evaluation.

One time when I left to go back to Spearfish, the sunset and the moonrise occurred at the same time. It was a pleasant drive back, with a full moon showing the way. That was not the case on this trip. The weather didn't look that great. When I reached Faith, the weather had taken a turn for the worse. It began to snow. I hoped I could get back without running into any drifts. As I was driving, I noticed the lights of a pickup behind me. I thought the driver would not like to go as slowly as I was going, so I slowed down even further and drove near the edge of the road so he could pass. The pickup slowed down. I picked up speed. So did the pickup. Again I slowed so he could pass. Again the pickup slowed.

I decided not to be concerned anymore and concentrated on my driving.

I was almost to Belle Fourche when the windshield wipers weren't clearing the snow any more. I pulled over to the side of the road, so I could brush the snow away. The pickup pulled up beside me. The guy rolled down his window and asked if I was OK.

I told him I would be once I had cleared the windshield. He then told me he had seen that a woman was alone in a small car. He decided to follow me in case I needed any help. He asked where I was going, and I told him Spearfish and assured him that I would be safe. I thanked him, and he drove on.

The rest of the trip was filled with warm thoughts of the people who live in this area. They look out for each other and help their neighbors and strangers alike. This memorable experience happened before the days of cell phones. Having a "guardian angel" look out for me was very special.

Darlene Swartz, Spearfish

A Union County Farm Wife—1936

The sky will churn into a dark cloud of rage tomorrow afternoon, and they will come again, swooping over us, spitting and hissing, hideous yellow and green bodies clumping together, tearing apart the silk underwear I forgot on the clothesline, hordes of hellish beasts stripping paint from the fence posts—and then they will fly lazily into the farm fields, they're in no hurry, no one can stop them from their supper, feasting as they will on stalk after stalk, ripping, chewing, swallowing, laughing, dancing— destruction on every wing nestled south of the house. The July sun becomes a coward, reeling away and hiding, its long arms wrapped around eyes that cannot bear to see ten thousand grasshopper thieves stealing our lives. My husband runs into the barn to hide, I rock in the kitchen, dust floating everywhere, in my mouth, in my heart, in the baby's crib, settling over her ycllow blanket in tiny circular patterns of ash black roses. Sweat dribbles down my face, and I do not wipe away the thin tracks my tears make in the dust, god damn them, how many more times will they come. Later, he will bring a bucket filled with icy well water and go to milk the cows, but he will be afraid. Yesterday, he found me on the porch, my head sunk into the pail, the water darkening from the dust in my long, tangled hair, the sweet coolness as sharp as the first biting snow of October. I breathed in the lovely freshness, so cold, so silent, so peaceful, and for just an instant . . . he handed me a towel, black with dirt, black with fear, black yesterday and today. I wiped my face and put the wet towel on the porch window sill. It will not block out dust. In the morning, our footprints will mark our lives disappearing in the heat and plague of this awful summer. Tonight, I will fry clumps of cornmeal mush in hot lard, and we will sit in a sizzling kitchen, saying little, as we eat what we have eaten every day this week. We pray. He lifts my fingers to his lips and kisses the dust away. We cry. We will wait together for a day without dust, wait together for a day without the blackness of green and yellow war in the early afternoon.

Liz Merrigan, Burbank

Oncoming storm at Buffalo Gap, Custer State Park. By Nick Estes. Used with permission of Nick Estes.

What Makes A South Dakotan

Wild windy winds
hammering the grassy sea
at cyclonic speed.

Tornadoes!

Monstrous white mountains crawling
across the state,
kaleidoscopic collections of crystalline shapes
echoing ephrastic landscapes
stolen from Currier and Ives.

American ingenuity.

Stifling summer heat.
October orange nights.
Umber colored
torched
hills of grassless
drought.

All
kinds
of
tribulation
and
narcissistic resolve.

Daniel Snethen, Colome

~

What a South Dakotan Isn't!

Oh, you'll hear a lot of glowing attributes describing a South Dakotan. Not unlike Captain 11 (and every true South Dakotan knows who that is!), a South Dakotan "must be kind. He must be fair. He must be brave." But let me put a spin on this topic and tell you what a real South Dakotan *isn't*. A South Dakotan isn't a Snow Bird!

You've heard the old joke about the father telling his son that when he was a kid, he had to walk to school two miles—uphill both ways. I view my school days similarly. I grew up in Cresbard, a northern South Dakota community where the actual temperature often dropped to thirty degrees below zero. And that's not considering wind-chill! This was in the day when girls weren't allowed to wear slacks of any kind to school. This was the era of mini-skirts, and no self-respecting female would ever consider wearing jeans under those short, short skirts. Nor did we wear hats—they would smash our teased hairdos. No scarves—they were dorky. No boots—they weren't cool. If we were lucky enough to be the first ones on the school bus, we would choose the seats nearest the heater; if not, we just stayed chilly for those endless rides.

We played outside at recess and after school—skating and sledding, making forts and snow angels, and enjoying endless games of Fox and Goose. When our toes and fingers were so cold that we could no longer feel them, and our noses and ears actually hurt, we'd head inside for hot chocolate and toast. When blizzards raged and school was canceled, we'd play board games or curl up with a good book.

Looking back on those childhood days, we South Dakotans may wonder how we stood the cold and wind and snow and ice. We survived and even thrived because we were "hardy pioneer stock," we told ourselves. We were born and raised in an environment so harsh that only the strongest could endure it. We didn't buckle when the going got tough. We slept in unheated upstairs bedrooms where we could see our breath. We'd be cut off from civilization for days when the roads were blocked and when the power was off. We'd slog to the barn through thigh-high snowdrifts to feed our 4-H calves. And it is that "hardy pioneer stock-ness" that still stands us in good stead in our adulthood.

Each year, more and more of my friends become Snow Birds. "It's too cold; we don't like the snow; we're tired of shoveling," they say.

"Hah!" I reply. "And you call yourselves South Dakotans?!"

I am a runner and, thanks to a finely tuned wardrobe of light, yet warm, duds, I run nearly every day, regardless of the temperature. "How can you stand the cold," I'm often asked. "Simple," I say, "I'm a South Dakotan!"

Maxine Swanson, Madison

Photo Courtesy of the State Archives of the South Dakota State Historical Society.

⁂

An Icy Welcome

Huddled in homes side by side on the prairie, we're isolated yet connected in shared solitude when a blizzard strikes. That mindset is the foundation of an interdependence that starts with our neighbors. The heart of South Dakota is grounded in our geography, and we all live with nature, even if we reside in town. The force of the seasons provides change and variety which enhance life but demand adaptability.

In spring and summer, the perfectly aligned marching rows of green cornstalks that edge every road leading to Brookings are an encouraging promise of bounty. After the fall harvest, the absent crops leave the flat land stretching unbroken to the horizon, until the winter snows create an infinite sheet cake frosted with meringue peaks and dips.

In winter, South Dakota takes endurance. Some say it keeps out the riff-raff, but it might be what forges our social consciousness. The cold weather tests its inhabitants and guides us to value and protect those within reach. We're all vulnerable when below zero temperatures grip the area, and snowstorms close schools and businesses, bringing movement to a halt.

Proud owners of our first house in Brookings that August, my husband and I looked forward to summertime, which would draw the neighbors outside and allow us to get better acquainted. We underestimated their hardiness. As the snow piled higher and the winds blew roads shut during the first snowstorm that winter, our next door neighbor heaved his powerful snow blower over our sidewalk and driveway, clearing the way for the stalwart mailman's arrival and allowing us to optimistically imagine driving our car out of the garage if the storm ever let up.

The coziness of our small home, as I peered out the frosty panes of the kitchen window, inspired me to cook up a kettle of soup and set the oven roaring with cobbler and cookies. On the third day of the blizzard as the snow started to reach the windows, my husband surveyed the counter full of baked goods, now expanded to pies, cookies, and coffeecakes. "We won't be able to eat our way out of this house, if you keep this up," he laughed.

"My mother always baked during blizzards. It's just so comfy inside when the house smells like cookies."

"But she had enough teenagers to plow through that bounty."

Strapping on my boots and tightening the hood of my parka, I grabbed a basket of cookies and high stepped through the drifts to the neighbors—who had teenagers. They hustled me inside, tugging the door closed before the wind-driven ice crystals filled their entry. Their kids cheered gratefully and attacked the treats. Smiling with satisfaction, I invited them to forge their way over to meet my husband, if they liked pie, and scurried back home.

That evening with flashlight in hand, Bill and Janie lit the way as their children shoveled a tunnel from their back door to ours. They came bearing whiskey and board games. Dusting snowflakes off their woolen shoulders and freeing their children from layers of winter duds, I directed them toward the kitchen table for monopoly. The kids set up the game and scoped out the house when I encouraged them to look around. The men shook hands and organized drinks, while Janie and I served pie and set out slices of cheese, cold meats, and crackers. We all gathered around the table and started a succession of lively games that never really ended. From then on, the path between our back doors was always cleared first, and my baking had a market. A friendship that had a stormy beginning spanned a lifetime on the South Dakota prairie.

Mary Flemmer Husman, Brookings

The Burning Snow

I felt bad waking Mom from her nap, as she seldom lay down during the day, but the smoke was surrounding us. We dressed in our warmest clothing that had earlier been placed by the stove to dry and warm. Each layer of clothing could mean the difference between warmth, frostbite, or death. It took only seconds for Mom to instruct me to take the radio and place it on the table outside the door, then continue to the barn using the life rope as a guide and open the west barn door when I reached it. The open door ensured the safety of the cattle if the barn caught fire, then I was to return to the wind mill and meet her there.

What had seemed like a short distance just a few hours earlier, now seemed twice as long. With each grasp, the guide, made of rope and barbed wire, was truly transformed into a lifeline. I returned to the well house, but there was no sign of Mom. I defied her order and returned to the shack. Daddy's homestead shack had a few studs that strengthened the outside walls. The walls were insulated with cardboard boxes, and there was a second layer of cardboard wrapped with tarpaper. The cardboard boxes were held together with lath and one last layer of cardboard, and a heavy, flowered wallpaper lined the inside walls.

Simultaneously, I felt the heat of the fire and the intense cold of the snow-packed north wind hitting my face with each turn I took as I went room to room. Again and again I called out to Mom to meet me at the well house, but there was no response. I was alone. Someone else was missing. It was Pooch, who never left my side. Now, when I needed him the most, he was gone. I was alone in this dark, cold, smoke-filled place we called home. I repeatedly called out, "Mom!" I felt a protective touch. I wasn't alone. A wet kiss touched the tip of my fingers. Pooch had stayed between me and Mom.

Holding on to each other, Mom and I staggered out the only door to the south and past the radio sitting on the outside table. We stood in the center of the yard facing the north wind and felt the rush of heat and saw the ash dance skyward as the shack collapsed into the hand-dug dirt cellar. This was the beginning of a life which would never be the same. We stood quietly at the well, only a few feet away from the flames, tears frozen to our faces. When the rubble fell, the radio was gone, but the shoebox Easter rabbit was tucked gently under my mother's arm.

The rope, which led from the house to the windmill and then to the cattle tank, was lying in the snow. The fence was being buried quickly beneath the drifting snow. Mom told me to find the end of the rope, pick it up, and wrap it around my waist. Without question, I did as I was told. She took my hand until we found the other end at the cattle tank. She untied that end and placed it around her waist. After we were tied together, we walked to the car, and she placed the shoebox Easter rabbit on the front seat. Together, the three of us set out to find the fence that would begin the mile-and-a-half walk to our closest neighbor.

Sally Damm, Brookings

By Les Voorhis. Used with permission of Les Voorhis.

ACTIVITIES

Courtesy of SDSU Archives & Special Collections, Hilton M. Briggs Library, South Dakota State University, Brookings, S.D.

Living the South Dakota Life

Listening to the old men talking and drinking coffee in the gas station every morning. Learning to drive when you're fourteen on the empty dirt road. Driving down the highway for miles without passing another car. Knowing every individual in your town. Watching the sunset while working in the combine. Walking in your field right behind your house to hunt pheasants.

Slowing down, smiling, and waiting for a deer or some ducks to cross the road. Cracking open the windows to enjoy a fall breeze when it's in the 50s. Needing just a sweatshirt when it's in the 40s. Starting your car twenty minutes before you leave for work so you can be warm. Packing up the camper on Friday to take a short vacation. Rolling up your jeans to wade in the water for fly fishing. Tubing on the lake is a water "joyride." Lighting up fireworks on the Fourth of July in your front yard. Marrying your high school sweetheart. Grilling on your deck every other night. Passing a tractor on the highway going five miles an hour. Racing snowmobiles in the ditch after a fresh snow. Picking the vegetables from the garden and eating them a couple of minutes later. Growing up on the farm your great, great grandpa grew up on. Passing on tradition for many years to come. I'm proud to have a South Dakota life.

Brianna Kunkel, Humboldt

Craig Howe, Executive Director, Wingsprings, home of the Center for American Indian Research and Native Studies (Cairns), Martin. By David Michaud. Used with permission of David Michaud.

Running

Running along a lazy "L" just south and east of our home is Bear In The Lodge Creek. It rises in the west near Allen, a town named after my mom's mother's father's father, and after bending around our place it meanders northward, emptying into the White River a little over a mile east of the town of Interior.

When my brother and I were still in grade school, Dad would encourage us to run to the barn to do chores, run to the granary to get feed, run to the shed to get parts, run and run to get in

216

shape for sports, especially basketball. We participated in fall and winter sports, football, cross country, and basketball. But because spring and summer were the labor intensive periods of ranch work, we did not compete in track and field events nor join softball or baseball teams. During my final three years of high school, cross country was my fall sport. I ran cow trails across our pastures from the slanting light of summer evenings into early fall. Training, I thought, for the upcoming cross country seasons. Being afraid of snakes kept me focused on the land. Any slight incongruence of color or pattern in the grass might indicate a bull snake or rattler.

But running on the earth, in the high plains landscape of our reservation ranch, unconsciously tethered me to its undulating curves and rolling hills, its steady winds and ancient sky. A thin sole of rubber, sweat pants, and tee-shirt were all that mediated the interaction between the environment and me. I felt a deep, maybe genetic, resonance from being in motion at that pace and place. Had my ancestors long ago followed these trails tracking game? Grandpa Ross, whose Dakota name was *Wamniyomni Hota* (Grey Whirlwind), said that spoken words hang in the air forever at the places where they are voiced. Were old stories nourishing me with every breath? To run in that landscape was exhilarating.

Cross country meets typically began with runners standing abreast in a golf course or park. Five miles later they end on a cinder track as runners sprint the final 400 yards or so hugging the inside lane around the final turn and down the home stretch before leaning across the finish line. I enjoyed running in the golf courses and parks. They felt similar in many ways to my home pastures. But finishing on a track filled me with apprehension. Tracks were flat and man-made. They encircled a manicured field and had bleacher seating for spectators. They felt like foreign places.

When I left home to attend college out of state, it, too, felt foreign. To avoid homesickness, I didn't hang pictures of home or family on the dorm room walls. Even when I moved out of the dorm, and then to Milwaukee, Ann Arbor, Chicago, and Washington, D.C., home and relatives were in my heart and imagination, not on end tables, shelves, or walls.

Arriving home the first time from college is still a vivid memory.

217

Though the journey from Lincoln to our home along Bear In The Lodge Creek has long since been forgotten, I remember clearly getting out of a vehicle near our yard gate. It was late afternoon in the fall. Mom and Dad were there, and I believe my brother was, too. Suddenly, overcome with emotion at being home, inexplicably I began running. I ran down to the creek, across the culvert and along the alfalfa field, staying near to the barbed wire fence. When I passed through the gate and into the horse pasture, the trail curved and climbed into the familiar native landscape that I had missed so much. Breathing deeply and in tears, I ran and ran and ran.

Craig Howe, Martin

Bridge Game

At eight tables, the young-old, old, and old-old shuffle, bid, play their hands, and keep score in the Senior Center card room. Well into the second hand, Fern calls out, "Robert, do you know why we haven't been able to get in touch with Margaret?" From another table, Robert answers, "No. Why?" Answer: "Because she died." A wave of titters washes across the room in response to the surprise of Fern's answer, some probably thinking, "One of these days someone will say that about me."

Marian D. Peters, Sioux Falls

South Dakotans Are . . . .

South Dakotans are not an unusual lot; it's just that many of us were born here, married, found opportunity adequate for our needs, and stayed here. Some have parents or even grandparents nearby, so our roots go deep. Some have ventured to faraway places only to realize that our placid life style, low population density, and freedom from stress make South Dakota a desirable place to live. They then return to raise a family or simply to retire.

We are products of one-room schools, consolidated schools, and reconsolidated schools which meet the needs of our children, some of whom have gone on to outstanding careers in-state and nationally. We are products of small towns and cities; of farms and ranches; and of a state divided into East River and West River, each with a distinctive life style.

South Dakotans are compassionate and noted for helping a neighbor in distress without expecting anything in return. It's just the right thing to do! We go for a walk and a passerby invariably stops to ask, "Do you need a lift?" Recently our youth chose a girl with Down's syndrome to be their high school prom queen, and the most popular boy in her class graciously served as her escort. He then politely posed on his knees for a class picture so he wouldn't tower over her.

Small-town South Dakotans attend church, sporting events, and card parties to fill their needs for social interactions in fall and winter. For the hardy outdoor type, ice fishing provides a welcome respite from being house-bound on cold winter days. In the summer, local lakes and Missouri River reservoirs provide some of the best walleye fishing in the country.

South Dakotans enjoy nature and frequently go on Sunday drives to see the changes nature has wrought to the prairie that surrounds us: waving fields of grain; grazing cattle; corn and beans in different shades of brown; native grasses of different colors; and when seen from above, fields and shelterbelts which add a geometric design to our countryside. Yes, we even see snowy marvels in wind-sculptured snow drifts in winter. And occasionally we come across a whimsical sign such as, "Astoria, Population 150, next 4 exits," that adds to our pleasure on these drives.

South Dakotans love their state with all of its sometimes extravagant weather patterns and its diverse terrain varying from rich farmland to the Black Hills; all populated by a compatible assortment of ethnic nationalities, including a large segment of Native Americans, which make South Dakota a unique place to live.

Bob Foster, Brookings

Christmas Gift of Friendship

I had lived in Oglala for four months, and one day on my way to the Oglala Post Office, I saw Elva One Feather walking and picked her up. Elva walked to and from the Post Office, a central gathering place, every day from her house, a ten-mile round-trip hike along US Highway 18. Someone would always stop to give her a ride there. Nearly six feet tall, Elva wore clothes as distinctive as her personality. During the winter months, she would wear a cotton dress over men's pants and sometimes a sweat shirt under or over the dress and a long wool coat over that. A cap covered her head but not the braid she wore down her back.

She was barely in the car before she asked if this was the first Christmas I wouldn't be spending with my family. I said it was. "Then you come to St. Peter's Christmas party with me. Pick me up that evening." Christmas was more than a month away.

Christmas night I went to Elva's and picked her up. We drove through downtown Oglala, which is comprised of two small stores and a post office, turned at the top of the hill, and drove half way around Oglala Dam on a dirt road. We entered St. Peter's church, a long, narrow room which also functioned as a hall and a kitchen, but tonight it was packed with children and their families. I felt shy and very white, despite the immediate smiles and Merry

Christmas greetings from everyone. At first I saw just a blur of faces and wished that I could hide behind Elva. Gradually I began to see individuals, some of whom I knew.

Garlands swooped across the ceiling, and a large decorated tree with piles of wrapped presents beneath it stood in a corner. People sat on folding chairs and backless wooden benches along each wall. We sang Christmas songs, and Santa came. The children and the elderly received gifts, and everyone received fruit, nuts, cookies, and cake. Months of everyone there playing quarter-a-card bingo for homemade prizes had raised most of the money for the celebration, yet I wondered how the church people had managed this party. Six months before, a shooting had occurred on Jumping Bull's land. Since then the Oglala community had experienced daily retaliation by FBI agents carrying M-16s and being a threatening presence. Few people had jobs, and many had relatives in jail because of the shootout. Yet that Christmas night, St. Peter's overflowed with laughter, generosity, and resilience, among the greatest gifts of the Lakota.

Thirty years later. St. Peter's means close friendships, kinship, and sharing at Thanksgiving, baptisms, Easter, and always Christmas. With easier times, Santa brings more gifts, many still bought from the proceeds of quarter-a-card bingo. We share food, fun, and laughter. I've seen a generation grow up, and now they bring their children, the fourth generation of St. Peter's families.

Last year we didn't know that we were enjoying our last St. Peter's Christmas. The following spring the Episcopal Diocese of South Dakota announced it was closing nine Pine Ridge reservation churches because of costs and expenses, and St. Peter's was one of them.

I wonder about sharing this story in a book about being a South Dakotan because I've never connected it with South Dakota. We live within the boundaries of the state, but the Pine Ridge Reservation is a sovereign nation. Few, if any, Oglala think of themselves as South Dakotans, because too often beyond the reservation border is an unwelcoming, unfriendly place. Perhaps someday this reality will change, a gift to all, like St. Peter's Church.

Candy Hamilton, Rapid City

Mountain Majesty. By Paul Schiller. Used with permission of Paul Schiller.

Memories of a Prairie Dweller

It recently occurred to me that I have lived in South Dakota for more than two decades, which means I have lived here as long as I resided in my home state of Michigan.

That's a lot to consider because there are certain responsibilities associated with settling in Sioux Falls. It helps to know your way around a video lottery screen, for instance, and you need to be able to become one with the wind. Embracing the wonders of chislic is optional, but recommended.

Ideally, this sense of "being a South Dakotan" isn't tied to a street address or occupation. It stems from a succession of experiences that foster familiarity and make you feel right at

home, regardless where you started.

From one proud prairie dweller to a host of others, it's time to let those memories roll:

■ Visiting Mount Rushmore at night, trying to give my kids insight on each illuminated face as the fatigue from a six-hour drive set in.

■ Sitting with a Mitchell High School sophomore named Mike Miller on a snow day as he picked through a stack of recruiting letters, stopping to show me the good ones.

■ Witnessing the transformation of Sioux Falls from a meatpacking town to a credit-card and then health care mecca during the course of a few decades, meaning less instances of "Morrell smell" in my nostrils.

■ Sitting at Gunner's Lounge in Sturgis during the motorcycle rally and finding myself a few seats down from an emergency meeting of the Bandidos biker gang.

- Working in the *Argus Leader* newsroom and hearing the roar of cars racing around "the loop," a bygone tradition that symbolized a city that sometimes goes in circles.

- Engaging in friendly East River-West River banter and marveling at how the state's two largest cities can be so different in so many ways.

- Sitting in Bob Burns' living room and hearing him spin tales of his life as a Golden Gloves boxer, World War II fighter pilot, master promoter and , yes, legendary football coach.

- Spending a languid evening playing Frisbee and listening to music at the McKennan Park bandshell, where it's possible to believe that summer nights can indeed last forever.

- Attending the Lakota Nation Invitational in Rapid City, where White River star Louie Krogman drained a free throw to become the state's all-time leading high school scorer and was honored with the Lakota name Nagi Ohitika, meaning "fearless spirit."

- Chatting casually with a member of Los Lobos at the Pomp Room, which exuded a raw energy and unpredictability that doesn't exist in Sioux Falls nightspots anymore.

- Scraping ice off my windshield on a bitterly cold Monday morning, taking solace in the fact that living through South Dakota winters builds character along the way.

- Climbing Harney Peak in the Black Hills with my wife and kids and feeling that satisfaction of reaching the summit, where chipmunks frolic and fellow hikers swap stories of past adventures.

- Seeing former NBA star Darryl Dawkins walk out of the Arena after practice with the Skyforce, holding an airline ticket. When I asked him what was in his hand, he responded, "Bye-bye."

- Interviewing Bill Janklow and feeling like I had just emerged from a 15-round championship boxing match when the verbal jousting was over.

- Learning that Pierre is pronounced "Peer" and always being able to pinpoint an outsider when they mess that up.

- Stopping for ice cream (and free ice water) at Wall Drug on the way out west, helping my daughter count all the license plates from different states.

■ Watching election returns until the wee hours as Tim Johnson held off John Thune in a U.S. Senate race, then seeing Thune storm back to knock off Tom Daschle two years later. For a state with three measly electoral votes, South Dakota packs a political punch.

■ Spending time on the Pine Ridge Indian Reservation, talking to basketball players whose hoop dreams fizzled as they found themselves drawn back to their cultural core.

■ Bristling when outsiders make fun of South Dakota, knowing that I was once one of them, and now I'm one of you.

Stu Whitney, Sioux Falls

By Chad Coppess/www.travelsd.com. Used with permission of Chad Coppess.

Top Twelve Observations about What It Means to Be a South Dakotan

One – In what other state could a big chain store leave merchandise outside overnight?
Two – When a disaster strikes, our governor works besides prison inmates with chainsaws!
Three – Where a person's word is just as good as a signed contract.
Four – We can take sixty below, freezing cold—sometimes eighty degree differences—in a 24-hour period.
Five – We go to church on Sunday and practice what we learn all week.
Six – When we work, we make sure we do everything the best we know how, and usually more.
Seven – We treat our livestock like they are our children.
Eight – On politics and religion, with a handshake, we disagree with another's opposing opinion.
Nine – The color of your skin don't matter as long as you don't cheat, lie, or steal!
Ten – When flying in from a big city to a small airport, where my car sat for a week—no charge—I got down and kissed the South Dakota soil!
Eleven – We are a proud, fearless, independent people.
Twelve – To sum it up: You mind your business, I will mind mine, and we will get along just fine.

Lillian R. Misar, Estelline

Clothespin, Please

Yipee! I was home in Box Elder from my country school and skipping off to do my evening chores. South of our driveway we had a humongous chicken coop with over a hundred Leghorn chickens. It was my job to gather the eggs every day. I entered the aromatic coop with my yellow wire egg basket in hand. Some nests had been vacated, and the eggs were easily accessible. On I went, bounding from nest to nest and humming the Lone Ranger song. I knew when I completed my task I could rush to the house, turn on TV, and stare at the test pattern until the Lone Ranger show started. Periodically, a ruffled chicken would protest and try to peck my hand as I attempted to acquire her precious egg. I robotically continued the egg gathering process.

I was almost done with my task when I went to reach into the next nest. My fingers did not sense feathers, but rather something very hairy. I jerked to attention and gazed into the nest. It was occupied by a large black and white mass . . . called a SKUNK! The closest escape was the feed room on the west end of the coop. The side door entrance to the feed room was locked. How could I escape? I was petrified! I could not get back to the main exit without prancing right past the skunk. I decided to just wait in the feed room until someone in my family came to rescue me. After an eternity of waiting (anyway it seemed like an eternity to a nine-year-old), my dad came to look for me. He let me out the side door. I hugged him and told him about the skunk. To my utter amazement, he lured that skunk out of the hen house with no odors emitted. My dad was my hero, and from that day forward I was a lot more alert when I gathered the eggs. I missed my favorite show that day, but having to do chores daily and continue to do them even after my skunk encounter helped make me a true South Dakotan. My dad's calm reaction to a scary situation added one more piece to forming my South Dakotan personality. Thanks, Dad.

Kay Smeenk, Newell

Scotty Philip Memorial Ride hosted by Verendrye Museum Association and sponsored in part by a grant from the SD Humanities Council. By Justin Koehler. Used with permission of Justin Koehler.

Railroad Days in South Dakota

My parents, Walter and Therese Fenske, and their five children moved to the Lars Austin farm one and a half miles east of Hetland, beside the railroad track, on December 15, 1935. (At that time there were four passenger trains each day.) My parents bought this farm from the Northwestern Insurance Company in 1941 and lived on it until August 21, 1981, when they moved to Arlington. My father, Walter, died on July 5, 1983, at the age of eighty-nine. He was survived by his wife, Therese, to whom he was married for sixty-two years, and eight children—seven girls and one boy. My mother died on August 28, 1999.

Because we lived by the railroad and that was the shortest route to Hetland, we walked the tracks each morning after helping milk cows and feed the calves. By the time we were ready to leave the house to walk to school, our mother would have our noon lunch packed in a pail, which we would carry to school. After school was dismissed, we would walk back home along the railroad track. We learned to listen for the trains, as there were places along the track that were very difficult to get off because of the high banks or because of places with water. I liked to walk with my brother and sisters, because I hated walking past the stockyards, which were right by the tracks. Bums or tramps, as we called them, often slept in the stockyards or the depot, and I was afraid to meet them. They often walked the railroad tracks, and we would encounter them. They never paid any attention to us; they just went on their way, and so did we.

Some of the tramps rode the freight trains, and some walked the tracks. Often the tramps would come to our place for food. They would offer to chop wood, carry water, or do other odd jobs, but our mom never had them do anything. She would give them food, and they would sit out on the porch steps and eat. They never wanted to come into the house. When they finished eating, they would leave and continue their walk to Hetland. We kids were scared of them, but our mom was brave. She knew they wouldn't hurt anyone. We would have felt safer if our dad had been there, too, but he was out working in the field.

The depot agent in Hetland sold tickets, handled passengers' baggage, and took care of inbound and outbound freight, which included the shipments of grain, coal, lumber, potatoes, and livestock. He also was in charge of the telegrams—receiving and delivering. He also handled the train orders and getting the passengers on the train. The waiting room in the depot had benches along the walls, a pot-bellied stove in the middle of the room, a ticket office, and a freight room. The depot agent used a dray cart to take the freight from the train to the freight room.

There was a section crew that consisted of the section boss and his men, who rode the "hand car" or the "section car" to check the rails and ties and did the repairs to keep the track safe for the train so no cars would derail or "jump the tracks." Once in awhile, the section boss would stop and ask us if we wanted a ride, and, of course, we always accepted! This was a real treat for us.

When the weather was bad or when it was very cold and the snow was deep, our dad would take us to school with the horses and the bob sled. Dad would braid the horses' tails and wrap them around in a big "bun" so they wouldn't get all iced and heavy. This was always a fun trip. We would have blankets to keep us warm.

My brother and a couple of his friends were asked to unload the coal cars. What a dirty job that was. Their faces and clothes would be coal black. They looked so funny when they would finish the job. This gave them a little hard earned money!

Irma Fenske Peterson, Mitchell

Independence Day

Each year on the Fourth of July, the county sheriff drove his police cruiser out to Uncle Sam's House of Explosives, the fireworks shop at the edge of Brookville, and requested the most expensive assortment. That year it was the Contraband Collection, a name that made the sheriff snicker and grin, and it came in a big white box with illustrations of rockets and stars rendered in navy and red down the sides. The sheriff used a dolly to roll the box out to his cruiser, where he loaded the rockets into the backseat and delivered the stash to the volunteer fire crew assembled to supervise the events.

By Pheasant County tradition, the works were set up and ignited in the gravel lot of the elevator. Thirty-ball Roman Candles and Sonic Booms and spider-like, neon explosions traveled up from the base of the elevator lot and into the black night sky, bursting and twinkling down on Burg. Residents lined the streets, leaning back in their lawn chairs, necks flopped back like u-shaped hot dogs, marveling as shapes mixed with stars, mixed with the moon and the Dipper. Many flopped down right on their lawns just like sunbathers, letting the cool dew of the grass moisten the backs of their tanks, acquiescing as spiders and ants crawled across their ankles and bellies. Some cracked open silo cans of Coors Light, letting the cool golden liquid slowly seep into their stomachs. Others drank homemade lemonade out of tall, plastic glasses.

By day, they'd sunburned themselves at the lake while trawling for lunkers or racing each other on Jet Skis. They'd eaten grilled burgers at picnic tables. Bowls of potato salad and coleslaw. They'd thrown fun snaps down on their concrete sidewalks and lit big strands of firecrackers out on the dirt road, touching the punk to the wick before sprinting back toward the grass, giggling like children, eager to hear the explosions. They'd ignited purple smoke balls. Written their names in the air with silvery sparklers.

Dani Johannesen, Vermillion

South Dakota Senior Citizens—Today's Pioneers: Still Breaking New Ground

"Join us for a round of golf or a game of tennis! Come for a swim or go kayaking. Bike, walk, or jog along miles of trails! Join the baseball team, or play racquetball! Hunters can pursue South Dakota's wild game. Winter offers skating, snow-shoeing, and skiing. For the more adventuresome, try skydiving, mountain climbing, weight lifting, zip-lines, or rock climbing! Learn to fly a plane! For relaxation, practice yoga."

This may sound like a promotion for a vacation spa or a fitness club, but it's not! According to a survey of senior citizens, these are some of the activities that occupy their busy lives. Some are merely continuations of what these people have done for many years; others are new pursuits that fail to intimidate the "mature learner." Since people over sixty-five comprise about 15 percent of South Dakota's population, the impact of all of their activities is both broad and deep.

Of course, not all "senior" activities demand physical energy; many could be described as "brain boosters." Learning something or producing something is integral to the lives of these so-called "retired" citizens. You could easily find them engaged in crafts such as scrapbooking, painting, photography, basket making, woodworking, needlework, glass crafts, and home improvement. It's a good time to learn to play the piano. Other relaxing activities include taking classes, reading for a book club, and researching genealogy. Travel is not only entertaining, but also another avenue to learning.

Sixty-five does not translate into real retirement for these South Dakotans. Many are still working at their old jobs, though perhaps not full time any more. You will find them at the office, in the classroom, at retail centers, at restaurants, and in health care facilities. Some serve in public office. Fortunately for thousands of South Dakotans, these senior citizens volunteer their services in a multitude of venues: in caring for family members, in schools, in food pantries, in hospitals, in museums, in churches, with Scouts, with charitable organizations, and with people who need food or transportation.

Seniors are building ramps for the handicapped, helping with Habitat for Humanity, sending care packages to our military, and replenishing the supplies of the Children's Home Society, the Ronald McDonald House, and other domestic refuges. Contributions of this group extend beyond services; tangible evidence of their crafts can be found throughout the community. Thanks to senior handiwork, hospitals have hats and quilts for newborns, burp cloths, Teddy bears, prayer shawls, and lap robes. Needy children have school kits, scarves, and caps. Homeless people have quilts, pillowcases, and hygiene kits.

Like their pioneering ancestors, today's senior citizens continue to explore new worlds, develop new skills, rise to new challenges, and continue to make good things happen for South Dakota.

Members of the Osher Lifelong Learning Institute, Sioux Falls

_^\)^_

A Lovely Life in South Dakota

The air smells fresh with a hint of burnt leaves. The birds are always present and chirping. My dog bursts through the cracked open door and begs me to throw her Frisbee. The party-house girl speeds up and down the road. The gravel crunches under her Mitsubishi's tires. My two best friends live down the street and their door is always open. They and I played Barbies in their basement when we were younger. We modeled their whole basement into our own Barbie town and had no cares in the world. I grew up in a pretty house and had my space to play. My brother and I fought and yelled on a regular basis. I got tucked in by my mommy every night, and my daddy woke me up for school every morning. It's still the same way it was back then, except my brother and I don't fight, and my friends and I don't play Barbies. Instead, we shop and watch movies. And most of my time is dedicated to work and my boyfriend. I work at Auntie Anne's, a pretzel shop in the Empire Mall. We make the best pretzels around the state. I work twenty to thirty hours as a shift manager, so I'm in charge. I have the privilege to put people in their place. During the summer, on Saturday nights, I pay twenty-five bucks to go to the pits at the I-90 Speedway to watch my boyfriend race. Joe's number twenty-nine, and I cheer him on. The gravel crunches under my flip-flops. My hair flows in the summer breeze. The smell of fuel and tires fills my nostrils as the drivers rev their engines. I live in the state of South Dakota. I get to see the stars every night. I know I probably won't live here forever, but this state will always hold most of my memories.

Tori Kock, Hartford

South Dakota State Agricultural Heritage Museum Photographic Collection.

A State Full of Musical Tradition

Music has always been important to me, which is why I am studying to be a music teacher at the University of South Dakota. I was taught piano from my mother, a music teacher, from the age of seven. I fell in love with the beauty of the French horn in fifth grade, and I discovered just how much music connects people in high school.

I was not the first in my family to be taught piano by my

mother, and I hope to certainly not be the last. I am a fourth or fifth generation pianist on two sides of my family. There have been generations of Mogen and Dannenbring families in South Dakota that have taught piano, and some have continued on to teach band, choir, and elementary music or become professional musicians. South Dakota has meant home for my family ever since my ancestors settled here from Norway and Germany, and music is what connects us.

When I entered high school, I started attending music camps and honor bands in the Black Hills. These are some of my greatest memories because of the friends I made, the music I learned, and the chance to become a better musician in the beautiful setting of the Black Hills. Now as a college student, I am attending honor bands and music events and meeting some of the same people that I met back in high school. There are some fantastic college music programs in this state.

Last week the USD symphonic band performed at the South Dakota Bandmaster's Conference in Brookings the day after the Coyotes beat the Jacks in men's basketball. Our director, Dr. Rolf Olson, ended our performance with "Go Yotes," and our band joked about incorporating the school song into the program.

Many of these musicians at the conference are people we have known from previous music camps, honor bands, honor choirs, and all-state events. Though we opted to attend different schools, we are still connected by music. South Dakota is a place full of traditions in music. The power of music connection is what South Dakota means to this 21-year-old college student.

Emily Mason, Vermillion

By Christian Begeman. Used with permission of Christian Begeman.

Living a Dream

Electricity fills the air on this hot, summer day in late July. The sun is beating down on our backs and consuming us with its warm rays. My anticipation grows, and my excitement is beginning to overwhelm me. Finally the calming tune of our nation's anthem begins to play, and abruptly it ends. Adrenaline shoots through my veins, and I break into a nervous, clammy sweat. I quickly scoop up my cool, leather baseball mitt and begin trotting to shortstop. I feel the smooth, green grass below my feet, and then the hard, crunchy dirt as I arrive at my destination. I'm ready. It's Game Time.

Jacob Ellens, Hartford

Backyard Rink, Version 1.0

I can't say with any authority what makes a South Dakotan, because I am such a recently minted one, having lived in Brookings for only six months as I write this. But I do know one thing: being a South Dakotan has something to do with the hockey rink I built in my backyard.

"You'll all be happier here if you find something to love about winter," a doctor told us in September, but I was one step ahead of him. By then, I had already priced out plastic sheeting and lawn edging, and spent hours researching rink-building techniques on the internet.

I'm not a tool guy, and my relationship with the accoutrements of machismo is tenuous. I don't hunt, and I only fish when my sons drag me. I don't have a big truck, and actually don't even drive stick. But hockey has been a part of my life since I caught the bug at age nine, and it's the lone skill among the manly arts that I can pass on with pride.

I can't teach Lucas and Landon how to shoot a buck or tie a fly or plumb a pipe, but I can teach them how to lean into a check when somebody thinks they're about to flatten you. I can teach them how to frustrate the heck out of a winger who loves his big slap shot by making the smallest little poke check at the right time.

But in order to do this, I needed a backyard rink. Needed it this year, because I had to show South Dakota that the Wingates are serious about making it our new home. That we aren't fly-by-night, that we are tough enough and inventive enough for the state to call its own.

Of course I didn't plan for the warmest winter in anybody's recorded memory. I started building the rink in November, laying down my plastic the second we had single-digit temperatures. I discovered that South Dakota is not flat, but has rolling hills on my very own lawn that made an even sheet of ice impossible. By the time we drove to Colorado for Christmas, I had every inch of the rink covered in ice that would, I believed, be thicker when we got home.

I returned to find my neighbors wearing T-shirts and my rink, its ripped plastic sheeting blown over on itself like a clamshell, less than half its former size. So I changed its shape, making it sort of kidney-ish, and redoubled my efforts to lay down ice. Every night I added water. Every day it would leak out from some unseen tear, or a new imbalance in the surface would reveal itself.

"I'm giving up!" I shouted many times to my wife.

"Don't give up!" Jenny always said back. She knew I needed the rink to work, not merely to salvage what remained of my crushed non-tool-guy ego, but to tell South Dakota that my family and I are for real. That we won't blow away and we won't chicken out because of a simple fact like weather—cold or warm. That we'll deal with things, because generations here have done exactly that without complaint.

By early February it finally got cold enough to maintain ice. I got it as level as I could, smoothed down its bumps, and filled its holes. Now my sons can skate on it, try slapshots, and score the game-winning goals to many Stanley Cups.

Now I can look at the window and watch them and say, We're here.

Steven Wingate, Brookings

In Pursuit of "Logger the Big One"

On January 5, 2012, Maynard Greenfield and I went from Pierre to Lake Pocasse near Pollock, South Dakota, to catch the big fish I've named "Logger the Big One." I had had this lunker on my line and lost it twice over New Year's. Here is our story.

One evening when I was shore fishing behind the hospital in Pierre, Maynard comes walking up and asks, "Are you catching anything?"

"Nothing, so far," I say.

"Maybe we should go up to Pollock and see if we can catch that big fish you say got away, the one you call 'Logger the Big One.'"

"Thursday will work for me. Will it work for you?"

"I'll pick you up about nine," I say.

Thursday morning I picked up Maynard, and we arrived in Pollock after eleven with plans to fish the open water under the east-crossing bridge over Lake Pocasse.

We parked, and Maynard pulled out his "Go Army" chair and his antique Bronson 63 rods and reels—one was gold and the other, red.

In anticipation of catching "Logger the Big One," he had purchased a net with a sliding handle which could be extended.

"Where should I go?" says Maynard.

"Any place you like," I say.

"But, I don't want to take your spot," he says.

"Just pick a spot," I say, "the fish are all over." He picked the spot where "Logger the Big One" had gotten away from me twice over New Year's.

No live bait for us. We started casting with spoons. Before long, I had a nice sized fish.

"I got one, bring the net!"

Maynard hobbled to the car to get the net while I worked the fish close to shore. I landed a nice sized northern and had it in our catch pail before he came back.

When I went to the car to get something, Maynard moved to where I'd caught the fish.

"I see you moved," I say.

"Just a little," he says. "You know, on the edge of that ice over there might be a good spot." He points to the other side of the road where the ice was closer to shore. I got the sense he was trying to lure me away from this spot.

I decided to give it a try. I caught some fish, so it wasn't a bad spot. Maynard, however, was reeling in the big ones. He'd set up his chair and was casting while sitting down.

I caught a 27-inch northern and put it in the catch pail. "Are we keeping little ones, too?" He'd caught two 33-inch northerns and was rubbing it in. I went back to the other side of the road where I caught a couple of walleye, but no "Logger the Big One."

I got a snag and walked over the bridge to the other shore to get it loose. From this vantage point, I could see Maynard rocking back and forth in his chair.

"Maynard, you need to get out of your chair when you get a big fish on the line," I holler.

"Do you need help?"

"I can handle this," he says. His pole is bent, and he's reeling.

I decided to help, but by the time I got there, the fish was off his line.

"That was a big, big fish!" he says excitedly. "I thought it might've been a snag, but it was a big fish!"

"That's the same one I had twice! Now do you believe me?"

"You bet I do. There's a big fish in these waters," he says.

"Logger the Big One" still stalks the clear waters of Lake Pocasse, but Maynard and I think that fish's days are numbered.

James Pollock, Pierre

By Jim Pollock. Used with permission of Jim Pollock.

༝ᛗ༝

Game Hunting: A South Dakota Family Tradition

It's been said that my husband, Gary, and our son, Dave, are part of a dying breed—the South Dakota game hunter. It won't happen if Gary has anything to say about it. He's making every effort to see that a four-generation tradition lives on.

Gary was eight years old when he started walking the corn fields with his father and grandfather on opening day of pheasant-hunting season. Dwarfed by the tall, dried stalks, he tramped alongside the others in the hopes of flushing those beautiful, elusive birds. He would thrill at the sound of that first rustling signal, as a flock of pheasants flew out in front of them, soaring toward the horizon, as shotgun blasts echoed all around, breaking the silence of a crisp autumn day.

His rite of passage occurred when he turned twelve. His father gave him his first shotgun—a Mossberg, 20-gauge, single-shot—and he joined the ranks of South Dakota hunters. This is a treasured pastime that he has enjoyed for nearly six decades now. He's rarely missed an opening day of pheasant-hunting season with all its accompanying memories of family togetherness and sportsmanship.

As Gary advanced into his teen and college years, he also enjoyed hunting ducks and deer, in and around the farm he grew up on near St. Lawrence. His two younger brothers also inherited this love for the outdoors and hunting. As they grew older, Gary, his dad, and two brothers, Mike and Den, did a lot of hunting together. It truly became a family affair. In addition to hunting, Gary's dad taught his boys how to trap, how to respect the land and the animals they shot, and how to track and find a wounded animal at all costs.

The love of hunting took root in our son, Dave, at an early age. When he was just a little shaver, Gary took him along on his goose and duck hunts. On cold, frosty mornings he'd comfortably sleep on the floor of their cozy camouflaged duck boat while waiting for the sun to come up and the birds to take flight. I guess you could

241

Photo Courtesy of the State Archives of the South Dakota State Historical Society.

say he cut his teeth in a duck blind! Dave still loves to tell the story of how he shot his first deer at thirteen and how they had to drag it up out of the ravine it had fallen into after he shot it.

Between fishing on the river during the warmer months, and bird and deer hunting in the fall, Gary and Dave have spent many companionable hours together enjoying all that South Dakota has to offer, whether the sound of the morning dove at daybreak, or a breathtaking sunset that stretches across the spacious horizon at the end of the day. It's always been Gary's dream to have one of his grandchildren carry on this wonderful South Dakota legacy, but it's not been without a challenge,

Our two grandsons live in St. Paul. It's a bustling city with an urban lifestyle, far removed from the rural prairie setting that so defined their grandfather's childhood. They both have many interests which include numerous year-round sports, in addition to all the new electronic devices that keep them so mesmerized. Last August, after some juggling to get it into his busy summer schedule, our eleven-year-old grandson, Parker, came to South Dakota and took the youth hunter safety course. In October he and his dad, our son-in-law, Scott, came back for their first pheasant hunt. They both got birds. Grampa is encouraged. Who knows, maybe the fire has been lit, and Parker as well as his dad will find a passion for the hunt.

One can only hope that this proud South Dakota family tradition will be carried on into the next generation. This is one of the enduring legacies of being a South Dakotan.

Sally Kulm, Sioux Falls

Curbside Pickup

In Canton during the teens and early 1920s, there were many avid hunters who figured out all sorts of ways to enjoy their sport. Melvin Juel, an excellent marksman, was one of the most dedicated members of the group, which held an annual Crow Hunt in which the participants were divided into two teams: "Get 'em All" and "Never Miss 'em." The winners would be dinner guests of the losers and recipients of assorted prizes, including bragging rights.

For the autumn ritual, Lincoln County hunters met in the Canton Firehouse, where many of the men also served as volunteer firefighters. Although they were divided into two groups, each hunter was on his own in searching for and occupying the ideal location to guarantee a successful hunt with the greatest number of birds. This meant that Mel would take several trips into the countryside to scout out the best spot, watching for crows as they gorged themselves on valuable grain from the fields. Thus, the annual Crow Hunt provided not only entertainment for the hunters but also an appreciated service.

On the appointed day of the hunt, he would rise at four a.m., make his own breakfast, and fix his modest lunch, which consisted of a peanut butter sandwich, a thermos of tomato soup, a few cookies, and a jug of water. Then he would head for his privately selected place, organize the blind he had created, and set out his decoys. Two of those decoys were hand-carved and painted black, while the other two were made of cardboard. He would spend all day in that blind. That kind of patience and his skills as a marksman were what allowed him to hope for success.

During the 1960s, our family made frequent trips from Brookings to visit both pairs of grandparents in Canton. One day, I took our children from the Skyberg home to the Juel home, a few blocks away. As we drew to a stop, I noticed a small pile of what appeared to be discards at the curb. Normally, I would have paid no attention, but something made me take a second look. One item caught my eye, so I went to investigate. The item in question turned out to be a heavily tarnished silver loving cup, almost a foot tall, which could not stand on its base because the stem was badly bent.

Curiosity led me to pick it up to determine what in the world it could mean. There on its front I was barely able to read the engraved information on the blackened surface:

Trophy

1920 Crow Hunt

Canton, S.D.

Won by

M. P. Juel

36 Crows

Apparently Clara, Mel's wife, had been clearing out unused and misused items from the basement and had decided that the loving cup had not been appreciated for a long time. She did not enjoy polishing silver anyway, so to the curb it went. I rescued it, straightened the base, and happily spent a lot of "elbow grease" restoring it to its original shine.

Today that trophy is among our cherished family items along

with a wood decoy that Melvin Juel used for many of his crow-hunting adventures. Because Mel would never have taken advantage of the "bragging rights" associated with this accomplishment, we are thankful that these pieces can tell the story.

Mildred Skyberg Juel, Brookings

Photo submitted by Mildred Skyberg Juel. Used with permission of Mildred Skyberg Juel.

A Prairie Pastime

An early wakeup call, long before the breaking of dawn. Waiting at the breakfast table for the first signs of light to grace the tops of rolling prairie hills. Walking outside, I feel the tell-tale brisk, moist wind of morning during the early fall. The anticipation of what will come in the next few hours grips me. My uncle and I unpack our gear that will be needed for this morning and begin the long trek to our destination. Next comes the wait. All that runs through my mind is what actions I will take, and when will these actions be needed. Deafening silence overwhelms me as I notice the world around me wake up. Piercing screeches of red-tailed hawks, the chuckles of pheasants, and the calling and bleating of waterfowl ready to embark on their journey to the fields. As the sun is reaching the horizon of the beautiful slopes over the sloughs and lakes of the northeastern prairies, the skies finally come alive with the graceful flight of South Dakota's ducks and geese. My uncle signals for me to get ready, and our silent field comes alive with the sounds of flying waterfowl.

Paxton Steen, Sioux Falls

MEMORY

Playground, Oglala. By David Michaud. Used with permission of David Michaud.

Death of a Farmyard

The children left one by one
Called to a life of a different sort.
The animals left when the farmer
Could no longer care for them.
The fields were rented out
To the Big Machines.
The house burnt down
On a snowy day,
The farmer and his wife
Moved to town.

The weeds took over the yard
And claimed it for their own.
The tall and stately barn,
Once a shelter,
Now quiet and unused,
Sighed and settled down.

The years move by.
The farmer dozes and dreams.
The children return to the
Old family table on special days.
The talk is "remember when?"
The cows got out on Easter morning.
The snowstorm blocked the way
To the Christmas program,
To the climbing tree
And the playhouse in the grove,
Listening to the geese fly overhead,
Going barefoot after a warm rain,
The year of the big corn crop,
The time hail pounded it down,
Picking rocks and gathering eggs,
Company Sundays when cousins came,

Birthdays, confirmations, and graduations.

Memories live on and the farmer
Listens, sighs, and smiles.

Edna Angerhofer, Brookings

Easter 1961

Mournfully, I sorted through my mother's possessions a few months after her death. I came across a beat-up, brass bowl that was long past its use and beauty. Almost throwing it in the piles of discarded memories, I picked up that tarnished, dented bowl to give it one last look and realized why my mother had hung onto it for so long. That bowl took me back to the spring of 1961, when I had just turned eight. I was living in a small northeastern South Dakota town, and my dad had suddenly passed away a month earlier. My mother was left with four little kids under the age of eight. Easter was nearing, and we were eagerly anticipating the arrival of the Easter bunny. As kids, we just couldn't understand why mom wasn't as excited as we were. As I would find out years later, paying for a funeral and trying to keep a household going with four small children left my mother penniless. I am sure she wondered how she could fulfill our holiday expectations.

As Easter morning arrived, we sleepily wandered out to our living room to see what the Easter bunny had left us and noticed just a few pieces of candy in a small basket. Seeing our mother's sad but smiling face, we tore into what candy there was, just happy that we had a few treats. A short while later, it was time for church, so we dressed in our Sunday clothes and prepared to leave. As my brother opened the front door, he yelled at mom that the Easter bunny had come to our house. Of course, we all rushed to the door. There it was, sitting on our front step, a big, brass bowl filled to the brim with candy and small stuffed toys. We all jumped with happiness that the Easter bunny had really remembered us after all. As we brought in the bowl, we turned to see mom with tears streaming down her face and couldn't understand why she would be crying at such a happy time. We never found out who placed that bowl on our front step, and whoever the "Easter bunny" was will never know what it meant to four little kids and their grieving mother. And, as I was astonished to find, that fifty years later that bowl was still full of bittersweet memories of someone's compassion and love in a small South Dakota town.

Elizabeth Simons, Vermillion

Indian girl, Pine Ridge. Selected from Oglala Lakota College Archives photo collection, South Dakota State Historical Society.

250

December 29, 1890 – The Story Not Often Revealed

(for those mothers and their children who were massacred on this day)

The first sliver of light of this new day slowly reveals itself in this space where we are lying. The bitter cold grips me, and I pray that warmth will soon be upon us. My child lies next to me, snuggling as far under my side as he can, trying to steal heat from my body. I pull him closer into the curve of my breast and make sure he is fully covered so that the cold cannot get to him, but even so, I can see his frosty breath as it rhythmically flows in and out from between his lips. He sleeps soundly, seemingly unaware of this enveloping cold which threatens to take our flesh from us. I look down at his round little face, eyelashes, black, splayed across the tops of his cheeks, his eyebrows, perfect lines. I put my hand gently on his face and touch it as if to memorize its features. I marvel at this gift which has been given to me, a gift from the depths of my body and the depths of my soul. This child cannot know the completeness of my life because of his presence. He moves, as if to say, "Let me sleep, do not wake me." The milk in my breasts begins to surge against my nipples, and I uncover one breast and gently ease my nipple into his mouth. He takes it quickly and makes gulping noises as the first milk rushes from my breast.

Soon he is finished and lets my nipple slip slowly from his lips. I cover him, and we sleep again in each other's warmth as we wait for the time to rise.

A loud, sharp, cracking noise tears through the crisp, cold morning air, and jolts me upright. I am confused, what is that? Another sound which I cannot identify explodes outside my tent, and again, this time only louder, and again and again. Screams, I hear screams, I hear children crying for their mothers. I hear the voices of my relatives, hollering for each other and at each other, and the crunching sound of feet running on the frozen snow. Someone falls, a cry of pain, and then more cries. I hear my name

251

being called. "Run, run," they say. I am too frightened to move, but finally I grab my son and wrap him then move hesitantly toward the opening of the tent, not knowing what is happening or what I should do. I peek out—everyone is running away from the campsite. I pause for a second and then I run, my son in my arms.

Others run past me and beside me, frantic, some falling. I cannot stop to help. I am running and running and running until I stumble and fall. My son flies from my arms and screams as he lands on his back. His blanket opens, and he spills from it and rolls onto the hard, frozen snow cover. He cries, but his cries are indistinguishable from the chaos and confusion which encircle us. As I crawl desperately on my hands and knees to him, I look and see people lying on the ground all around us in this ravine, lying in pools of red, harsh against the white, that are growing larger and larger, and all with their faces in the snow. I pick up my son and pull him to me. I struggle to my feet and begin to run again as I follow those who are running toward the early morning sun. I hear whistling sounds fly by my head and see people fall. I continue to run, I cannot stop, I must not stop.

My chest is on fire, it is difficult to breathe, and I can no longer feel my feet, but I run, with my child in my arms, I run. There are screams, continuous screams. My child cries at the top of his lungs, but I hold him tighter and run. I am blinded by fear and by tears streaming down my face. What is happening?

Suddenly, a searing pain rips my breath away and stops me. I cannot cry out. I feel my child go limp in my arms. My breasts are awash in something hot and wet. I look down at my chest and my child and see the mingling of our blood. My knees buckle under me, and I drop softly to the ground but still hold my son hard and tight to me. I hear his breath, gurgling as it leaves his little body with red, bloody bubbles pouring slowly from his mouth. I hold him tight, but there is no life. I try to scream—*WHY?*—but my mouth will not make the sound. I feel myself getting lighter. I cannot see the sky; my thoughts are leaving me. I ease myself down and lie on my side on the frozen, snow-covered ground. My son lies in my arms; his tiny body stained red with our blood. Sleep overcomes me as a blanket of warmth covers me. My arms are heavy, but I hold him and touch his face as I sleep.

Lenora Hudson, Rapid City

~ഗ৲~

Kindled Memories: On the Burning of Kress Drug in Mitchell, April 1950

Standing in front of Schultz Paint Store, I watched the hotel fire jump the street, igniting Kress Drug's water-soaked roof. Dad's drugstore on the corner of First and Main, constructed of 1910 clapboard, burned quickly from rear to front. Freshman classmates clustered near me, but I scarcely noticed them as memories surfaced.

Flames engulfed the back room. In my mind's eye, I observe Dad laboring over his monthly statements at his roll-top desk. I perch on the stool beside him, quietly practicing my numbers on my own special black ledger. Dad reaches over and doodles tic-tac-toe on my page. Flames spread through camera and school supplies. "What color pencils for my girl's first day of school?" Otto, the hired man, spreads sweeping compound on the oil polished wooden floor, as he playfully pushes the broom against the toes poking out of my first sandals.

Flames invaded prescription drugs, patent medicine, veterinary supplies. Miss Suzie walks in and begins her Saturday ritual. She sits on the wire-rim ice-cream parlor chair and systematically takes out her apple, cheese, and Scallin Drug vitamins. This burns Dad; not even Kress Drug vitamins! Miss Suzy waits for water and helps herself to free napkins. Dad escapes across the street to the Town House for coffee. Suzie leaves; Dad returns. Dad scowls, "Pick up a dust cloth; I don't pay you to read *Seventeen*."

Flames poured out the side door. Bottles of spirits behind the fountain burst. Tom, the grease monkey from Max Motors, slips in the side door and eases a dollar twenty-two onto the counter. Instinctively I reach for a pint of Old Crow, remembering not to sack it as I set it on the counter. He swivels and leaves with the usual bulge in his right pocket. Tony, my first steady, hangs around, pretending to decide which soda flavor to order. Finally, Dad shrugs his shoulders and disappears into the back room. Tony grins and orders his usual—chocolate. I scoop in extra ice cream.

Flames blazed through cosmetics, jewelry, gifts. Out-of-state hunters rush in looking for souvenirs to take home to wives and children. Women's hats made from pheasant feathers fly off the shelves. Buyers snatch Indian dolls brightly colored canvas drums and toy covered wagons.

The meticulously decorated display windows exploded, shattering glass across Main to Schuty Paint Store. Hoddy Kress, Dad's elderly business partner, patted my shoulder. He whispered, "Don't worry; it's only money." Dad came to my side and gently took my hand. We walked home the fourteen blocks in silence. The stale smoke smell lingered.

Lynette Olson, Brookings

Sonnets from the Prairie

I. Wheels of Creation

Cold pre-dawn breezes catch the bleating cry
   of daughter born amidst tall seas of grass.
Paeans of praise from earth to heaven high
   with Conestogas creaking, slowly pass.
With corded arms and gnarled boughs he finds
   a home excluding dangers of the night.
Protecting and defending hearts and minds,
   he cherishes and loves with all his might.
Her needles fly amidst the miles of sheep
   to keep her family clothed and safely warm.
Her quiet grace and faith grow ever deep
   to keep her loved ones ever far from harm.
Here in this prairie fortress hope survives.
   Their daughter of the prairie grows and thrives.

II. Wheels of Change

As with the way of wheels and plans of men,
　　the hands and feet of Time do swiftly run.
The creaking of the prairie schooners then
　　in bringing change they ceased beneath the sun.
In time with raging fury's marching roar
　　regarding not the simpler prairie ways.
No room for bison's realm or eagles soar
　　people once danced for years, now counted days.
The iron horse screamed challenge for the land
　　taking peace and life from the Lakota
and spinning dreams with looming visions planned
　　for territory there, called Dakota.
And here the girl grew tall and full of grace
　　reflecting changes on a woman's face.

III. Wheels of Trial

Those early years, with pride and passion wrought,
　　found homesteads planted richly 'neath the sky.
While plow and famine, snow, and hoppers fought
　　to bring the harvest home with wheat sheaves high.
The decades rolled with cars, and folks, and trains
　　filled with the hopes and dreams of families more.
Then farmers and their kin came to the plains,
　　and soldiers left their fields against the war.
The dragons of the skies screamed out their roar
　　devouring plow boy knights beneath the sun.
The glory of their fire raged ever more,
　　and tore them from the sky, dead one by one.
She fell upon her knees there on the floor.
　　The letter there addressed: they were no more.

IV. Wheels of Triumph

They marched on pursuing prairie treasure
　　finding gold and jewels rare in their mine.
A golden sun shone down for their pleasure;

the silver orb graced all at evening time.
Tall sentries of electric marked the sky
    and prairie creeks were piped across the sand,
granting comfort, bringing hope where we lie.
Bold progress ever marched across the land.
    New schools of higher learning crossed our state
stretching young minds with their ideas bright.
    Fine goals shined forth there, and our dreams grew great.
Dakota prospered us with all her might.
    Her silver crown wreathed round a nobler face.
Though slow of foot she walked with deeper grace.

V. Wheels of Tomorrow

To be Dakotan speaks to certain breed
    with braver hearts for action clearly won.
To follow never ending is their creed
    from breaking of the dawn 'til work is done.
Though wheels of progress ever shift and grow;
    our minds and hearts and bodies clearly stand
defending rights and loved ones even now,
    and in the doing make Dakota grand.
The future we may never clearly see,
    but our children embrace with open arms.
The strong ones of Dakota they will be
    and walking in her light tread safe from harm.
Ten thousand dreams shine in our dear ones' eyes.
    Our hopes for these beloved ever rise.

C. R. Larsen, Mitchell

Photo by Greg Latza. Used with permission of Greg Latza.

Scotty Philip Memorial Ride hosted by Verendrye Museum Association and sponsored in part by a grant from the SD Humanities Council. By Justin Koehler. Used with permission of Justin Koehler.

Echoes from My Past

This summer I went back to a time when the prairie was not yet settled, back to a time when the simple life was cherished, back to a time when man rode alongside the buffalo, and back to a time where I could hear the voices of those who had gone before me over 200 years ago echo across the prairie. I participated in the Historic Bad River Trail: Scotty Philip Memorial Drive. This was a week-long journey by foot, horseback, and wagon from Philip to Fort Pierre, and it was the experience of a lifetime. My most useful tools were determination, tolerance, and resilience.

This week consisted of enduring the harsh South Dakota weather and the rough terrain that our ancestors settled years ago. On this drive we encountered every obstacle imaginable. We conquered triple-digit heat as well as violent thunderstorms rolling over the grasslands. We endured sleepless nights and dawn-to-dusk riding. There were mechanical malfunctions and animal mishaps.

I learned multiple life lessons throughout this adventure, but my ultimate experience was seeing South Dakota like my ancestors saw it every day so long ago. As we rode from day to day, I saw South Dakota as the nature-filled and beautiful state that it is. I can say that you haven't seen South Dakota until you've been on a horse on a cliff overlooking a valley below. You haven't seen South Dakota until you've risen before the sun breaks the line between land and sky and have observed nature, in all its glory, come to life. You haven't seen South Dakota until you've ridden alongside a herd of buffalo at dawn. You haven't seen South Dakota until you've jumped a horse across a river, and you haven't seen South Dakota until you've experienced the unity of complete strangers helping one another to make it through each day, sometimes hour to hour.

My goal was to help my grandpa achieve a dream. He lives barely 150 yards from my house and has been an important role model throughout my life. He gives everything and asks for nothing in return. He's taught me everything that I know about horses and has shown me how hard work will lead to a successful life full of happiness and love. As our week across the prairie progressed, amid tears and laughter, our bond grew stronger.

As the sun set on our final day, we climbed the last and tallest hill of the journey. As we made the slow ascent to the top, we could start to see the edge of civilization. Once we rode through town and our lives returned to normal, I would have the chance to reflect on my adventure. I had completed a week-long trip which consisted of obstacles, new experiences, and family bonding all without the presence of modern conveniences. This gave me a deeper understanding and knowledge of the simple life. This journey took me to my past and showed me how our ancestors lived and struggled when they first encountered this land. It was a memorable time that has made me appreciate the life that we all live today.

At the end of the trip I realized I had helped this special person in my life fulfill his dream, not just because we completed the journey, but because of the look on my grandpa's face. He had a smile that stretched for miles and settled in his eyes.

Madelyn Anderson, Webster

Radiomen

When my parents told me how they had met at First Lutheran Church during World War II, I naively envisioned my own version of the occasion. It was a simple setting with egg coffee and cookies, but the circumstances surrounding them were anything but an after-church meeting. Possibly because of that "aw shucks" South Dakotan mentality, I could not fathom what role Sioux Falls played in the war.

When my dad enlisted in Peoria, Illinois, he did not expect to be stationed in Sioux Falls, South Dakota. The far-sighted Sioux Falls Chamber of Commerce had recruited the radio training school to locate in the middle of America. This was one of only two such schools in the United States. Thus, one-half of the radio operator mechanics trained in Morse Code, radio theory, and identification of airplanes in the United States were trained in Sioux Falls.

The base was constructed in three short months by 6,000 Works Projects Administration (WPA) workers. The building plans had originated in the southern states, so the tar-paper-covered barracks were no match for the extreme South Dakota climate. The non-insulated barracks were not warm, and the coal stoves caused some of the soldiers to suffer from coal soot pneumonia.

The 42,000 citizens of Sioux Falls started welcoming over 27,000 soldiers in July 1942. Local families rented out rooms throughout the city, and many South Dakotans invited soldiers into their homes for home-cooked meals.

Dances were held at the Arkota Ballroom and on the base. Live, big-band music was the norm for these dances, and one special day the tennis court on base was the stage for the Tommy Dorsey band, as it played "Sentimental Journey," "A Train," "String of Pearls," and other popular songs of the time. Young ladies known as Tickette Girls were bussed to the air base to dance with the radiomen and were promptly whisked home at evening's end. The Egyptian, State, Granada, and Times theaters showed the latest films, and the Orpheum and Coliseum had activities also. There were several USO (United Service Organi zations) centers, one of them at the First Lutheran Church, which served the egg coffee and cookies for that fateful first meeting of my parents.

On VE Day, people formed a conga line and snaked down Phillips Avenue to celebrate the end of the war. Many of those Tickette Girls avoided this raucous celebration.

In December 1945, the Army Air Force Technical Command Radio Training School was deactivated. At war's end, my dad returned from the Philippines, where he had worked in General MacArthur's headquarters, and married the girl he had met at the USO meeting. They would build their lives in Sioux Falls. There are others throughout South Dakota who can trace their origins to this base in Sioux Falls.

After the base closed, some of the barracks were moved off the base and used in Sioux Falls as houses and churches and at Augustana College as dorms and educational spaces. I grew up with these buildings dotting the town, but until recently never really knew of their true significance in the formation of my family and the community.

Perhaps we should be a little more knowledgeable and vocal about our history. We need not be so shy about boasting about Sioux Falls or our radiomen and the impact they had on the war effort. Aw shucks.

Paula Tursam, Brookings

Igloo, South Dakota

Very few people know that in 1942 a new community was built in the southwest corner of South Dakota, a few miles from Edgemont. I was six years old, and my mother, sister, and I were living in Sioux Falls with my grandparents and waiting for our lodging to be built. Finally the day came, and we were waved through the gate, and I began my six years at the Black Hills Ordinance Depot at Igloo.

Igloo was an army base surrounded by barbed wire, where everything was painted brown. There was a community building, a BX, and a church. The school, swimming pool, and theater were built a few months after we arrived. During first grade, I had to ride a big brown army bus to Edgemont. I was so scared.

Igloo was named after the 900 earth-rammed igloos which housed bombs, mustard gas, and TNT on heavily guarded land. None of us was allowed on this part of the base.

As the war progressed, prisoners from Germany and Italy were housed in the barracks. We were too young to understand what being a prisoner meant (particularly because they sang and laughed as they marched to the cafeteria each day), and it wasn't frightening to us.

Very few people had cars, and the gravel streets were narrow. The town was built on gumbo, and when it rained, the base was a muddy mess. But we didn't know any different. It was home to us.

We were a close-knit community, and we were all in the same boat. Many of our fathers had gone to war, and we had the time to develop close friendships with each other. I remember when the playground, which had swings, slides, and teeter totters, was built. We had a place to gather and play. There were rattlesnakes, so we had to be careful where we played.

Occasionally my mother would give me little, round, red tokens, and I would go to the BX to buy coffee, sugar, or bananas. This was my life during the first through sixth grade.

In 1948, many of the men took jobs with the Bureau of Reclamation in Huron, and our family and some of our friends moved there. I remember my first impression of Huron when I walked downtown a few days after moving. I couldn't believe all of the stores, shops, hotels, and restaurants that were there. I was in heaven—particularly with the dime store.

Several years ago my son and I decided to go to Igloo to see what was there. During the '50s, there had been a pig farm, but no one lived there anymore; however, fifteen people lived on the hill where the colonels used to live. I visited with a woman who had lived in Igloo in the '40s, and she was so excited to talk to someone who was there "way back then."

We drove to the spot where our duplex had been. It was an empty space, but the two trees that my dad had planted soon after we had arrived in Igloo were still living and were large. I stood there and cried.

It was an unusual place to live, but it was "what made not only me, but some others, South Dakotans."

Rev. Lin Jennewein, Rapid City

Visitors At Black Hills Ordnance Depot, Igloo. Photo courtesy of the State Archives of the South Dakota State Historical Society.

This barn fire on Interstate 29 was captured by a Brookings Fire Department member December 29, 2011. Used with permission of Brookings Register.

Interstate

My thoughts of what makes a South Dakotan are memories that flooded my mind as I read the December 29, 2011, *Brookings Register* article, "Interstate Spectacle":

Travelers along Interstate 29 north of Brookings were witness to a dramatic roadside fire. A barn on a farmstead just a mile north of the White/Bruce exit caught fire and burned to the ground.

That barn was where my dad labored away on a daily basis. He milked cows by hand and sold a portion of the milk to the White Creamery for a few dollars to spend on me and my brothers. He pitched hay from the haymow to feed cattle so we could sell the milk and eat fresh beef. It was always rather sad for me each summer when we would fill the haymow. Dad knew his four sons liked to play basketball, and he had installed a hoop in the haymow. The excitement to start shooting hoops would build as we cleared hay each fall. Dad always said that we wore holes in that old barn floor. He loved watching us shoot. He even patched up the holes and would occasionally shoot a basket himself. It wasn't Frost Arena, but for the Smidt brothers and other family members in the area, that barn was an arena like no other. We used haymow floor braces to wipe out defenders and get a good shot. Many times, the fierce competition would result in bloody noses and hasty retreats out of the barn.

That old barn taught me many lessons about what it means to be a South Dakotan. Places matter, but the development of a solid work ethic, a strong sense of competition, the love of family, and responsibility define in a greater sense what it means to be a South Dakotan.

Orv Smidt, Brookings

Finding a Place Called Home

Eight words resonated through my high school walls:
"I can't wait to get out of here."
And we left.

We all went out to aspire to great heights,
To learn new thoughts, to think new things,
To do better than our parents,
Who had raised us in a podunk town.
There was the world to explore,
And we did.

We saw great museums, historical sites,
Cultures upon cultures and more.
And then we aged.

We, one by one, realized
What that podunk town did for our hearts, and our minds,
And our souls.
And we found our own versions of our small town,
Some of us closer than others.

Courtney VanZanten, Colton

A
South Dakota
Inventory
1989

(Centennial Poem)

Snow ticking on cornstalks; honking v's of geese at 3 a.m.
pulling spring back over farms, over neighbor-
hoods; wind rattling through corridors of stubble;
the sound of claws on bark; corn *pinging* from a
shovel's lip; the *caw caw* of crows; redwinged blackbirds' fierce metal warbling; the two clean morning
notes of the chickadee—

Deer hightailing it; the badger looking up suddenly from
his half clawed hole; the snapper orbiting from mud
to pasture to mud; a hawk's slow-motion glide;
paddle-fish vacuuming the gloomy floors of dams;
crows flapping away from road-kills with plenty of
time on their wings; cattails swaying like car an-
tennas; pine limbs weighed down by snow—

The sudden tug on a fishing line, the rod-tip divining;
bullheads sucking air in shallow pails; hunters'
boots crunching snow; cottonwood leaves shimmering in windy sunlight; moon-faced cattle; hog
houses, hog grunts; dead-end roads; auctioneers
in white Stetsons; graveyards on hills; the iron level
sound of trains; the rough softness of milkpods;
seed hats—

That second sun, the October pumpkin; those yellow
ventriloquists, the meadowlarks; the Missouri swirl-
ing around bluffs; December's frozen sun; flat stones
skimming lake water; the probing headlights of
tractors in night fields; silver water towers; rodeos,
the smell of alfalfa; quick draw packinghouse hands;
the grim smile of a possum really dead—

Names of towns: Sinai, Eagle Butte, Deadwood, Aurora,
Willow Lake, Ipswich, Blunt, Faith, Lake Andes,
Mound City, Buffalo Gap, White River, Elk Point,
Wessington Springs, Potato Creek, Redfield, Win-
ner, Woonsocket, Fort Pierre, Trail City, Pine Ridge,
Bonesteel, Sisseton, Wall, Tea, Lead, Hayti—

Dogs chasing rabbits zigzagging across fields; ice houses
with portable tv's; the sun rising in alleys; one hundred blackbirds suddenly flying up as one black
wing and away; garage sales; pow wows; the earnest
swing of lunch pails on sidewalks at 6 a.m.; white
country churches; swivelling owl-looks; farm
ponds; prairie grass; nine sparrows neatly spaced
on a power line . . .

David Allan Evans

David Allan Evans, Brookings, one of the nine official Centennial poets, wrote "South Dakota, 1989 (Centennial Poem)" as a commemorative poem to mark South Dakota's century anniversary. Evans is a professor in the English Department at SDSU. An author of three books of poems and two books of prose, Evans has published his poems in over 40 anthologies. Jim Taggert, Brookings, designed the poster. (courtesy of David Allan Evans)

Photo Courtesy of the State Archives of the South Dakota State Historical Society.

Going Home

A South Dakotan never leaves home. It does not matter how many places he or she lives; that person will say, "I am going home." We know that is true because it has happened to us. We grew up in central South Dakota at Rockham and Carthage. We went to schools from one-room buildings to colleges in Brookings and Aberdeen. Then we found work in Nebraska, Iowa, Illinois, and Minnesota. Our careers allowed us to travel around the world and all over the United States. But twice a year during those fifty-plus years we have gone "home." People will ask, "Isn't this your home?" It is and it isn't.

Going home is the trip back to South Dakota to attend a family wedding, to cry at a close relative's funeral, to laugh and recall funny events when attending high school reunions, to drive the back roads trying to find familiar farms, to stop again and again at cemeteries to look at family and friends' tombstones, to drive the main streets of small, desolate towns, wishing a café was open or that we could buy an ice cream cone, waving to every car and pickup we meet on dusty roads, and standing in awe at Mount Rushmore and the Corn Palace. We don't ever get tired of or bored with "going home."

Joyce and Delmar Wittenhagen, St. Cloud, Minn.

Music and Barn Dances

I was born and raised in the Roscoe-Hosmer area on a farm eighteen miles east of Hosmer or nine miles north and nine miles east of Roscoe. My parents, Gottfried and Eva (Dockter) Adam, were married in 1913 and raised nine children. At the present time only my brother Gottfried (ninety-two) and I are living.

I've lived in New Mexico since 1965, and many times I've been asked: "How could you stand those long cold winters?" Easy. We were young and had plenty of food, and if there was a problem, mom and dad never let on. Instead dad would pull out his little accordion, and before long, someone would have alerted all the neighbors that there was a party at the Adam farm. Within minutes, the house would be packed, and the table moved outside so there was more room for dancing. These parties happened quite often, and after school programs, our house was the target. I had three brothers who each had a band and played for dances almost every weekend. Our dances ended up being in the hay loft of the barn. I remember dancing the polka all by myself as one of my brothers was playing until, bang, I was gone. I had fallen through one of the holes that led to the floor below where we would push hay down for the cattle and horses. The day after a dance my two younger sisters and I would head for the barn because we usually found coins that had been dropped the night before from people climbing the stairs to the loft.

I recently had a book published entitled *As Bob Would Say, Thanks for the Memories*, which includes many short stories about growing up in South Dakota. I have many happy memories of growing up in South Dakota, but my happiest memories are of all the parties we had.

Clara Hoffer, Las Cruces, N.M.

CULTURE

By David Michaud. Used with permission of David Michaud.

‿ℐ‿

Culture of South Dakota

South Dakotans are a combination of many factors, including genetics, family, environment, community, and others. But what we all have in common is how much we have been influenced by the "Culture of South Dakota." This culture may vary a bit from area to area; in my case, it was the culture of farm and small town.

I was born in the early 1930s and remember well what went on in our farming community. We were poor, but no one knew it or cared. Family was most important. You helped your neighbor if they needed it. You trusted everyone. Hard work was expected.

Family expectations were to wear hand-me-down clothes and not to complain. You would clean your plate and not fuss about leftovers. You would take a bath once a week and share that same water with your siblings. You wouldn't fight with your school mates or siblings, and you would learn to share. You would always think of others and never be selfish. The strong message to me from my parents and extended family was, "Always do your best and don't complain."

I got to go to town (1,000 people) on Saturday nights, and I was given ten cents to spend on anything I wanted. Once in a while, I might even be given a quarter. I quickly learned to budget and control impulse spending.

When I went away to college, my parents could not afford the tuition, so my uncle loaned me the money. During my college years, I always had at least two part-time jobs, and a portion of my paychecks went to pay off the loan to Uncle John. I had learned from my South Dakota culture that if you wanted something badly enough, there would always be a way to accomplish it.

So how did that culture affect me? It affected my choices, values, priorities, behavior, and attitudes. Even though I moved far away, I retained the effect of that culture in which I was born and raised. My career choice was psychotherapy, and I have a doctorate in psychology. The major part of my career was spent at a university teaching hospital before I entered full-time private practice. I am now retired but volunteer at a hospice, helping people deal with terminal cancer and impending death.

Even though I have not lived in South Dakota for many years, the South Dakota culture has always been a part of my being and my behavior. It is my hope that I have instilled that culture in my children and grandchildren.

Marvin Johnson, Glenview, Ill.

Reading, Writing, and Really Good Times— Education Memories

Country School—what an experience! It included eight or nine grade levels, one classroom, one teacher, and two outhouses, but so much more. Those of us lucky enough to have attended one of them will remember the recitation bench, older students assisting struggling young students, YCL (Young Citizens League) conventions, all-county eighth-grade graduation ceremonies, the scary visits of the county superintendent, and the year-end achievement tests. We had multi-aged teams of students competing in games of 23 Skidoo, Tag, baseball, Keep Away, Fox-and-Goose on that perfect stretch of new snow, and snowball fights from elaborate snow forts with tunnel exits. Yes, we had a swing set, but that pastime was so tame compared to chasing a drowned-out gopher. The activities were driven by our imaginations, and our imaginations were unlimited.

Town school had its hot lunch program, but so did we. It was the saucepan with the daily collection of hot dogs boiling on the hot plate, the foil-wrapped potatoes baking on the heater all morning, or the thermos of soup which challenged you to entice that last noodle from the narrow-necked container. These items were eaten with apples or bananas and cookies, all a bit bruised or damaged from their dinner-pail journey to school that day.

We had music and art once a week, *real* field trips, Arbor Day tree plantings, drama performances, daily flag raising and lowering, the Pledge of Allegiance without controversy, energetic recess time, and much more. We learned, we shared, we lived. What more could we have asked for?

Sperlich School
Aurora County, Aurora Township
1956-1962
Karen E. Clark, Mitchell

_ʃ1ʃ_

South Dakota's Best Investment (Part I)

A few of us have been guilty of that old refrain: "When I was in high school. . . ." We go on to bemoan the current shortcomings of today's young people, convincing ourselves that things just *aren't* like they used to be. A recent, informal survey of small-town juniors and seniors indicates that things really aren't like the way they used to be (and that's likely a good thing!).

Typical daily concerns for these young people are probably the same as in the "old days": family, friends, girls, movies, shopping, cars, music, money worries, boys, school pressures, sports, or the latest fads. But these students consistently expressed serious concerns about preparing for their futures, getting homework finished, earning money through their jobs, taking tests, and finding scholarships.

They worry about what others think of them, how to be responsible, and how to accomplish their goals. Some readers might be surprised to learn that many of these students are putting constant pressure on themselves to "try to be the best of everything," "to get my grades up," and to excel in whatever sport they are in. Some expressed their non-school concerns about their spiritual lives and sharing their beliefs with others.

Obviously, these students also have some familiar goals for their future, which probably mirror the same ones of previous generations: a good career, a home of their own, being on their own, a spouse to share things with, and just plain "loving life."

But compare the following item with how things were one or two generations back! Out of the seventy students surveyed, 88 percent indicated plans for college. (How many years ago was it that parents were happy if their children had plans for *high school*?) Many already have specific career plans: dentist, zoologist, nurse, musician, paramedic, realtor, comedian, farmer, doctor, teacher, military, physical therapist, "chopper" designer, missionary, ultra-sound technician, or car designer. One has already begun his agriculture career as he muses about "the best time to sell my cattle." Almost all have planned to further their educations to prepare for these jobs.

Interestingly, not one of those surveyed had a career goal of "making lots of money" or "finding something easy to do." Notice how many of these careers pertain to being of direct service to people. The recurring theme was working hard right now to achieve future goals! This should come as no surprise, considering the influence of their parents, schools, churches, and communities.

Beresford High School Students

South Dakota's Best Investment (Part II)

After the students shared their dreams and concerns, their teachers weighed in on what factors would have an impact on their students' future successes. Not surprisingly, the teachers recognized the same challenges that get featured in the media: cyber-bullying, unexpected Facebook disclosures, and pressures from a myriad of anonymous sources. Disasters and threats—both near and far, real or imagined—accost students with the click of a button.

However, while all this might constitute sensory overload to an older generation, one teacher marveled at the informational multitasking skills of today's young people. While taking students to a school activity, he witnessed "kids texting two, three, four other kids at one time, keeping up with the conversation in the vehicle, visiting with my questions, and managing all that information."

Other teachers reiterate similar observations about student "tech savvy." Yesterday's teenagers accessed information in "slow motion" or not at all, while today's students have instant coverage of every sporting event in the country, any disaster in the world, or pictures from a Mars exploration rover. They glide smoothly from cell phone to iPad to face-to-face online correspondence. A New Zealand earthquake report arrives as easily as a fashion update. Yet, today's student learns how to sort through this cornucopia of data!

It is the *personal traits*, however, that equip today's young people to manage their lives in a complicated world. Teachers observe students' "inner drive to complete the task set before them," then "seek out the next venture to conquer." They display a "willingness and hunger to gather information." Being so connected to the world with technology, students "are more sensitive than they want us to know, care about the world and its environment, are champions of the 'underdog,' are adventuresome, have kind souls, are curious, creative, out-spoken, and fun to be around."

One student story serves as a micro-example of what hundreds of teachers could report. A sixth grader with musical talent and ambition went to New York to audition for *Annie*. She didn't get the part but continued to develop her voice with every opportunity available: show choir, church choir, contests, and oral interpretation. This young woman eventually became Miss South Dakota. As her former teacher reports: "I see a poised, confident woman. It will not matter how much money she makes, but what matters is who she has become."

Perhaps one of today's students might become the next George McGovern, or Ernest O. Lawrence, or Laura Ingalls Wilder; the next Joe Robbie, or Mary Hart, or Billy Mills. Their teachers have every right to expect it!

Beresford Jr./Sr. High Teachers

The Big Read Egypt/U.S., a collaborative project of the U.S. Department of State and the National Endowment for the Arts in partnership with Arts Midwest, the U.S. Embassy in Cairo, the Institute of Museum and Library Services, and the South Dakota Humanities Council, brought eight Egyptian students from schools in Cairo and Alexandria to South Dakota in 2010. SDHC's South Dakota Center for the Book coordinated the cultural exchange activities ranging from museum visits and a buffalo tour in Custer State Park to presentations at rotary clubs and the festival, as well as visits to Sioux Falls and Red Cloud high schools. After the Dave Eggers and Valentino Achak Deng presentation at the 2010 South Dakota Festival of Books, Egyptian students converse with Sioux Falls Sudanese residents. By Toby Brusseau. Used with permission of SDHC.

Egyptian students with the Big Read Egypt/U.S. project pose with author Dan O'Brien at Zandbroz Variety in Sioux Falls. Dan O'Brien's book, Buffalo for the Broken Heart, *was selected as the 2009 One Book South Dakota. The book was given to the Egyptians at the 2010 book festival to gain a glimpse into South Dakota culture. Used with permission of SDHC.*

2009 One Book South Dakota

Though western South Dakotans can be a surprisingly tolerant bunch, there is something in the way Erney and I live that offends some. For them this land is a sort of factory and it should produce wheat and beef. The idea of enjoying the natural features of the country, minimizing human impact on the land, and deviating from the way people have traditionally lived out here simply does not compute. And what really puzzles some of them is that by managing the land for wildlife and grass we end up raising more and better-quality livestock than many.

When I first moved here some of the neighbors were suspicious of my intentions. It took almost two years to become friends with my closest neighbor. Those were in the years when parts of the West were dotted with missiles pointed at Russia. They are gone now, but back then there were a dozen within ten miles of the ranch. Steve Bestgen has become a good friend, but at first he seemed to avoid me. He farmed a field that had no good access except through my yard, and for a week or so in the spring and fall Steve passed back and forth outside my office window several times a day.

The road he took is not a public thoroughfare, it is our mile-and-a-quarter driveway, but I didn't mind. I would be at my desk trying to write, but since I welcome every opportunity to stop writing, I waved as he passed. He would pretend not to see me, and after a few trips past my window I was so desperate to stop writing that I would run out to flag him down when I heard the tractor straining to climb the hill. Once he was stopped, I'd crawl up on the tractor and attempt a chat with him. For the entire first year it did not go well. I got monosyllabic answers to my questions, but I refused to be dissuaded. I kept right on with my chatter about the weather and livestock prices and he slowly loosened up.

Finally he began to ask questions about the falcons perched in the yard, and one particularly beautiful autumn day he came out with a confession of sorts. "You know," Steve said, "you're really all right."

"Yeah?"

"We weren't too sure, you know."

"About me?"

"Yeah. I mean all this stuff." He waved a hand at the falcons, the bird dogs pistoning up and down in the kennel. "Some people said it was a front."

I grimaced, afraid the local gossip was that I was a drug dealer. "A front for what?"

"Well, nobody can figure out what a guy with an education is doing out here. We kind of figured you were a spy."

"A spy?"

"You know, a Russian or something. Keeping an eye on these missiles. But, heck, you just like birds."

Dan O'Brien, Hermosa

Dan O'Brien's contribution to this book is an excerpt from *Buffalo for the Broken Heart*, first published by Random House.

The Formation of a Church Community

Around 1910, the area west and south of Clark was being settled by pioneers. As the community grew, the residents felt the need for a church. One farmer donated the land, and soon the sound of hammers filled the air. The men of the community built the Logan Township Methodist Church, which was affiliated with the Clark Methodist Church. There was a sidewalk about twelve feet long leading out from it and a raised block of cement at the end of it to accommodate people getting in and out of their buggies. In addition to church services, Sunday School was held for all ages. Epworth League was held in homes on Sunday evenings for the youth of the community. This consisted of a lesson, a social time, and lunch. Young people from all religions were included. The ladies of the community organized Ladies Aid, which also met in homes. At Christmas time, a church Christmas program was held, and afterwards every child received a paper sack filled with an apple, hard candy, and peanuts in the shell. That was a very special treat!

By about the 1930s, attendance was down so much that the church was closed, and the congregation joined the Clark Methodist Church. My father bought the church for one dollar and had it moved one mile to the farm where I lived with my family. We lived in the basement for years, saving money to have the church remodeled into our living quarters. We had a kitchen, living/dining room, bathroom, and three bedrooms on the main level, and an upper level remained unfinished, as the church was so tall! Once finished, it served as our home for forty-five years, and if you go upstairs today, you can still see the original wallpaper from the church and the shapes of the tops of the church windows. Due to health reasons, I now live in a care center in Yankton, near my daughter, but my son still lives in the house which had been the Logan Township Methodist Church! Early churches and schools helped form the backbone of the community and bonded the families together.

Melba Olverson, Yankton

Looking West

When people in South Dakota step outside and look around, they tend to look to the west. It isn't so much a wanderlust they have inherited from the settlers who came from Europe to homestead. It isn't that they are looking west to where they may be going. They are looking west for what may be coming. Here, the weather comes mainly from the west. For decades, people have cut hay and looked to the west, hoping for clear skies. People walking through fields of parched corn and wheat have leaned their eyes into the west, hoping to conjure up a bank of rain clouds by sheer force of will. Children have stood transfixed by thunderheads that pile one dark billow on another and then craze the sky with lightening above fields of ripe grain. Clear days, needed rain, dangerous storms, or fierce blizzards—we look to the west to see what's coming.

In the southern part of Day County on a pleasant day in 1904, Tomina Sannes looked to the west to get an idea of what was coming. Tomina was a unique person in her own right, one of the pioneers who had crossed the ocean to build a new home on the empty prairie. The day would come when she would be remembered for her grandson Hubert, who spent summers playing on the porch of her farm house and who would, at length, become vice president of the United States. But such grand possibilities were not on her mind that day in 1904 when Tomina looked to the west and frowned at what she saw.

It was not a tornado, tearing a path of destruction, or a raging blizzard she saw. Less than a mile across the section was a gang of her neighbors engaged in the project of building the sanctuary for Highland Lutheran Church. It was close enough that if the wind were right, she could probably hear the pleasant sounds of neighbors working together, hammers, saws, laughter, and talk. But for Tomina these were no pleasant sounds. She and her family belonged to Hosanger Lutheran Church, some three miles to the north and east, and Tomina loved her church, loved it so much she didn't want another congregation crowding in and dividing potential members, making the way harder. Whether it was doctrine or piety or just proximity, her distaste for the church going up to the west was such that she pulled the shades on the west side of her house so she and her household would not have to look at that church.

Even though Tomina wouldn't look at it, the Highland church kept going, just to her west, and the weather kept coming from the west. On July 3, 1920, a great black cloud came from the west, and a tornado reached down like the finger of God and leveled her beloved Hosanger church.

When the members of Hosanger surveyed the wreckage, they decided that there were enough other churches to accommodate them, and they chose not to rebuild. All that is left of Hosanger now is the cemetery, where the old members lie and wait for the resurrection.

What happened to Tomina? There was no logical alternative for her and her family other than the Highland Church just across the section, the church she had not wanted to even look at. So, like thousands of other South Dakotans who have watched towns, churches, and schools they loved dwindle and die and then started over, she turned to her new church home, Highland, and put her hand to the plow there.

I can't tell you that this move was easy for Tomina. I suspect it was not. But I can tell you that before her days on these prairies were done, she was the lady at Highland all the children sought out because she carried candy in her purse for them. I can also tell you that she no longer looks west in frustration and anger. She is buried in the Highland cemetery in the Christian custom, facing east, waiting for the resurrection.

Rev. Terrill Sorensen, Britton

Congregation B'nai Isaac, Jewish Synagogue in Aberdeen

The Synagogue in Aberdeen was purchased in 1917, when the active group that was meeting here formally incorporated. Our long history means that Jewish visitors to town, whether they inquire at the local hospital or the University, are told there is a Jewish community and given our phone number. The Synagogue continues as our center of Jewish life today, although our numbers have declined substantially over the decades. As Jewish children grew up here, they did not follow their parents into the family business, but instead left home to seek opportunities in large cities. Many Jews also intermarried or remarried and did not raise their children in the Jewish faith, a common problem in Judaism as in other religions.

Our congregation welcomes anyone who wants a place to worship, Jewish or not; for many years, one of our "regulars" was a Quaker. We offer Hebrew School for children when needed, and we celebrate a bar mitzvah (the coming of age of a Jewish boy) this year, the first in over twenty years. There have also been a few people who converted to Judaism while living in Aberdeen, although we never proselytize, in keeping with a firm tenet of our religion. Our weekly Torah Study group is attended by both Synagogue members and those from other churches, and the discussion is always lively and informative. Community holiday meals are often attended by as many as fifty people, many of whom are not Jewish. Food is always plentiful and prepared in the Synagogue's kitchen under strict Kosher rules, which prohibits mixing meat and dairy foods.

One of the difficult parts of being Jewish in Aberdeen is that we must do without traditional Jewish foods. If someone wants challah—the egg bread served on Friday nights—it must be made from scratch. Lox and bagels are a rare delicacy, available only when someone brings them back from a visit to a larger city. Nor do many people understand Yiddish words, so when you complain that you have to "schlep" to the store in the snow and ice, no one knows what you are "qvetching" about. Beyond that, many people have difficulty understanding our religion, because they know so little about it. We therefore invite community groups, especially from local schools, to tour the Synagogue to learn about our beliefs and traditions.

Our membership list has fallen over the years, so it now numbers no more than ten families. The small size of our congregation means that each member has a key to the door of the Synagogue. We cannot afford to hire staff, so one of us leads services, which are cancelled in the winter when many of us are gone. We also cooperate on the work needed to keep the building running. Maintenance, landscaping, and kitchen work are voluntarily divided among the members. We are in fact a very close family, each with our share of chores. Above all else, we are there for each other, for anything and everything. If one of us needs something, all we have to do is ask.

In keeping with our religious values, the local Jewish population has long been involved in community projects; civic participation and volunteerism are important in our way of life. We all feel very fortunate to be an active part of this community, and we want to give back to it, like any South Dakotan.

Members of the Congregation, Aberdeen

No Place Like Home

I devise a test of community connection.

Waving in the country has been the subject of too many humorous essays, often written by city folks, so I want my signal to be simple and clear. With my right hand at the top of the steering wheel, palm out, I raise my index finger and middle fingers. I make this gesture when I can see the oncoming driver's face, allowing time for a response.

My first waving experiment lasts twenty-eight miles, from my turnoff to Hot Springs, South Dakota and includes eighty-four vehicles. Greetings are returned by six.

For the next few miles, I review my data. My headlights are on, a universal signal for "Passing is dangerous." Many of us in this neighborhood adopted this custom after losing relatives and friends to accidents on two-lane highways; therefore, the cars showing headlights may have been local. The school bus driver waved, but the highway patrol trooper didn't. I waved three times at three cars too close together, and got no response. The first driver was nervously watching the two behind him. Both of them were riding each other's bumpers, zigzagging, peering ahead and trying to pass in the no-passing zone.

Intrigued by the results, I repeated the experiment from Edgemont, South Dakota, to Lusk, Wyoming, on two-lane SD 18 and WY 18-85, famous for lurking troopers, leaping deer, and speed traps.

The first vehicle I meet is a battered pickup with local plates. The driver's arm is extended along the back of the seat. Surprised, he waves, grins, and waves some more. No one waves first. When I wave at two semis hauling hay bales, the first driver looks astonished; the second is talking on his cell phone. A dozen dead deer decompose in the ditch; speeders have made this road a death trap for wildlife. Covering sixty-six miles in sixty-two minutes, I wave seventy-four times and receive only four salutations.

Experiments summary: 158 waves, 10 returned. What might

we learn from this waving experiment?

At the very least, my research may indicate plains folk are dangerously out of practice in the traditional friendly western wave. If they just moved here, maybe they don't understand the custom. And perhaps longtime residents aren't feeling friendly in these challenging days.

A friend with whom I discuss my trial suggests that my waving is an aggressive act, and compares it to the traditional New York third-finger wave. She suggests that my waving symbolizes my refusal to adapt to "modern" ways, and calls me "a holdout, a living old westerner practicing neighborliness." (I suspect she wants to say "old fossil.")

If this is aggression, why not? Let's all start waving at each other on two-lane highways. If your wave expresses your hostility to bigger highways and look-alike communities, that's fine. If it's pure friendliness, that's ok too. Maybe the jerk tailgating that oncoming car will be so startled he'll drop his cell phone and drive with both hands.

Perhaps we'll start choosing to drive where people wave, relishing the relaxation of lower speeds limits on two-lanes the way we adjust our lifestyles in wilderness, the way we are rediscovering cooking under the banner of "slow food." When increased traffic on narrow roads encourages highway planners to push for wider routes, maybe we'll take the next step: discussing with neighbors whether we need a bigger highway before we leap on the bandwagon of support.

Waving certainly won't solve the problems of growth and development in western communities, but we have to start somewhere. Waving a hand is better than brandishing a firearm and maybe our ulcers won't flare up.

Linda M. Hasselstrom, Hermosa

Linda M. Hasselstrom's contribution to this book is an excerpt from "The School Bus Driver Waved," an essay first published in *No Place Like Home: Notes From a Western Life*, Reno: University of Nevada Press, 2009. www.windbreakhouse.com

Participants in the 2012 Crazy Horse Ride enter the Pine Ridge Reservation from White Clay, Nebraska. By David Michaud. Used with permission of David Michaud.

The Crazy Horse Ride: More Than Just A Fun Trip On Horseback

Not many men have a buffalo head mounted in their living room, but then again there aren't many men like Bamm Brewer. Charles "Bamm" Brewer is a character of a man: outgoing, warm, open, and one of the greatest storytellers you may encounter. He sat us down below the giant buffalo head sandwiched between two antelope mounted on the wall in his living room, overlooking the rolling hills of the Pine Ridge Reservation.

Brewer is the original organizer of the Crazy Horse Ride, an event that takes place over the course of four days during the second week of June where people of all ages follow the trail on horseback from Fort Robinson in Nebraska to Pine Ridge in South Dakota. The ride is meant to honor the warriors of Lakota society— from the past to the present and even the future. Great warriors like Crazy Horse, for whom the ride is named, and modern day warriors serving in the armed forces. The Lakota used the horse as their main mode of survival—the buffalo and the hunt associated with it. The horse and its rider are of one spirit, and during a hunt this was apparent. It is still visible, even in this day and age, how intertwined the spirit of the horse and the rider are; especially on the Crazy Horse Ride.

The ride begins in Fort Robinson with a smudging ceremony to bless the 200 riders on their journey and the ride itself. Fort Robinson is the place where Crazy Horse was murdered during the surrender of the Lakota people in the late 1800s. The first day the riders cover thirty miles, and not all of the riders who begin the first leg of the journey will finish in Pine Ridge. Day two, they travel eighteen miles, which takes the riders to the Beaver Valley Camp, where Crazy Horse had camped once before. A Youth Dedication Ceremony takes place here because the area holds significance for the Oglala Lakota Oyate. The Youth Dedication ceremony is a special event because of what takes place during the ceremony. Many young people are given their Lakota names—a big stepping stone into adulthood—and war bonnets are awarded to certain riders. There are dances, songs, and stories told during the ceremony to accompany the ceremonial awards.

The final stop for the weary riders and horses is Pine Ridge, South Dakota. The sight of the riders coming into town is a thing to behold, hundreds of riders coming through town on their horses, carrying elaborate, colorful staffs and flags representing the tribes, the United States and the POWs. One horse is left without a rider to represent Crazy Horse's spirit. Brewer said, with awe in his voice, "We would just let it run free, and it would always stay at the front. It was like Crazy Horse was actually with us."

Dusti Michaud has been on the ride for ten consecutive years. Michaud said she has learned more about her culture as she has grown older because of her participation in the ride. The grueling ride helped her through Army Basic Training due to the high mental strength necessary to endure boot camp. The Crazy Horse Ride helps to remind younger Lakota about who they are as a people and what they represent. "During the ride, the older riders will ride next to you and tell you stories," Michaud said. "They tell you stories about not only our people but about what alcohol and drugs have done to us. It makes you think that maybe you shouldn't do those things because then you can help keep the culture alive."

In 2010, the governor of Nebraska dedicated U.S. Highway 20 in Nebraska to Crazy Horse. Crazy Horse Memorial Highway stretches from Hay Springs to Fort Robinson and was actually an effort by Chadron residents to recognize Crazy Horse's importance in the region. Brewer not only organizes the Crazy Horse Ride, but also helps troubled youth. He hopes that the ride will help them feel connected to their culture and also help them avoid the things that are destroying Lakota society. Despite being a ride that was supposed to only last four years, Bamm Brewer's Crazy Horse Ride has continued for fourteen years and will continue for many years to come.

Keeping the spirit of Crazy Horse and Lakota warriors alive is the main aim for it all, but underneath the obvious reasons, it also teaches Lakota youth the power of the horse, the power of their people, and the importance of their way of life.

Julia R. DeCook, Brookings and Seoul

Julia R. DeCook's contribution to this book was previously published in *The Lakota Times*, 2012

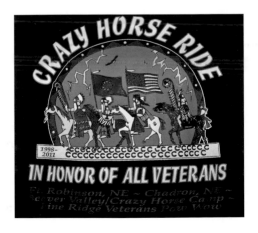

A Retired Farmer Working as a Greeter at Walmart

The store went up last year outside of town.
There was a cornfield where I'm standing now,
smiling, saying hello, and handing out ads
for plastic purses, towels, and microwaves.
The job doesn't pay much, but neither did farming.
Pete, my old neighbor, wearing clean overalls,
comes in. I say "Hey, you lazy fart, I see
you're taking a day off to loaf in town."
And Pete says, "You should talk, getting paid
for standing around in an air-conditioned store."
While we talk about the rain last night,
the possibility of early frost, the price of hogs,
a dozen customers pass by ungreeted,
and I feel uneasy about not doing my job.

In one way, it's like farming – spending hours
on the tractor, with lots of time to daydream.
Now, I invent secrets I'd like to tell customers.
"Every third mineral water bottle is filled
with Russian vodka. Snakes have been found
in the cups of the imported brassieres."
But I only say, "Hello, how are you,"
and send them on their way down the aisles,
which are nothing like rows of corn.

Leo Dangel, Yankton

Leo Dangel's contribution to this book is an excerpt from *Home from the Field*, first published by Spoon River Poetry Press.

Photo by Greg Latza. Used with permission of Greg Latza.

Note on the indexing. Locations (if known or identified by contributors) of essays or poems, proper names of places and people (including contributors' names) and residences of contributors are indexed. Generally the page number refers to the first mention of the subject. Any errors or omissions are not intentional.